Lives and Letters of an Immigrant Family

Lives and Letters

of an Immigrant Family

The van Dreveldts' Experiences

along the Missouri, 1844–1866

Written and translated by

KENNETH KRONENBERG

in association with C. Hans von Gimborn

University of Nebraska Press

LINCOLN AND LONDON

Library of Congress Cataloging in Publication Data
Kronenberg, Kenneth, 1946–
Lives and letters of an immigrant family: the
van Dreveldts' experiences along the Missouri,
1844–1866 / written and translated by Kenneth
Kronenberg in association with C. Hans von
Gimborn.
p.   cm. Includes bibliographical references
(p.) and index. ISBN 0-8032-2741-8 (alk. paper)
1. Van Dreveldt family – Correspondence.
2. Germans Americans – Missouri River Region –
Correspondence. 3. Immigrants – Missouri
River Region – Correspondence. 4. Van Dreveldt,
Anton, 1804–1859 – Correspondence. 5. Van
Dreveldt, Bernhard, 1835–1866 – Correspondence.
6. Missouri River Region – Biography. I. Van
Dreveldt, Anton, 1804–1859. II. Van Dreveldt,
Bernard, d. 1880. III. Van Dreveldt, Bernhard,
1835–1866. IV. Gimborn, Carl von. V. Title.
F472.M7K76 1998 978'.00431'0092–dc21 98-19559 CIP

Contents

Illustrations

Foreword

In 1929, when I was six, I received two cigar boxes filled with American postage stamps from my Aunt Franziska van Dreveldt as well as a stamp book from my parents as Christmas presents. On the first blank page of the book, my father wrote in large letters "U.S.A." and explained to me that this was the English abbreviation for the United States of America.

That was my first encounter with the English language as well as the United States, a country with which six generations of my family have had a special relationship to date.

There were plenty of stories about our family's experiences in that vast and wonderful land, which I found nothing short of magical as a little boy. These stories planted the idea of America firmly in my mind. I learned about my great-grandfather Theodor van Dreveldt, who emigrated to America, and about his adventures. Then there was his elder brother Anton, who settled in Missouri after Theodor returned to Germany, as well as our cousins, the von Weises from Cologne, who had emigrated on Theodor's advice. I was always excited when our "uncles from America" came to visit.

Uncle Carl van Dreveldt, Theodor's oldest son, had emigrated as a young man to escape Prussian authoritarianism, much like his father had before him. He returned to Germany to take over Voorthuyzen, the family property, after Theodor's death in 1880.

When our U.S. relatives visited, I would hear stories about "little Charley" from Rockford, Illinois, and his cousin "big Charley" from Oklahoma, the branch of the von Weises that lived in San Antonio, Texas, and particularly about Louis von Weise from St. Louis, Missouri. Some of the stories were funny, others amazed me. When we asked an uncle whether Americans hunted rabbits, he answered "no." Further probing elicited the explanation that American rabbits were the size of a calf. I'm sure my eyes must have bulged. In any case, the memory has stayed with me all these years.

"Little Charley" came through Emmerich during the summer of 1936 on his way to Baden-Baden. It was my birthday, and he gave me three dollars. I coveted them like a rare treasure, even though the Nazis forbade possession of foreign currency. During the war, my "treasure" burned along with my parents' house.

Like many young Germans, I read James Fenimore Cooper's rather misleading stories about the American frontier. These only served to fuel my interest. And because my father had spent a year in the United States in 1912 after finishing his studies and returned there after the war to travel all over the country on business and in search of family, America remained a huge topic of discussion at home.

But America wasn't the only subject that piqued my curiosity. Every once in a while, older family members would whisper about someone they called "Uncle Provost." My old Catholic aunts from Elten, the daughters of Theodor's sister Annette, never talked openly about this person in the presence of us children. Their religiosity was such that my father used to joke that when they walked in, the room went black. And because we perceived a secret, every little bit of information became interesting. For the aunts, the official genealogy was the final word; it was simply impossible for a Catholic priest to have children, as turned out to be the case.

Later my father, who even as a student had tried to put together a family tree, told me that he had noticed contradictory documents and other things that made him question the official genealogy. In particular there was almost no mention of Theodor's parentage. As he worked on completing the family tree and got closer to the truth, matters became somewhat acute. There is a German proverb that probably gave him pause:

Bist edlen Blutes Du, vergiß es nicht
und handle recht wie Deine Ahnen taten
daß nicht die Nachwelt von Dir spricht
"Der Stamm war gut, die Frucht mißraten".

If you are of noble blood, do not forget it
but act properly as your ancestors did
so that posterity will not say of you,
"The family was good; its fruit was not."

When it came time for me to take over the family tree, my mother, who could be a very critical person, pointed toward a picture of the Provost and to the change in name from Goossens to van Dreveldt and made a rather acerbic comment about the goodness of the family and its fruits.

My father also showed me an entry in a breviary that belonged to "Uncle Provost" and told me what conclusions he drew from it. It was only later, when my father foraged through the family archives more thoroughly, that he came up with conclusive evidence that "Uncle Provost" was Theodor's father.

There is a room in my home in Emmerich am Rhein with a long table that holds boxes and folders containing what is left of the family archives. Miraculously, this particular trove, especially the letters, survived the war more or less intact in Voorthuyzen—minus the stamps my aunt had given me, of course. These archives also contain Provost Goossens's notebooks, Rhine ship schedules, and records of real estate transactions and agricultural cultivation as well as maps and drawings of Voorthuyzen. However, a large part of the letters, mementos, and other records that I remember from my childhood were destroyed.

As we tried to put our lives back together after World War II, other matters were more pressing. When I returned home I received packages of clothing and food from my American cousins. We also exchanged countless letters that paved the way for my visit the United States. Given our family history, it was only logical that my father and his cousins in the United States would do everything in their power to enable me to travel to the United States to reestablish family and business connections that had been broken by the war. In 1950 I followed the route taken by so many of my ancestors and arrived in New York, where I was met by my cousin Louis von Weise.

That year in the United States furthered my development after the horrible events I had lived through during the war. I will never forget the acceptance and hospitality shown me so soon after those events. I traveled throughout the country visiting relatives and reestablishing bonds in New York, Rockford, St. Louis, and San Antonio. Because of this experience I was able to complete my father's work of piecing together and transcribing the family correspondence by making it available to family members living in the United States.

The New World has also tugged at my own five children. Three of them have spent significant time in Boston and in California. My daughter Jacoba has settled outside Boston. And so, a fifth-generation descendant of Theodor van Dreveldt has "shaken the European dust from her shoes." The first member of the sixth generation was born in 1995.

C. HANS VON GIMBORN

Preface

VAN DREVELDT

BERNHARD VAN DREVELDT	TER GEDACHTENIS VAN	HUBERT T.A. VAN DREVELDT
GEBOREN AUF VOORTHUYZEN	ANTON VAN DREVELDT	GEBOREN AUF VOORTHUYZEN
RHEINPREUSSEN	GEB. TE UTRECHT	RHEINPREUSSEN
DEN 22 NOV. 1835	DEN 16 SEPT. 1804	DEN 10 JUNI 1837
GESTORBEN ZU ST. LOUIS MO	OVERLEDEN TE ST. LOUIS	GESTORBEN ZU ELKVILLE ILL
DEN 18 SEPT. 1866	DEN 28 JUNY 1859	DEN 3 MAY 1913

These are the inscriptions on the gravestones I found in Bellefontaine Cemetery in St. Louis in October 1996; the headstone with the family name and three small memorial tablets set into the lawn, the father flanked by his two sons. The van Dreveldts are not my ancestors. Nonetheless, I could not suppress my tears when I found them, such good friends had they become.

I was introduced to the van Dreveldts in 1995, when a descendant living outside Boston approached me about translating some nineteenth-century family letters in her father's possession. What began as a small sheaf of letters later ballooned into more than 130,000 words.

It may well be true that there is no closer reading than translation. In the process of interpreting and retelling, one soon finds oneself at a sort of meta-level where words are linked together into chains and meaning is created. And although one can never be entirely certain whether that meaning is one's own or that of the original writer, particularly when the writer is no longer around to protest, a very close dialogue and friendship develops. This book was born of that friendship.

At some point in the translation the idea for a book began to crystallize in my mind, and I proposed a few ideas to my then client, Hans von Gimborn. Since that had been his intention all along, his response was very positive. As it became clear that a closer collaboration between us was likely, I decided that I needed to broach a very difficult issue. I wrote a letter to him in which I explained that my family, born in Germany, had been largely destroyed in the Holocaust. Would this make a difference to him? Could he, a member of the generation of perpetrators, work with a Jewish collaborator? Could I with him? I was

xiii

awakened by my fax machine at 4:00 the next morning with von Gimborn's answer. Among other things, he had involved himself since 1951 in bringing together former Jewish citizens of his town, Emmerich. He was eager to work with me. In May 1996 I visited Emmerich.

As I came to know Hans (Theodor's great-grandson) and other living members of the family better, it became clear how important Theodor van Dreveldt, Anton's younger brother, was as a model in the family mythology. While the life of the uncommunicative, irresponsible, and manipulative Anton could serve as a cautionary tale, Theodor's was worth emulating. The golden boy Theodor was outgoing, concerned about people and justice, enlightened, a good friend, and worthy ancestor.

And in fact, as I read and translated Theodor's letters and put myself in his place, I found his story irresistible. When I read his final letter, written two days before his death in 1880, I grieved the loss of a man now dead 116 years and pondered how different things might have been for my family if something like his sensibility had become the dominant tradition in Germany. Part of that letter is quoted in the conclusion.

KENNETH KRONENBERG

Acknowledgments

This book might never have been written without the immense work of transcription and genealogical research undertaken by Hans's father, Carl von Gimborn.

Hans von Gimborn and I wish to thank all those who supplied photographs, documents, and letters as well as advice. They include Carl Hugo van Dreveldt, Xanten; Karla Lensing-Hebben, Moers; Jo Dewerpe, Brussels; Liesbeth Weselaar, Amsterdam; and Jane Trautmann, Palo Alto.

We also want to thank Walter Kamphoefner, Steven Rowan, and Erin McCauley Renn for their careful reading of the manuscript and translations as well as their encouragement and very sound advice.

I owe a particular debt to Doris von Gimborn for her unfailing patience and gracious hospitality and to Jacoba von Gimborn for her steady hand and encouragement.

Finally, the support and friendship of my partner in this endeavor, Hans von Gimborn, has meant the world to me. Throughout our work together, his wise counsel and encyclopedic knowledge of local and European history kept me from going too far astray. We weathered some storms together, and I have learned a great deal from him.

Introduction

The promise of America has been a lure to Europeans seeking to escape poverty, persecution, or personal demons virtually since its discovery. It was always a new beginning under unimaginably difficult conditions, but settlers invariably believed that they would be remade or redeemed by the New World. Early letters, narratives, and travelogues frequently expressed this theme of renewal.

Although there had been German immigration to America in the eighteenth century, the mass migration began in the 1830s, prompted by a combination of increasing poverty and Prussian authoritarianism.[1] Of the more than 150 pieces of "immigration literature" published in Germany from 1827 to 1856, the most important and influential was undoubtedly Gottfried Duden's *Report on a Journey to the Western States of North America and a Stay of Several Years along the Missouri (during the Years 1824, '25, '26, 1827)*, published in 1829.

Duden, a Prussian lawyer and civil servant, settled for a time in Montgomery County, Missouri. He had given a great deal of thought to the problems facing Germans in an authoritarian state such as Prussia with its oppressive class-based codes and laws. Duden believed that overpopulation was a major obstacle to democracy: "It is overpopulation that causes the passionate grabbing for the lowest offices, and the mere fear of poverty gives rise to a whole horde of acts of servitude that even in family life serve as an excellent preparation for unquestioning obedience to the demands of political despotism."[2] In his book he made it clear that unsettled lands promoted the opposite. Coming to America would give Germans a new start.

Implicit in this conception is the idea that people can leave their old selves behind. Duden's book had an enormous effect in Germany, influencing thousands of men and women to try their luck in America. Those immigrants found conditions to be much less favorable than Duden had described. Many of them, for a variety of reasons, were not up to the task and returned to Germany. Nevertheless, Germans continued to make the journey, becoming the largest immigrant group during the nineteenth century. Theodor van Dreveldt was almost certainly influenced by Duden, as was his brother Anton.

In 1844 Theodor's old university friend Gerhard Lensing, in a letter from Montgomery County, Duden country, made clear what attitudes

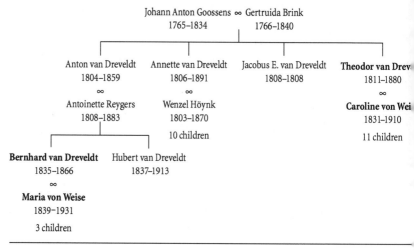

The van Dreveldts (connections with the von Weises shown in bold type).

he believed should be left behind in Europe. Lensing, who as a university student in Bonn had been active in the same banned political fraternity as Theodor, escaped Prussia to avoid prosecution and prison in the mid-1830s and came to America to farm the land. He was successful, and his great-grandson continues to this day to farm essentially the same Missouri bottomland as he did. So intent was Lensing on leaving the past behind that he refused to correspond with his family in Germany, even about financial matters. Family legend has it that he was afraid that Prussian agents would come over and arrest him if they knew where he was. Tellingly, Lensing's letter was addressed to Theodor in London, to where Theodor decamped while deciding what to do next:

> I have always believed that you do not belong in the Old World. . . . However, test yourself to make sure that you really are a republican and a democrat and will be able to leave at home any aristocratic notions by whatever name they are called, whether birth, wealth, or education. That alone is necessary for happiness here.

If only it were as simple as a "geographical cure." The fact is that whatever they left behind in the Old Country and whatever else they may have brought with them to the New, immigrants always brought themselves.

The letters that Theodor and Anton (and later Anton's son Bernard)

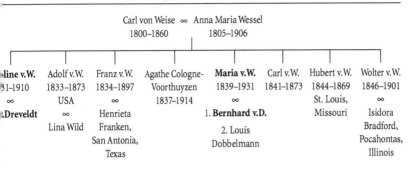

Carl von Weise ∞ Anna Maria Wessel
1800–1860   1805–1906

| line v.W. 31–1910 ∞ .Dreveldt | Adolf v.W. 1833–1873 USA ∞ Lina Wild | Franz v.W. 1834–1897 ∞ Henrieta Franken, San Antonia, Texas | Agathe Cologne-Voorthuyzen 1837–1914 | Maria v.W. 1839–1931 ∞ 1. Bernhard v.D. 2. Louis Dobbelmann | Carl v.W. 1841–1873 | Hubert v.W. 1844–1869 St. Louis, Missouri | Wolter v.W. 1846–1901 ∞ Isidora Bradford, Pocahontas, Illinois |

The von Weises.

wrote from America are extraordinary in that they unselfconsciously reveal their personal flaws as well as their strengths, in other words, all the character traits they brought over with them. The van Dreveldts wrote very articulate letters and appear to have made little or no effort to censor themselves. What was on their minds reached the page. We are fortunate that these letters were saved and that the heirs to this patrimony preserved them as they did.

But if we only had letters from America, the background from which the brothers came could only have been expressed in generalities and possibilities. We are doubly lucky, because the record of family letters and documents reaches back to the late eighteenth century. We therefore can get a distinctive picture of the family as a whole over time. Of course, this is not to say that there aren't huge gaps about which one can only guess. There is a question attached to this: If the peculiar circumstances surrounding Anton's and Theodor's births had been lost, would it make a difference to our appreciation of their story? And what exactly do these details add?

In short form the story is as follows: Anton and Theodor van Dreveldt were the illegitimate sons of Johann Goossens, a Catholic priest in Emmerich on the lower Rhine in the former Duchy of Cleves. Their mother, Gertruida Brink, was Goossens's housekeeper. Goossens ac-

quired properties called Voorthuyzen as a result of Napoleon's secularization of the churches in 1811. While Anton was the first-born and
therefore the inheritor of his father's lands, Theodor was his father's
favorite. Anton developed into something of an alcoholic ne'er-do-
well, while Theodor became involved in the liberal politics of the 1830s,
joining a political fraternity (*Burschenschaft*) at the university in Bonn
in 1831, where he studied law.

The fallout from this involvement led directly to Theodor's decision
to emigrate in 1844. His attempts to put down roots in Missouri might
have been successful if he had not contracted malaria and if his brother
had been more dependable. As it was, Theodor languished in a log
cabin he built near Hermann, Missouri, unable to work and waiting
for money, which did not arrive until he was too discouraged to make
use of it. In 1849 he returned to Germany, where he took over Voorthuyzen from Anton.[3] Anton, in turn, came to America with his young
sons Bernhard and Hubert, after having his wife committed to an insane asylum.

Theodor became the sort of concerned democrat whom a friend
sought to lure back to Germany in 1847 with the following tidbit:

There's just one thing that I would like to mention, namely that
all members of the state Parliament [*Reichstände*] are infused with
such a liberal and good spirit that I really expect the best in the
future. At the last session, a majority voted for the emancipation
of the Jews. The debates are altogether so interesting that if you
haven't read them already in your newspapers, I will send them as
soon as they are published.

After Theodor moved back to Germany, acquaintances were more apt
to write to Theodor about Anton's behavior in America:

I expect that you already know that he [Anton] and Noot split
up. You are probably in a better position than I to judge who was
in the wrong. I have heard that Noot is demanding several hundred dollars from your brother and has even threatened to sue. He
has spoken very bitterly about him. I'm sure that you have also
learned that your brother has since split up with Westhooven as
well. Westhooven and his father-in-law are just as bitter.

However, all right was probably not on Theodor's side. Success or
failure in immigration often turned on support, both financial and

emotional, from home. There is some evidence in the letters that Theodor may have acted vindictively once his brother was in the United States and he had control of the purse. On the other hand, Anton's continuing inability to get either his personal or financial life under control would have been ample reason for Theodor to keep his brother on a tight leash. And so we have a picture of conflict between the brothers. The heir and the favorite son, in effect, undermined each other's immigration.

Eventually, Anton sold Voorthuyzen outright to Theodor. With the proceeds from the sale, he was able to buy a farm near Waterloo, Illinois, which he and his sons worked until his death in 1859. Bernhard, who died at age thirty-one in 1866, developed many of his father's traits. Arrogant and self-righteous, Bernhard left a full picture of himself in his letters, and given what we know about Anton, we quickly come to recognize Bernhard as his son. Aside from running the farm, he also opened a general store near Waterloo. Had he lived, the van Dreveldts might well have become established on these shores, but a few years after Bernhard's death, his widow, Maria, returned to Europe with her two young daughters.

At Voorthuyzen, Theodor became the focal point of a large, extended family, the much-loved rock to whom everyone turned for advice and help. Although not directly involved in politics, in part because he had sworn allegiance to the king in 1837 to avoid a lengthier prison term for his student activities and perhaps also because he now had much to lose, he remained interested and even hosted the radical Jewish politician and parliamentarian Johann Jacobi at Voorthuyzen in 1869. It has been suggested, though evidence has not been found, that Theodor was not a particularly effective steward of the property and that the income he generated was insufficient to support his family's lifestyle. Bits and plots of Voorthuyzen were sold off to cover financial shortfalls, and it finally went out of the family in 1932.

This book is primarily about the relationship between Anton and Theodor and its effect on their immigration. Immigration was not, and is never, an easy matter, even though we may tend to credit only unabashed success stories. Mid-nineteenth-century customs statistics show only the numbers flowing in; there are no hard figures for those who returned to Germany. Yet there were many, and each returnee had a story, just as much so as those who remained. The van Dreveldt letters give evidence of the fate of two brothers, one who returned and one who stayed. Their fate in America is much more representative of the immigrant experience than most of us care to admit.

I have tried to place the van Dreveldts in historical perspective so that the reader may gain some sense of the external pressures and circumstances that surrounded them.

While focusing on the brothers, I have also written about Anton's son Bernhard, in large part because, as mentioned above, the behavioral connections between father and son were too striking to ignore and because his ideas and character traits stand in such contrast to Theodor's. Although Theodor had eleven children, and a total of four sons emigrated to the United States at his urging, I decided not to include them because they added little to my understanding of the brothers.

I have skimped in other areas as well. For example, I have focused little on the women in the family, although their lives and thoughts are no less interesting than the men's. Bernhard's wife, Maria von Weise, for example, married him over her father's initial opposition, leaving a very comfortable life in Cologne to follow her husband to a small town in western Illinois. Although she seems to have shared some of his racism, though without his free-floating but controlled rage, she became peripherally involved in suffrage issues when she returned to Europe after his untimely death. At one point she considered going to medical school; however, Jacobi, who was a physician as well as a politician, advised her of the difficulties she would face. She also realized that although the family would not stand in her way, she would not be able to count on their support, not even Theodor's. Maria's letters to her sister Lina (Caroline), Theodor's wife, as well as to other family members, give a good sense of how she saw herself and how she thought. These have been largely left out. The story of Maria, who lived until 1931, deserves to be another book.

The letters included in this book are translations of transcriptions made primarily by Carl von Gimborn, a grandson of Theodor's. Carl's son Hans has also transcribed numerous letters written in German and Dutch script. Without this labor of love, my job as a translator would have been well nigh impossible; I am not fluent in the old script. Most of Anton's and Theodor's letters are included in this book, although some of the letters have been excerpted. Many of Bernhard's letters, which tended to the interminable, repetitious, and annoying, have been cut down.

Unfortunately, many of the original letters, along with photographs, Theodor's drawings of America, and contemporary American newspapers, had been misplaced and were found again only after this book was completed. In his later years, Carl von Gimborn edited four books of letters, primarily for family consumption, and my chronology of family events and early family history are based largely on his work. The books include *Johann Anton Goossens, eine Familiengeschichte* (1965), *Als der Großvater die Großmutter nahm* (1967), *Aus der neuen Welt, Familienbriefe 1844–1869* (1968), and *Theodor van Dreveldt, aus dem Leben meines Großvaters* (1969). However, the books omitted a great deal of material that was deemed "unimportant" but was nonetheless revealing of the motivations and personal traits of family members. I have endeavored to restore this material as appropriate where complete transcriptions could be found.

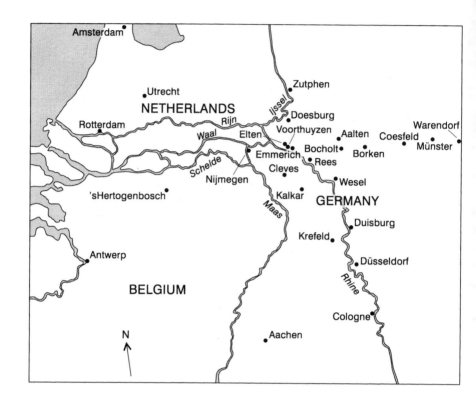

Above: Map of the lower
Rhine from Cologne to
Rotterdam, and including
Emmerich, Elten, and
Voorthuyzen.
Right: Portion of Lloyd's
Official Map of Missouri,
1861, including Hermann,
Loutre Island, and St.
Louis, Missouri, as well as
Waterloo, Illinois.
Courtesy of The Trustees
of Boston Public Library.

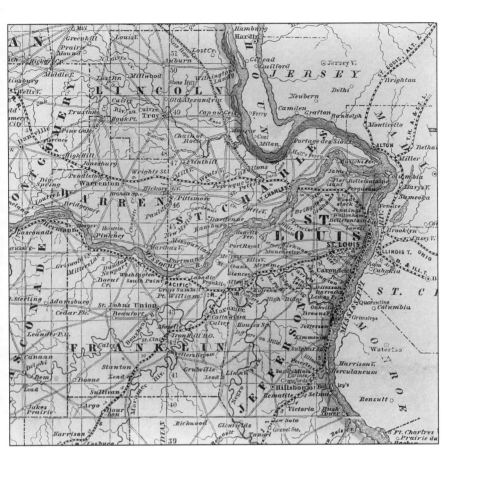

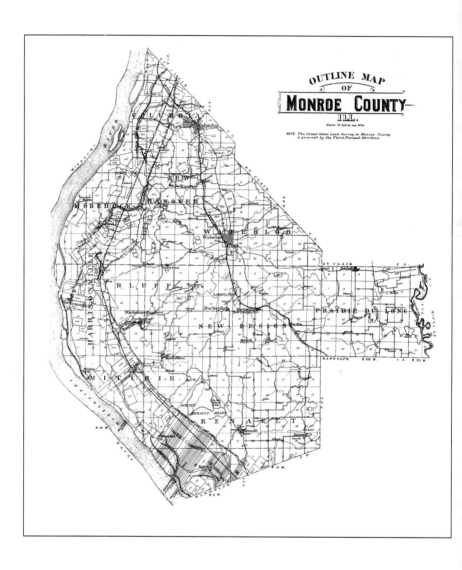

Monroe County, in *An Illustrated Historical Atlas Map of Monroe County,* Ills., W. R. Brink & Co. of Illinois, 1875. Courtesy of Monroe County Historical Society, Waterloo IL.

The Town of Emmerich

The town of Emmerich, or Emmerik as it is sometimes spelled on old maps, lies on the right bank of the lower Rhine just above the point where the river's delta, consisting of the Ijssel, Waal, Schelde, and Rijn (Rhine) Rivers, begins. It has profited from its geographic position for nearly one thousand years. The settlement was first mentioned in documents in 697 when a church was built in Villa Embricensis, and it was elevated to the status of town in 1233, with all attendant rights and privileges. In the seventeenth and early eighteenth centuries, it became a port of some importance; because Emmerich lay on the border with Holland, river sailboats known as *Beurtschiffe* that plied the stretch between Wesel in Germany and Amsterdam or Rotterdam had to unload there. Market boats, *Marktschiffe,* took goods from Emmerich to the towns of Cleves and Kalkar via canals. Rights to this commerce belonged to Emmerich as well. The harbor, a pouch that lies outside the stream of the river, was a valuable asset because it offered protection to boats during floods and icy conditions.

Farmers from the interior brought grain, wool, and livestock to market in Emmerich either for local consumption or to be transported upriver toward Cologne or downriver to Amsterdam and Rotterdam. The town itself bustled with economic activity related to river trade and agriculture. Emmerich was a lively center for cottage textile and leather industries. Farmers who lived outside the walls of the town often had pastures in the town where they could keep their animals in times of war or high water.

For hundreds of years, the commercial, political, and even social life of the town were dominated by an oligarchy of independent mercantile houses. All major decisions regarding trade were made in their counting offices. Because of their centrality, these houses pulsed with the important news of the world brought by shippers and businessmen, especially news that affected local business.

This oligarchy was heavily involved in foreign trade. As a member of the Hanseatic League from about 1300 to 1600, Emmerich enjoyed all the advantages of trade with outposts of the league, including far-off Nizhni Novgorod in Russia.

Early on, the mercantile houses founded guilds and associations which, among other things, came to regulate trade in the delta region.

Although *Beurtschiffe* were in use as far back as the fourteenth century, as Emmerich and other towns grew in importance, shipping on the river came under the regulation and control of these guilds.

Shipping usually began out of Emmerich in early February and continued into November. River traffic stopped during the winter. The town magistrate put together a schedule that regulated the eight official Emmerich shippers in such a way that there was no conflict between them. For example, certain shippers did the Rotterdam run and others the Amsterdam run; they were not permitted to carry goods destined for the others' port.

Timely service was crucial, but given the technology in use, it was not always possible. The wind could come from the wrong direction, be too strong, or, rarely, not blow at all. As on all meandering rivers, there were constantly changing sandbanks to watch for. There were also toll collectors — as many as twenty toll stations on the lower Rhine below Cologne — to slow progress. If a shipper delivered his goods late, he was charged a fine. On the way back, horses on shore pulled the *Beurtschiff* upstream. A *Beurtschiffer* working out of Emmerich could count on a fourteen-day trip from Amsterdam back to his home port, a distance of just eighty miles. Typically the trip downriver delivered such products as grain, iron and steel, tallow, down feathers, glassware, linen and other textiles, wood, beets, and apples. Dutch ports sent wine and brandy, herring and salted fish, vinegar and oils, soap, rice, tobacco, dried fruits, coffee and tea, sugar, and pharmaceuticals back upstream.[1]

Beurtschiffe continued to work the Rhine until the middle of the nineteenth century. In times of war the river had provided a safer means of transporting goods than the overland routes, but British-built steam engines and the railroads put the *Beurtschiffe* out of business. But even as early as 1776 the magistrate in Emmerich wrote in a report to the Chamber of War and the demesne in Cleves about the competition from overland routes: "The changes that were undertaken in the Münster and Cologne districts cut off trade through the Rhine province, and it no longer came through our territory. The people in Warendorf, Münster, Coesfeld, Borken, and Bocholt sent their wares through Cleves."[2] The report reveals how large Emmerich's catchment was; Warendorf was a good seventy-five miles to the east.

The river had more than just economic importance. The Rhine winds through the lowlands of northwestern Germany and Holland. Residents along the river have been building dams and embankments or dikes since about 1200. In the past, despite the dikes, the lower Rhine created islands where it broke through a loop one year and erased this land again the next. In the winter, high water combined with ice floes damaged piers and houses; in the spring, flood waters spread across the lowland and polders, flooding homes and fields. To this day earthen embankments surround some low-lying towns; there are grooved sluice gates where roads pass through the dikes, and sluices can be slid into them in times of flooding. The river's vagaries affected the Dutch and the Germans equally and leavened their competition with an understanding of the need for cooperation regardless of borders. Thus, at a meeting of Hanseatic cities in Lübeck in 1439, Emmerich agreed to pay for the upkeep of the Rhine dike between Emmerich and Dornick. This dike helped protect territory as far off as Zutphen on the Ijssel River in Holland.[3] Yet farmers also realized that the floods renewed the soil by depositing tons of organic silt on the land, despite the simultaneous destruction of crops.

Soil and river: just as these elements affected their forebears in the Rhine region, they would also come to figure prominently in the lives of the van Dreveldts in the New World.

Provost Goossens

As a result of trade and interdependence, cross-border marriages were not uncommon. Dutch settled in Emmerich and Emmerichers moved to Holland so that even today more than 40 percent of townspeople have Dutch names. So it was with the parents of Johann Anton Goossens.[1] His father, the Emmerich lawyer Everard Joseph Goossens, was descended from a Dutch family that had lived in town for more than one hundred years. His mother, Anna Maria Theresia Braem, was born in Den Haag, Holland; her family, however, was originally from Emmerich. At home the families spoke Dutch and the local variant of Low German.

Johann Goossens was born 25 March 1765; his father died when Johann was only five. Family legend has it that Everard tripped over his long coat while boarding a boat on the Rhine, fell into the water, and drowned. Although the elder Goossens had property, the land did not bring in much rent. He was cash poor when he died, and the family — Johann, his younger sister Hendrina, and his mother — depended on Anna Maria's brother-in-law, Arnold van den Sanden, for support. Johann's mother died in 1779.

From 1783 to 1788 Johann Goossens studied for the priesthood at Douai, France, the city where the Old Testament of the Vulgate Bible had been translated into English in 1609. Arnold van den Sanden kept meticulous records of the cost of his nephew's education: 1783 — 153 thalers, 10 stüber; 1784 — 222 thalers, 10 stüber, and so forth, amounting to a total of exactly 1526 thaler and 14 stüber.

In 1793 the young priest became a chaplain in Doesburg, Holland. As it happened, that same year, the St. Martin's Church Foundation in Emmerich lost its provost (*Propst*), the official responsible for overseeing the church's properties and monies. These were quite considerable, having been amassed over many years. A number of cloisters in Germany and Holland were also administered by the church. Emmerich was also notable for the Hohe Schule, a school that had trained the bishops of Cologne and Münster since about 1200. For all these reasons a position in Emmerich might well be coveted by an ambitious young man. The young chaplain applied for and got the position.

From that moment on, every little expenditure of his was duly noted in his ledger book, and so, even in the absence of surviving correspon-

4

dence, we are able to piece together those parts of his life that could
be quantified. What follows is a small sample of expenditures from the
years 1794 and 1795:

	Thaler	Stüber	Pfennig
Tip for delivering an orange			27
2 lbs. of carbonate		15	
To Frau Gras for 2 dozen stools	74		
2 bottles of French white wine from Kok	1	18	
¾ lb. of salmon		15	
1 lb. of tea—the best	3	22	
Contribution from the provostry for 1795–96, sent to Wesel	853	7	
To Roeder, the printer in Wesel, for 5 volumes on gynecology	15	14	
To the quartermaster of the regiment in Cologne, sent to the war chest in 4 different currencies	421		

If it seems unclear from these figures which were personal expenditures
and which had to do with his duties, that is because he used one set
of books for both, a practice that would land him in court today but
would not have raised eyebrows then. At the end of the year, he simply
made a separate accounting of church transactions based on this yearly
accounting.

One item in the list might have raised eyebrows, however: the five
volumes on gynecology. It is not known to what purpose he put these
books, whether it was a personal or church-related expenditure. Was
it adolescent curiosity appearing belatedly in a twenty-nine-year-old
who had spent years studying for the priesthood? Was it for a hospital
endowed by the foundation? Given his later behavior, the former seems
more likely. We do know that the personal library that he built up indicates that he was a man interested in the world outside of Emmerich,
particularly travel and history.

Goossens also bought "the best" tea—an indication of the life he
would come to live as a *grand seigneur*, surrounding himself with beautiful objects and books, not to mention property. In later years he would
sign his name "Goossens tot Voorthuyzen," "tot," being the Dutch
equivalent of the German "zu" or "von," a designation of nobility.

The French Revolution

In 1789 the French Revolution shook Europe and even came to have profound effects on tiny Emmerich. As the original goal of *liberté, égalité, fraternité* degenerated into the Terror unleashed by the Jacobins, refugees spilled into neighboring countries. More than ninety-four French families, mainly nobility, took refuge in the area around Cleves, just across the Rhine from Emmerich.[1]

On the eve of the French Revolution there were approximately 150 distinct political entities along the Rhine, many of them ecclesiastical states, in what would eventually become the Prussian Rhine Province. Some of them were sizable duchies that exercised considerable influence; others were parcels of land reasonably measured in acres. Because power and land were so diffuse, the region formed a weak western flank for the Holy Roman Empire. It was also largely unable to determine its own destiny; decisions affecting the region were made far to the east, in Prussia.

The Holy Roman Empire, founded in 962 by Otto I, had by this time become largely a fiction. It had once comprised all of what is today Germany, Austria, Switzerland, Burgundy in France, and northern Italy. However, by the end of the eighteenth century it had not only lost most of this territory but had also become completely hollowed out. In Germany the Protestant Hohenzollerns who had ruled Prussia had begun to concentrate their military power. Aside from their territories in eastern Germany, they also controlled a few tiny pockets of land in the west, including the Duchy of Cleves, which straddled the lower Rhine adjacent to Holland and included Emmerich. This exclave had been ceded to Prussia in 1614 as a result of a complex struggle with the Austrian Hapsburgs. But Prussia's sights had always been set to the east; this little parcel of land was not its primary concern.

Almost all of the emperors of the Holy Roman Empire came from the Catholic Hapsburg family. In the course of a succession struggle in Spain from 1702 to 1713, Austria had won control over what was then called the Spanish Netherlands, now approximately Belgium. In 1740 a succession struggle took place over the right of Maria Theresia to become ruler of Austria after the death of her father. Taking advantage of this temporary power vacuum, Frederick the Great of Prussia took Silesia away from Austria.

After the revolutionaries took over France, all the European powers, realizing that the institution of the monarchy was at stake everywhere, decided they must act. Austria and Prussia, the two preeminent but competing and distrustful German powers within the empire, signed a treaty in 1792 that underscored their resolve "to act promptly, in mutual accord with the forces necessary to attain the proposed common objective." To the French, that language was clear. On 20 April 1792 revolutionary France declared war on Austria. Shortly thereafter, Prussia formally joined its ally.

Throughout the summer, as the Austro-Prussian army prepared to attack, France was in turmoil. During the night of 9 August, revolutionaries overthrew the existing Paris city government and declared the "Revolutionary Commune." The Assembly immediately voted to suspend the monarchy. The entire country was put on a war footing. Then, on 2 September, news reached Paris that Verdun was about to fall to the Prussians. This news unleashed a frenzy of massacres in and around Paris in which more than eleven hundred people, including Catholic clergy who had decided not to side with the Revolution, were butchered.

In spite of the chaos in Paris, on 20 September the French army (Revolutionary France had introduced mass citizen mobilization) faced the Prussians at Valmy, less than one hundred miles from Paris, and the superior Prussian force retreated, stunning the other European powers. The Revolution, which had been on the defensive, now went on the attack. They went into Austrian Netherlands (Belgium) and occupied it in November. They also pushed east, taking the German cities of Speyer, Worms, Frankfurt, and Mainz. By March 1793 these territories were declared part of France. Although they were forced out of most of these territories a few months later, the French forces retook them in 1794. The treaties of Basel (1795) and Lunéville (1801) finalized these conquests. Thus, in 1794, France controlled the entire left side of the Rhine. Prussia promised to protect the right side, which included Emmerich, something it was not in a position to do.

In fact, Prussia stayed on the sidelines until 1806. Prussia's passivity allowed the French to push the Austrians around various battlefields in central and southern Europe, defeating them everywhere and incorporating the land into the French Empire. Then, in mid-1806, Prussia declared war on France because of some actions it had taken in northern Germany. But on 14 October the French defeated the Prussians at both

Jena and Auerstädt; two days later Napoleon was sitting in Berlin. By June 1807 the French Empire extended all the way to the Russian border. Germany was completely demoralized. However, it was precisely at this point that an awareness of German nationality came to the fore as a reaction to Napoleonic victories. This new nationalism took various forms, some of which will be important to our story; some were to have terrible echoes in twentieth-century Germany.

How Provost Goossens was affected by and what he thought about these events is not known; there are no records or correspondence. We do know that he wore a wig with a braid, which, after the French Revolution, would have identified him as a political reactionary. We also have an official report written from Emmerich to King Frederick William II of Prussia, which began with the following words: "6 November 1794 was a day of terror in Emmerich. In the morning at about 10:00, shots were heard below the city, and we were informed that shots were being fired at a scouting vessel heading upstream." Later that day a French soldier crossed the Rhine for the purpose of negotiating with the town. Before he even got back to the other side, the French began to shell Emmerich with four 8-pound cannons and three howitzers. More than 120 shots were fired, starting numerous fires and causing much damage. The Provost's ledger book for that date contains the following cryptic entries:

½ pitcher of gin: 16 stüber
Powder and buckshot: 1 thaler, 4 stüber

Emmerich came to be known by French authorities as "that nest of emigrants." But even earlier, the town had hosted fleeing Huguenots as well as Spanish and Dutch Catholics. The town was an ideal place to flee to because it was separated from French territory by the Rhine, so if matters deteriorated, there would be somewhat more time to retreat further inland; Emmerich was also the headquarters of General Blücher, the commander of the Prussian observation army who would come to play a decisive role in Napoleon's ultimate defeat at Waterloo in 1815. Consequently, in 1796 eleven Catholic priests and a nun, whom Provost Goossens would have come to know well, sought and were given refuge by the town. There followed a procession of French and Belgian refugees, many of high social or clerical rank and standing. For example, the primate of Belgium, Cardinal von Franckenberg, was deported by the French and stayed in Emmerich for several years, from where he continued to be in close contact with his community in Belgium. In early 1801 Napoleon sent the following note to his advisor and Citizen Minister Talleyrand: "You will find enclosed a letter detailing the unrest which clerics living in Emmerich have incited in Mecheln, Antwerp, and other towns. Demand that the Prussian government hand these individuals over to the French authorities." With that, the cardinal was forced to move on to Borken in Westphalia and later, when that became unsafe, to Holland.[2]

Even though war might be intense in one part of Europe, life continued much as usual in other regions. In the discharge of his duties the Provost often took long trips to oversee properties owned by his church, some in Westphalia and Holland. Partly because of the pressures of the position and partly because he liked to live well, he set about hiring a housekeeper. After nine candidates failed to meet his standards, he asked Gertruida and Aleida Brink, sisters of a local priest, to take over the household duties, which they did at the end of 1798.

The "Little Mishaps"

What began as a relationship of employment blossomed into intimacy with Gertruida, the younger sister, and in the spring of 1804 she found herself pregnant.[1] Such a *"Malheurchen"* (little mishap), as later generations would call it, might have social drawbacks if it became known. Even for a priest with a position of responsibility in the Church, the problem was simply one of keeping the mishap quiet, as the Church was in the habit of covering for its own; such was the morality of the period. On 9 September 1804 Goossens sent Gertruida to Utrecht to have the baby. His church, St. Martin's in Emmerich, was under the Bishopric of Utrecht. On 16 September the following name was entered into the baptismal book of the cathedral: Antonius Josephus Everardus Joannes van Dreveld. The parents, who supposedly did not live in Utrecht, went by the names Antonius Gosuinus van Dreveld and Gerarda Julia de Beautxant. Needless to say, these names were fabricated out of whole cloth. Antonius Gosuinus is an amusing little word game on Johann Anton Goossens, and it is believed that the name Dreveld (a final *t* was added later) came from a piece of land Goossens oversaw, the "three fields."

Mother and son stayed together in Utrecht for several months. During that time the Provost sent money regularly, duly recorded in his ledger, to an addressee in Utrecht named Martens whose actual identity is unknown, but who was most probably someone connected to the church.

In 1806 Gertruida Brink became pregnant again, and again she was sent off to Utrecht. On 6 September she gave birth to Anna Alijdis Maria Theresia van Dreveld; again, the same fictitious parents found their way into the baptismal book. Annette, as the baby was called, was sent to live with a family named van der Schoot in Anholt along with her two-year-old brother. In 1808 Anton was sent to a Jesuit school in Anholt, and Annette followed him there in 1811.

The couple's last child, Karl Theodor Ferdinand van Dreveld, made his appearance on 24 January 1811 in Zutphen, Holland. The same names were used to identify the parents.

Anton and Annette are first mentioned as living in Emmerich in 1813; Theodor joined the family several years later. All three were separated from their parents for crucial early years of their lives. Apart from any effects they might have suffered from the separation, when they joined their parents' household they were at a tremendous disadvantage at school because they spoke only Dutch, the language spoken in the Jesuit school in Holland and in the Provost's home. Most townspeople spoke Low German; the upper classes preferred High German and French.

The Provost told the children that he was their uncle and Gertruida their Aunt Truijke. This fiction was carried on for years. Nevertheless, the older two children, at least, had to endure endless teasing from schoolmates who ran after them calling them *"Pröpstkes"* (provostlets), which would seem to indicate that the townspeople suspected the truth. Presumably, this caused the children some insecurities about their parentage.

The hypocrisy of the children's lineage was eventually given official cachet in 1833, a year before Goossens's death. He wanted there to be no question concerning inheritance rights, and so he filed the following document, a small masterpiece of creative family-building:

Family attestation made by the former Provost of the Foundation, presently owner of the estate Voorthuyzen, Joh. Anton Goossens, concerning his three wards Anton van Dreveldt, born in Utrecht in the Kingdom of the Netherlands on 16 September 1804; Annette van Dreveldt, born in the same place, 6 September 1806; and Theodor van Dreveldt, born in Zutphen on 24 January 1811.

The youngest sister of my maternal grandmother, Henrietta or Hendrina van Loosbroek, born in 's-Hertogenbosch, was named Julia or Julietta van Loesbroek. She married a trader, Thierry de Beautxant, who came from Charleville in France. Their youngest daughter, Gerarda Julia, married the French colonel Antonius Gosuinus van Dreveldt, who came from around Dunkirk.

In 1812, when the French army under Napoleon fought its way across Europe, he was ordered to Spain. Because his wife had relatives in Bayonne in the Department of Basses Pyrennées, she intended to follow him there and stay with her relatives. Upon her departure in May 1812, she left her children, at my recommendation, being her only relative in these parts, at a school in Anholt. She gave me 300 guldens toward their education in the firm hope that she would soon return and resume care of her beloved children. To date, she has not returned. As far as I know, the family had no money and lived from his military pay. All attempts made thus far to track them down have been in vain, and it is more than probable that these good parents were killed, perhaps assassinated, in the chaos that engulfed that region.

Emmerich, 17 January 1833

J. A. Goossens
tot Voorthuyzen
Former Provost of the abolished Capitulum
Canonicorum ad Sanctum Martinum in Emmerich

The painter Francisco Goya immortalized the cruelty and chaos that engulfed the Spanish theater of the Napoleonic Wars in his series of etchings *The Disasters of War*. Goossens put these disasters to an entirely different use.

Voorthuyzen

Napoleon did transform Goossens's life completely, but not in the manner he suggested in the attestation. Not content with the left side of the Rhine, Napoleon's army swept into central Europe and by 1806 controlled large swatches of land east of the river. France created the Confederation of the Rhine, completely eliminating the ecclesiastical states and winnowing the number of states down to thirty-nine. With this act, the Holy Roman Empire can be said to have disappeared. Suddenly Emmerich found itself in the newly formed buffer state, the Grand Duchy of Berg. Although thalers and guldens were acceptable currency, entries in the Provost's ledger book began to be made in francs.

Napoleon attempted to change the entire social fabric of the region. Over the centuries, cities and towns gained substantial rights to self-government in exchange for supporting the king in time of war or emergency with soldiers, provisions, and money. Napoleon completely wiped out that ancient system of mutual obligations and replaced it with a dictatorship run from Paris. However, within this dictatorial framework, he introduced reforms that were liberal and democratic. Serfdom was abolished. His administration replaced a legal system favoring the aristocracy with the French system, the *Code Civil*, which made all citizens equal before a court of law. Germans, especially those along the Rhine who had suffered under the arbitrary and unfair Prussian legal systems, welcomed many of these reforms. The French tried as much as possible to keep those Prussian bureaucrats in their administration who could adapt to the French system, which resulted in lingering liberalization in the region even after Napoleon was gone. The esteem in which Napoleon was held can be gauged by the fact that even after his death, his portrait was not uncommon in German homes along the Rhine.

Napoleon's dictatorial power can also be seen in his road building policy. By fiat Napoleon created a system of ruler-straight roads "from church spire to church spire" that greatly facilitated travel and commerce as well as troop movements. Especially on the left side of the Rhine, the roads simply cut through the properties of the aristocracy and the churches. The Prussians could never have done this because they needed the aristocrats and clerics as allies. The Provost's life, however, was most changed by the policy of secularization of the churches, particularly the Catholic ones. The French Revolution had been profoundly anticlerical, seeing in the Catholic Church a key prop of the old order. Beginning in 1806, church properties in the confederation were sold off and the churches converted to other uses. In 1811 secularization reached Emmerich, and Goossens's position was abolished. The church became the seat of the French administration, and sales of church property began in 1813.

Given Goossens's accumulated knowledge of church properties in the region and their values, this was his big chance, and he cashed in. He was particularly fond of a property called Voorthuyzen, an ancient allodial estate just north of Emmerich at the foot of the Eltenberg, a 260-foot-high moraine. It originally belonged to the House of the counts Wichmann, whose property extended well into the delta of the Rhine, Maas, and Schelde around the year 1000. Beginning in 1793 Provost Goossens had ordered houses built or remodeled, fruit trees and poplars planted, fields cleared, drainage ditches dug, and roads and bridges constructed. Now, parlaying his pension, rents from properties he already owned, and his own assets with a sizable bank loan, he was able to purchase parcels of this land. His records show that he paid out 20,256.68 francs in 1813, 19,938.22 in 1814, 12,802.40 in 1815, and 21,482.84 in 1816. In 1817 he added a garden house and garden for 122 thalers; the asking price had been 800. By 1860 (twenty-six years after Goossens's death), Voorthuyzen came to cover about one thousand acres, mainly on the Prussian but also on the Dutch side of the border.

Goossens does not appear at first to have resided at Voorthuyzen, but rather at the old provostry in Emmerich opposite the church. Voorthuyzen was his retreat as well as a source of income from crops, sales of wood, and land rental to small farmers. Whenever he visited, he stayed in a relatively small house, Alt-Voorthuyzen, just south of the stream called the Wildbach.

In 1943 the artist Elizabeth Terhorst described Alt-Voorthuyzen, which she called "das Eyland" (the island), in a book by that title. And although this is a twentieth-century description, much of it would have applied in the last century as well.

> The darkly glittering canal is like a belt enclosing the island; a narrow dike running through a depression in the meadow leads to the only entrance. A levee on which age-old giant oaks grow protects

the entire enclosure. These oaks have grown together and, like tree soldiers, serve as a protective wall. It is as if one had placed a rare jewel in a multiple setting; the dike surrounds the canal, the canal the path, the path the grass, the grass the house, and the house the courtyard. It is like a small fortress whose peaceful bulwarks are oaks, levees, and water![1]

Many Germans suffered economic privation as a result of the continental blockade that Napoleon imposed on trade with England beginning in 1806. But even before that, goods were embargoed and trade with France restricted by Prussia. In 1804 the Emmerich magistrate wrote the government the following:

> One of the main reasons for the local lack of food is the embargo on all trade with the other side of the Rhine as a result of French trade laws. Nothing would be more desirable for our town than the reestablishment of free trade with the left side of the Rhine and the lifting of French bans on certain wares as well as the lowering of the high import tariffs on banned goods. . . . There used to be manufacturers of woolen socks here in Emmerich who were able to sell their goods in Holland and the Brabant. Manufacturers have become impoverished ever since France-Holland levied exorbitant taxes on the import of these manufactured goods. It used to be that subjects on the other side of the Rhine bought their consumer goods in this town, thereby promoting the local economy and the sovereign's taxes. However, since this trade has been forbidden by the French trade laws, this contribution has ceased.[2]

These vicissitudes in the local economy do not seem to have affected Goossens very much. Then as later, his ledger books hint at a rather more than adequate lifestyle. After losing his position in 1811, he attended balls, entertained, enjoyed good food and wine (which he bought by the cask), hunted, and bought tapestries and statues for his estate. He was also well connected to the local power structure; in a ledger entry, he noted, "On my 11-day trip to Münster with Herr Lebrun, the tax receiver, along with 2 horses and a servant, I spent 400 francs for food and 60 francs per day for transportation."

The now ex-Provost seems to have been very devoted to his "wards." They were given a full education. All three children took music, dance, and drawing lessons; the expenditures were duly entered into his ledger.

The Two Brothers

Aside from the Provost's ledger, records and accounts that have come down to us give very few clues about the upbringing of the children. This is particularly true of Anton. What we do know is that Anton seems to have been an indifferent student; his father enrolled him in several schools in an attempt to find the right place for him. As he grew older, Anton gained such a reputation for irresponsibility with money that his father kept him on a very tight budget even as a grown man. When he was called up to do military service in Berlin in 1824, his father sent him only small sums, and then only occasionally. This undoubtedly led to a great deal of bitterness. Even after Anton married Naatje Reygers from Doesburg in 1834, Goossens gave money intended for Anton to her.

Despite his financial carelessness, as the eldest son Anton was groomed to inherit Voorthuyzen. In preparation he was sent to agricultural school near Stuttgart, and after military service he took over operation of the farm. Unfortunately, relations between father and son continued to deteriorate. In one letter Goossens accused Anton of physically threatening him and his "aunts." Finally, in 1834, he wrote his son, "We just don't fit together," and suggested that Anton rent a small farm elsewhere; he would support him in this endeavor with 1500 guldens per year. Goossens even went so far as to appoint a farmer to take over Anton's duties at Voorthuyzen. It was during this time that Goossens, who was very ill and would die before the year was out, wrote:

> Your letter of yesterday, which you apparently think suffices for Aunt Truijke and me to forgive you for the persistent and intentional insults you have aimed at us, contains once again the most far-fetched and shameful accusations against Aunt Leijke. They are just as groundless and wicked as the accusations you have been making for some time against me and Aunt Truijke. Aunt Leijke, who has been your chief benefactor from your earliest childhood and even before you and your sister and brother were born, so important to your mother's welfare, you now accuse of trying to cheat you out of your inheritance and honor. You, who have no other clothes on your back nor bread to eat but through my and your two aunts' goodness . . . Pfui Anton, Pfui Anton! Aren't you ashamed in your heart of this indecent ingratitude. . . .

Listen to me, Anton. If we are ever to become good friends, then you must give up once and for all your obstinacy and these baseless notions. You must ask Aunt Leijke for her forgiveness and promise to behave differently toward her. Under these conditions, I will forgive you everything and you may return to the loving arms of him who calls himself a well-meaning friend and caring father.

Apparently realizing just how much was a stake, Anton wrote back:

Dear Father! Where there is love, peace, and harmony, there is heaven ... wouldn't it be advisable to do what we can, since we are in a position to prepare for heaven on earth and have the means at hand. In my opinion, we should set aside our impulses and passions; as a father, I'm sure you will agree. As a son, I ask forgiveness from my father and mother for any misdeeds and as a nephew, I ask the same of Aunt Leijke, my benefactress. With all respect, I call myself your most obedient son Anton van Dreveldt.

This formulaic insincerity would characterize much of Anton's later communication with his brother as well. We should not be surprised that a week later, he could write, "That you have for a long time not treated me as a father should is something only your honor and conscience can tell you." Apart from the glimpse we gain into the bitter struggle between father and son even at the end of the father's life, we can gather from this exchange that Goossens may have finally told his children about their true family identity.

Theodor's early adulthood, which certainly included crises, unfolded very differently, and more is known about it because he was more communicative. In many ways, he was much more representative of rebellious youth coming of age in the new post-Napoleonic Prussia.

After Napoleon's defeat, the diplomats of the major powers met at the Congress of Vienna in 1814 to decide how to put Europe back together. Napoleon had changed Europe forever; the Holy Roman Empire no longer existed and the relationships between the states were unclear. French rule had also spread very dangerous ideas about nationalism and liberal government. The representatives who met in Vienna enshrined the old political realities as much as they could; for example, they reinstalled the Bourbon monarchs in France.

However, the two major German powers, Austria and Prussia, were often in competition. Could a state be created that unified these countries, as many ardent nationalists wanted? Not if Count Clemens Metternich, the Austrian diplomat at Vienna, could help it. "I hope with the help of God to strike down the German revolution, as I have defeated the Conqueror of Europe," was the somewhat overblown way he put it.[1] He understood that because Austria (i.e., the Hapsburg monarchy) comprised a number of nationalities it could be blown apart by the forces of nationalism. In addition, neither the other German representatives of the aristocracy nor the Prussian king wanted to give up their particular powers to any central government. The idea of popular democratic rule by an elected parliament was not even worth considering. In the end, the Treaty of Vienna (1815) created a German Confederation, a loose alliance of thirty-nine sovereign states. Prussia (minus Prussian Poland and East Prussia) and Austria (minus its non-German areas such as Hungary and Croatia) were the most powerful German states in the confederation.

The ideals of liberal democracy had no place here; bureaucracy and authority were the order of the day. This was particularly galling to university students, many of whom had heeded the call to drive Napoleon out of Germany. Interestingly, it was the French model of nationalism that fueled their opposition to Napoleon. In 1815 students in Jena formed the first of the *Burschenschafts,* student unions or fraternities with an openly political agenda. The students who joined were a very mixed group. Some believed intensely in the idea of the *Volk* or were so rigid in their interpretation of Christianity that they excluded Jews and others not considered German.[2] While demanding liberty for themselves, they had little problem denying it to others. Nevertheless, when the anti-Jewish Hep! Hep! riots broke out in 1819, students in Würzburg and Frankfurt tended to side with the beleaguered Jews, believing that all who lived in Germany should have civil rights, a very un-*Volkisch* idea. These destructive riots, which stemmed in large part from resentments over economic competition, raged on and off for years.[3]

Many of the students who joined *Burschenschafts* were firmly committed to constitutional democracy. Some believed that only a new beginning along the model of the French revolution could ensure justice for the people; others hoped to work within the monarchical system for change. Love of the fatherland was a common theme. But, above all, as Heinrich von Gagern, a nineteen-year-old student who had fought at Waterloo at age fifteen wrote, "We want a constitution for the nation that conforms to the spirit of the age, to the Enlightenment, not one that each prince gives his people to suit his fancy and serve his private interests."[4]

Such sentiments (and they were not even the most radical) were dangerous; Metternich, King Frederick William III of Prussia, and the other rulers in the confederation had no sympathy for them. Frederick William had promised Prussians a constitution, but he had no intention of implementing one: "It is I who shall determine at what time the promised constitutional representation will be granted. . . . It is the duty of the subjects to await patiently the moment that I shall find opportune."[5] Under such circumstances, they could wait a very long time.

In 1819, using the murder of the playwright August von Kotzebue by a *Burschenschaft* member as a pretext, the government issued the Carlsbad Decrees in an attempt to suppress the *Burschenschafts*. They mandated that the *Burschenschafts* be dissolved and provided for prior censorship of newspapers, pamphlets, and other publications.[6] These sweeping laws forced at least some of the *Burschenschafts* to turn into secret political societies. The severity of repression often depended on the political leanings of the university trustee. In general, these decrees crippled political discourse within Germany, making reasonable new solutions to social problems nearly impossible to voice.

In addition to the students in the *Burschenschafts,* some professors became increasingly radicalized, often leading to their dismissal. These dismissals fed student discontent. Although the student movement did not change much in Prussia, many of the future leaders of the March Revolution of 1848 came out of the *Burschenschafts.* For example, von Gagern played an important role in the political ferment that preceded the revolution and in 1849 was elected president of the National Assembly in Frankfurt, a body that hoped to frame a constitution for Germany.

There were other sources of discontent as well. In June 1830 the French middle classes once again overthrew the Bourbon monarchy. The effects of this revolt were almost immediately felt in Germany. Riots broke out in a number of towns; in Brunswick the duke's castle was burned and he was forced to flee. Demonstrations were organized in many German cities in support of a revolt by the Poles against Russian rule; Germans sang the "Marseillaise" and chanted "Freedom!" Army discipline broke down when soldiers faced popular mobs.

This was the atmosphere in which Theodor began his studies for the law in Bonn in the spring of 1831. He immediately joined a *Burschenschaft*, a forerunner of the Burschenschaft *Alemannia*. It was one of the few *Burschenschafts* still functioning—possibly because the university trustee vouched for its loyalty to the king and the Prussian state. Nevertheless, during the winter semester 1831–32, the academic senate began disciplinary proceedings against the members, probably a reaction to the social unrest in Germany occasioned by the 1830 July Revolution in France. As a result, ten students were permanently expelled and six, including Theodor, were advised to withdraw in order to spare them expulsion. The report he received upon leaving in September 1832 stated:

> As a result of his participation in a banned organization, namely a student union, although without political tendencies, he has been turned over to us and as of 30 June received the *consilium abeundi* [advisement to withdraw] as punishment. However, he may continue here until the end of this semester. . . . It should be noted with regard to his behavior that he received a warning for disturbing the peace at night. Other than that, nothing has been found that would be to his detriment. He was investigated concerning destruction to a local resident's house but was cleared by a competent court.[7]

Burschenschaft members were not only involved in politics; drunken rowdiness was a frequent complaint among locals.

That might have been the end of the matter, except for the fact that, unbeknownst to Theodor, a criminal investigation of the *Burschenschaft*'s activities was begun in Berlin. After spending the summer at home in Emmerich hunting and relaxing, Theodor went off to Berlin with the intention of continuing his studies there. At this point the Ministry of Education blocked his path, denying him enrollment, but left open the possibility that "after six months you may be permitted to continue your studies under the condition that you produce credible documentation that your behavior has been impeccable, giving hope that you have attained that level of intellectual maturity that would allow you to recognize the sacredness of vows you made to the authorities."

The very language used by the various Prussian ministries and bureaucracies gives ample evidence of the high-handed paternalism on which they were founded. There is no sense that the individual citizen had meaningful rights to be treated fairly. The official police letter granting Theodor the right to enroll eight months later was just as peremptory:

To the Student of Law
Mr. Theodor van Dreveldt
Here
Krausenstraße 60

Berlin, 3 June 1833

Since the student of law, Mr. Theodor van Dreveldt, age 22, born in Zutphen, has led a life free from reproach during his stay here from 17 November 1832 to the present, his enrollment at this university will be granted upon demand.

Royal Police Commission
Dept. II

Thus, Theodor was able to continue his studies.

He seems to have stayed away from politics while in Berlin and he fulfilled his military obligations by volunteering for the Royal Guards. In 1835, having finished his course of studies, Theodor returned to Emmerich hoping to enter the civil service, but his application to the higher regional court in Hamm for admission to the civil service exam was answered as follows:

Hamm, 13 June 1835

From the enclosed letter from the Ministry of Justice dated the 27th of last month, you can see why your admission to the civil service examination cannot be granted yet.

Royal Regional Higher Court

That letter stated:

Berlin, 27 May 1835

The law candidate van Dreveldt from Emmerich, whose application for admission to the civil service examination dated the 22nd of last month, was a member of the *Burschenschaft* in Bonn that was investigated for disciplinary action in 1832. At the behest of the Appeals Court in Berlin, and with the highest authorization, these proceedings have been reinstated.

His admission to the examination may not be granted at this time but must await the outcome of these ongoing investigations.

The documents he submitted are enclosed.

Minister of Justice

By the time this news arrived in Emmerich, Theodor was already in prison. In spite of the fact that his membership was three years past, he had apparently led an exemplary life according to Prussian documentation, and he had even fulfilled his military duties, Theodor was placed in investigative detention at the citadel in Wesel, where he would languish for a full five months.

Not long after being released from the citadel, Theodor received word that he was to report for military maneuvers. He composed the following reply:

Emmerich, 6 August 1836

Most Esteemed
Chief Justice of the Higher Court
Istrich, Esq.
Berlin

I am overcome by a sense of melancholy when I think back on the unpleasant days I spent in Wesel. However, it is with joy that I recall those few happy moments which were granted me out of your humanity since you brought to bear on my case everything that was consistent with the law and your duty so that my heavy burdens would be lightened and I would be treated with compassion. In grateful recognition of this, I am convinced that you will listen to me now.

The letter went on to ask how he could be denied admittance to the civil service exam while being expected to appear for muster.

Just two days before he sent the letter, the Supreme Court in Berlin handed down sentences to the members of the Bonn *Burschenschaft* ranging from a terrifying "aggravated death penalty by means of the wheel from above" for the identified ringleader, K. H. Brueggemann, to prison terms ranging from six months to life for other members. Three members were sentenced to the "normal" death penalty "by means of the axe." A prisoner who was "broken on the wheel" was stretched out on a scaffold, often a wheel, whereupon the executioner smashed his bones with a heavy cartwheel until he was dead. There is no evidence that the authorities intended to execute any of the students. It is probable that this option was waved in front of the members to frighten them into submission and make them more pliant. Eventually all the sentences were reduced. Brueggemann's sentence, for example, was commuted to life in prison; Theodor received a three-year sentence.

Naturally Theodor instructed his lawyer to find any loophole that might be grounds for clemency. His lawyer's reply shows the workings of the court system:

> I take this opportunity to answer your letter. Unfortunately it is not possible for me to give you copies of your confederates' statements relating to your participation in the Bonn *Burschenschaft*. In spite of the fact that I spent an entire day just reading their testimony, I can only pass on a few notes to the effect that those who participated in the *Burschenschaft* up to Easter 1829 were not punished at all. Furthermore, those who had the status of *renommee* [nominal member, follower] also evaded punishment, nor were those punished who were in the inner circle of the association at the time of the disciplinary judgment of 7 July 1832. By the way, these exemptions are not based on the opinions of the court but rather come directly from his Royal Majesty and also from the ministerial commission. It is assumed that none of these exemptions apply to you:
>
> 1. because there is a well-founded suspicion that you belonged to the inner circle of the *Burschenschaft* even after the disciplinary judgment, and
>
> 2. because you were a member of the inner circle even before the disciplinary investigation, but were punished only as a *renommee*.
>
> You are now attempting to remove this suspicion. However, stating that your confession was the result of rough treatment by your inquisitors will not work because you never confessed to being in the inner circle but rather that you participated as a *renommee,* and so you were not punished.

The lawyer then went down the list of people who Theodor had hoped might provide testimony that he was not in the inner circle. Each of these members stated that he and his friends Arntz and Degenhardt were not only part of the inner circle, but served on the governing board as well. This evidence may well have been extracted with the wheel as a backdrop. Each of these members received six years. He then concluded:

> Therefore, I can give you no better advice than to declare yourself at peace with the decision . . . because I fear that intractability on

your part will deny you a merciful Royal clemency which many of those who are in your position have already received. I know that many who received six years got their sentences reduced to one; many with three years reduced to 6 months. In fact, the king sitting in cabinet has ordered that the punishments not be enforced in many cases. You must seek clemency immediately from His Majesty the King and at the same time ask that you be granted admission to the civil service examination.

Everything depended on the pleasure of the king. When German social critics of the period talked about the need for democratic reforms and a constitution, this arbitrary legal process is precisely the sort of problem they had in mind; punishments need not fit the crime and simple expressions of political belief could themselves become crimes. It must have cost Theodor quite some effort to force his fingers to form the following words:

Emmerich, 9 August 1837

The law candidate Theodor van Dreveldt of Emmerich most humbly requests merciful release from the punishment that has been pronounced.

Most serene King, most gracious King and Master.

Your Royal Majesty, in Your infinite mercy and gentleness You have already graciously bestowed Your mercy and pardon upon many young people who recently belonged to a banned association, thereby arousing Your justifiable displeasure.

The humble undersigned has also been sentenced to three years imprisonment and costs by the Royal Court for participation in banned associations which were active at the University of Bonn in 1831-32.

Trusting in Your Royal Majesty's infinite mercy, he ventures to approach Your Royal Majesty out of deepest reverence with a request:

Might Your Majesty be moved to extend to the undersigned the supreme mercy and forbearance which many others who were punished for the same crime have enjoyed.

When I was 21, I entered the University of Bonn in 1831. Only youthful folly and recklessness allowed me to fall into the company of the youths who have now also been punished for their illegal associations. Only later did I recognize my error which my

24

youthful recklessness did not allow me to see and which I now deeply regret.

I lost my parents during my early childhood; at a most tender age I was forced to attend school far from home and without parental supervision. Under such circumstances youthful folly caused me to make a few false steps without considering the consequences. They may be ascribed to youthful thoughtlessness. I now deeply regret this thoughtlessness, which has had unbelievable consequences for me. Nevertheless, I trust in Your Royal Majesty's infinite mercy and most humbly request that You might extend Your mercy and strike down the punishment pronounced against me so that the terrible consequences of my youthful folly thereby not endanger my existence.

I solemnly swear that I will always endeavor to prove myself Your Royal Majesty's most humble servant.

Theodor van Dreveldt

What Theodor's letter lacked in content it certainly made up for in attitude, and attitude was everything. Apparently His Royal Majesty Frederick William III was well pleased by his young subject's ritual act of submission: his sentence was reduced to six months and, once completed, he could indeed reapply for the civil service examination. This detention, again in the fortress in Wesel, was also much less harsh than his previous five-month investigative detention. He was occasionally permitted to go out into the town and he even managed to "get into trouble" with a burgher's maid. Nonetheless, he would never forget and never forgive his imprisonment.

By the time of his release, Theodor no longer wanted to work for the government; he probably had no idea what he wanted to do. Although life in Emmerich was easy, consisting of boozy hunting outings with his brother and friends as well as occasional administrative duties, things were not well on Voorthuyzen. Anton ran the farm poorly and did not get along with the aunts, who had been left the provostry in town as well as usage rights to Voorthuyzen when the Provost died. Theodor constantly had to mediate. In addition, Anton drank very heavily and his wife Naatje began to have severe emotional difficulties. As a result, their young children Bernhard and Hubert were badly neglected. Theodor also received frequent calls to military exercises, which he tried—often successfully—to evade by claiming medical disabilities.

Perhaps inspired by the travel books in his father's library, Theodor decided to get away for a while. But a young man in Prussia could barely stretch his legs without a permit to do so; he requested a permit from his regiment to travel. The permit read as follows:

10 August 1839

Landwehr Infantryman 1st Class Theodor van Dreveldt from Emmerich has stated that he would like to travel outside the country for a year. This has been certified by the military authorities and permission to travel is hereby granted.

The Major and Commander
of the 1st Wesel Battalion,
17th Landwehr Regiment

Shortly thereafter Aunt Leijke died, and in the early summer of 1840, his mother, Aunt Truijke, died as well. We do not know how he or Anton took these deaths.

In August of 1840 Theodor traveled through Belgium, his first trip outside Germany. After another missed muster, Theodor made a decision to change course and study in Paris. Having arrived there, he sent the following letter to the Prussian government in Düsseldorf:

Paris, 7 June 1841

The Most Praiseworthy
Royal Government in Düsseldorf

Application for a 6-year passport by Theodor van Dreveldt

Because I have been blocked in my legal career by investigations into my association with the *Burschenschaft* in Bonn, I have decided to take up forestry and agriculture. In order to pursue my education, I will be living outside the country for several years, and I therefore request that the Most Praiseworthy Royal Government grant me an emigration passport for six years. Should this not be possible, I would feel it necessary to request a permanent one.

Your most humble
Theodor van Dreveldt

This is the letter of a young man who has begun to take his life into his own hands. The fact that this request was written from Paris (although drafted in Emmerich) and contains an ultimatum tells us that he no longer cared what the government thought or did. He was denied an emigration passport.

During his stay in Paris the fault line between himself and Anton became more evident. Theodor sent his brother spirited letters bubbling over with details about his experiences in France, about architecture, about agriculture. Perhaps out of resentment that his younger brother had always been the favorite son or because his own joy at living was being blunted by alcohol, Anton rarely answered, and his letters showed nothing. In the winter of 1841, Theodor wrote:

> I have often brooded over the reason why you don't write and don't answer my questions. I left you feeling only brotherly friendship, and I know of no reason why you might be angry with me. I can't imagine that your silence is purposeful, but of course, only you know the reason. Is it procrastination? Perhaps you failed to answer and then got the annoying thought that you should write. Of course, that would make you all the more resistant to writing the longer you failed to do so. But I think that you would not lull your conscience to sleep if you thought about Aunt Truijke and how on her death bed she placed your, Annette's, and my hands together. The good woman could no longer speak, otherwise she would surely have said that she wouldn't tolerate any enmity between us. We must stick together, as she expressed it symbolically. We are not living up to her final wishes if we become indifferent and treat each other as we would a common stranger. She wanted us to stick together, and we promised her as much; at least I did. That is why I keep writing to you even though you pull back and haven't answered most of my letters. I want to see to it that even the slightest grounds for disunity between us are removed.

This letter tells us a great deal about Theodor. He was communicative, warm, very direct, and full of good sense. Already during his student days in Berlin, when Anton and his father exchanged vitriolic and accusing letters, Theodor defended his brother and offered to mediate between the two. It seems that although or because he grew up in a family that could not call itself that, Theodor, who was his father's favorite child, developed a strong sense of family and familial duty. However, these same circumstances appear to have engendered a deep sense of personal shame in his brother. Many of Anton's actions can perhaps best be seen as ways of responding to or recreating shame. Of course, there is no easy explanation for why one brother reacted to circumstances or trauma in one way and became a rock whom family and friends turned to and the other became a man who could only disappoint. Theodor's letter may have unwittingly played into his brother's shame, making communication even more difficult.

Theodor stayed in France for more than a year, studying and traveling. When he again wrote the authorities in Berlin to renew his passport, he was turned down because he had missed military exercises. He was called upon to justify his absence. Theodor thereupon went to the mayor's office in Marseille, the town he was passing through, and on 23 August 1842 was granted a provisional French passport. In the fall of 1842 Theodor briefly returned to Voorthuyzen. In the spring he left for London. There he made final plans to emigrate:

London, 12 Cecil St.

10 July 1843

Most Serene and Mighty King and Master,

In the year 1831 I studied in Bonn and participated in the *Burschenschaft* there, for which I was held in investigative detention in Wesel and where I was again incarcerated in 1837. As a result of these happenstances which halted my career, I intend to emigrate to America. However, in accordance with the law of 31 December 1832, my request has been turned down by the most praiseworthy military authorities in Wesel because although I served voluntarily in Berlin in 1841, I missed a 14-day exercise. I was away on a trip when the notice arrived. As a result, the most praiseworthy governmental authorities demand that I return and answer for my absence and possibly make up an exercise.

Since this would cost me more time and money, I humbly venture to request that Your Majesty extend His grace and consent to my emigration. Others who fled to Belgium and America during the period of demagogic investigation felt Your Majesty's grace without punishment nor the requirement of military service.

Your Majesty's most humble servant,

Theodor van Dreveldt

The Ministry of the Interior replied that Theodor would have to return and justify his absence before the consent would be given. And this he did.

Emigration

You will have received my answer to your letter from London. I'm hurrying to answer your last letter so that it gets to you in time. I was very happy to hear that your decision to come across to the New World will be realized. I have always believed that you do not belong in the Old World. I won't write anything about life here since you have already read my letters and you know enough about it anyway. I can hardly wait to call out my welcome to you here in the forests. However, test yourself to make sure that you really are a republican and a democrat and will be able to leave at home any aristocratic notions by whatever name they are called, whether birth, wealth, or education. That alone is necessary for happiness here. I have to tell you that I am completely happy and satisfied and that I never felt such pride in myself as now that I am a free farmer on my own land. You will also experience this and you should think of your entire earlier life as a child's game not worth playing into maturity.[1]

That was how his friend from university days, Gerhard Lensing, living in Hermann, Missouri, answered Theodor's request from London for information in 1844. Lensing also told him that it was extremely difficult for a European to make it in the United States without monetary support from the Old Country, so when Theodor returned to Germany to straighten out his military affairs, he signed over his property rights to Anton, who in turn agreed to send him money regularly. Because of his financial agreement with Anton, Theodor could have every expectation that his emigration would be a success. This sense of certainty would not have been shared by most Germans who emigrated to the United States in the early to mid–nineteenth century, most of whom were poor farmers.

The first wave of emigration from Germany occurred after the cold summer of 1816 when crop failure resulted in near starvation in southwestern Germany. Small farmers were desperate and all too often responded to tales spun by professional agents and others about the free land and easy money to be made in America. Many sold their properties at fire-sale prices to raise the fare down the Rhine to Amsterdam, where they had been promised that free passage across the Atlantic awaited them. Once in Holland, many realized their error; they were now stuck there, having had to renounce their German citizenship in order to emigrate, and their money soon ran out. They often languished in Rotterdam or Amsterdam. During this early period of emigration many became indentured servants in exchange for the passage.

Some managed to get back to what had been home, but they now had nothing and created additional pressure on their already cash-strapped towns, which they asked to support them. People with no place to go roamed the countryside and caused disturbances throughout the lower Rhine region. Once the continental blockade was lifted, the European market was opened up to cheap British manufactured goods, especially textiles, with the effect that manufacturing wages plummeted. By 1817 wages in Cleves, for example, had dropped to less than half of what they had been in 1815, creating great hardship and dislocation. The situation became so acute that officials in Cleves had certain roads declared *Wanderstrassen,* roads that nonnatives were not permitted to leave. And, in May of 1817, the entire Lower Rhine Province was closed to all emigrants from other regions who could not prove that they had the financial means to emigrate. This period of emigration ended with the bountiful harvests of 1817, but the bad memories of failed attempts to emigrate made people very cautious about setting out for many years.[2]

In northwestern Germany, most people involved in agriculture farmed on a small scale. Political reforms enacted after the Treaty of Vienna that freed the peasantry and gave them some rights were rolled back. Landless peasants often rented small plots from a landed peasant and had to give their landlord a percentage of their crops as well as pay rent. Even in the best of years, farming these small plots could only offer these tenant farmers a marginal existence. Most peasant families depended on cottage industries, such as linen weaving, to supplement their income.[3]

However, during the 1820s and 1830s, the effects of the Industrial Revolution began to be felt as mass-produced British textiles flooded the market and Germany began to build up its industries as well. As inexpensive cotton goods became more popular, the market for hand-woven linen collapsed. A fair number of farmers displaced by this process in the 1830s emigrated no further than to nearby cities to sell their services as laborers in the new factories. The collapse of cottage industries and the dislocations caused by industrialization combined with the often heavy-handed policies of king, aristocracy, and landed classes caused sporadic violent revolts. People had to pay taxes to support the royal court and their sons were taken into the military just as they grew strong enough to be a significant help on the farm. When they returned from war, these young men were often physically or emotionally broken. Thus, when crops failed or could not be harvested, farmers often held the king responsible. In this sense the peasantry and farmers, like the students, became politicized, even though many of them probably had little knowledge of abstract concepts such as "democracy" or "constitutional government."

At the same time, stories that reached Germany about America, most notably the *Report on a Journey to the Western States of North America and a Stay of Several Years along the Missouri,* published in German by Gottfried Duden in 1829, focused a great deal of fresh attention on the New World. Duden believed that the abundance of America would have a revivifying effect on Germans and ensure democracy. He saw America as a cure for what was ailing Germans and hoped that enough of them would come over to form a new fatherland. He came close to portraying Missouri as a land of milk and honey where crops were assured on cheap acreage and where winters were so mild that cattle could graze all year long. There may have been a few winters like that (Duden stayed in America from 1824 to 1827), but he certainly downplayed the considerable hardships facing new settlers. His descriptions have a lyrical quality that make America sound like the new Eden:

> The path from the house to the spring is shaded by tall oak, ash, walnut, and sassafras trees. The beautiful foliage of the white walnut trees bends the branches almost to the ground from a considerable height as is the case with weeping willows. In front of the hut, as I must call the place, a porch has been built. A few paces away, melons, cucumbers, and other kitchen plants thrive in a small garden.[4]

For Germans cramped into small plots and with hardly any place to move, Duden's musings about the land would have seemed near-miraculous:

> It is extremely alluring to settle down in regions where one has such complete freedom of choice; where one, map in hand, can roam through beautiful nature of hundreds of miles in order to select land and its cover of woods and meadows according to

31

one's own desires. Here attractive qualities are united with useful ones. Settling next to charming hills, near never-failing springs, on banks of small rivers near their junction with large rivers, all depends entirely on the option of the settler without taking the price into consideration.[5]

With such a promise of "complete freedom," a reader might well not heed the caveats:

> The basis for all the complaints about an unhealthy climate is almost entirely due to the situation of the dwellings in wooded river valleys (bottoms) and along swamps. If one constructs one's buildings on hills, far from swamps, one will be affected by the climate here as little as in Germany. And this procedure does not exclude one from utilizing the fertile soil of the valley plains. In no city in Germany can one lead a more healthful life than in St. Louis on the Mississippi because it is surrounded by several miles of open country. Also in St. Charles on the Missouri one seldom hears of diseases.[6]

The primary disease was malaria, an illness endemic to the Missouri bottomlands with which Theodor would become well acquainted. Duden described the pestilence of mosquitoes in both the previous and next paragraphs, but, of course, never made a connection between the two because according to prevailing medical theory, malaria was caused by bad air from the swamps. The true cause was not discovered until the end of the century.

Duden's vision of America presumed an influx of people of means. He estimated that a family would need a minimum of 800 to 1000 thalers to be successful. Duden himself received funds from Europe that allowed him to hire workers to cultivate the land, build buildings, and even do housework for him while he contemplated the splendors of the frontier. As he noted, "a porch has been built"; it is unlikely that he did the work himself. He paid both black and white field workers $12 to $14 per month—a considerable sum.

Germans who made the journey found vast uncleared forests, swamps, back-breaking work, and loneliness. Many gave up their dream of working their own farm and drifted to St. Louis to look for work or they returned to Germany. Criticism of the book mounted. In 1837 Duden felt constrained to write a counter-article, "Self-Accusation

Concerning His Travel Report, to Warn against Further Rash Emigration," the main point of which was that people did not take his advice and came unprepared. Despite the criticism, his *Report* continued to be widely discussed and acted on. It is almost certain that Theodor was familiar with it because he mentioned Duden by name several times in his letters from Missouri and seemed to copy Duden's style in places.

In his letter to Theodor, Lensing mentioned some rather large sums of money:

> Your capital is more than sufficient if it is handled in such a way that it lays the basis for valuable land holdings, namely about 10,000 thalers for 500 acres of the best land at about $10 per acre. Of this, an adequate amount of land will be cultivated to count on $800 income in the first year, assuming that you have two workers, two Negroes à $600 or a Negro family for $1000. Unless you prefer to work with whites. The good land in Missouri and in the United States in general is all bought up and can only be gotten second hand at between $1.25–12 per acre. Of course, the state sells a great deal of less fertile land at $1.25, but it is actually more expensive than land in the Missouri valley going for $10.

A thaler was worth slightly less than a dollar, and wages in northwestern Germany were extremely low. Male farm hands could bring in between 1 and 2 thalers per month; a chief farm hand might earn 30 thalers per year. A farm hand (*Heuerling*) renting from a landed peasant hardly earned more: 2 to 3 thalers per month for this seasonal work.[7] In the United States, letters reported, a skilled farm hand could earn 100 to 120 thalers per year. Still, passage to America cost about 30 thalers per person just for the ocean voyage. Lensing estimated that the cost from New York to Hermann would come to another $25. Still, Germans found ways to make the journey. Because land prices were so high and the plots tiny and fragmented in Germany, those who had a small plot could sell it at a price that might give them the boat fare. Those who had nothing but their hands to sell rarely emigrated. If they did, they were often forced to give themselves into indentured servitude for several years.

Even facing the prospect of indentured servitude, thousands attempted the trip with less than adequate means, and as more people were put out of work by industrial dislocation or crop failures, neither the Prussian nor local governments could come up with an adequate or unified response. In some towns, local governments decided to pay the boat fare of unemployed residents rather than have them begging on the streets, or worse, turning to banditry. In a few cases, local governments attempted to send convicted criminals to America so that they would not have the burden of caring for them.

At the same time, while Prussia never forbade emigration outright, it did try to discourage it by distributing accounts of negative experiences, among other methods. For example, in June 1833 the *Oldenburgische Blätter* printed a series of three articles ostensibly written by "a gentleman of education and experience" living in Pittsburgh, but quite possibly reflecting the heavy hand of a bureaucrat. The series was titled "Concerning the Sapping of Physical and Spiritual Vigor in America" and went on at length about American wood, which gave off little heat when burned, wildlife that was consistently smaller and less savory than European varieties, and horses that lacked energy. "The American," he declared, "is phlegmatic by temperament. He is completely apathetic; his intellectual powers are limited, and his moral values are nonexistent."[8] However, the credibility of the government was so low that this and other policies backfired. But there was little else that Prussia could do, because the emigrants were being recruited and organized by agents in small groups inside and outside its territory and because the free port cities of Hamburg and Bremen were not under its control.

Initially the main ports of exit were the Dutch ports of Amsterdam and Rotterdam, but starting in the 1830s, Hamburg and particularly Bremen vied for the lucrative emigration market as well. Boats full of human cargo sailed down the Weser River to Bremen and returned home with merchandise for sale.

Emigration tore people from their families and homes. No wonder that an article in the 9 December 1816 edition of the *Allgemeine Zeitung* in Augsburg called it "a sort of suicide, for it divides us from all that gives value to civilized existence." And so, it is also no wonder that emigrants did whatever they could to stay in touch with loved ones at home by sending letters in which they described, much as Lensing had, the land they were now inhabiting. Germans in America were particularly zealous letter writers, sending from 75 to 100 million letters between 1820 and 1869.[9]

The arrival of a letter from America was a major social event; friends and relatives would travel for hours to read the news. Discussion and argument would continue at home, on the road, even in chance encounters with strangers. In this way, the writer's new home and surroundings became associated with emigration, with the result that family, friends, and neighbors often chose the same destination when they decided to leave. Occasionally an entire village would pick up and resettle in America. The Prussian government considered these letters so dangerous and subversive of population stability that in 1836 the Ministry of Interior and Police ordered that letters arriving from America be given special scrutiny. Many letters were simply confiscated, something that Theodor, Anton, and, later, Anton's son Bernhard complained about bitterly when their letters home did not arrive. Both Theodor and Bernhard became so incensed that they asked their families to open a postal box across the border in Holland so that the "Prussian postal spies" could not get ahold of them.

Theodor's circumstances and view of the world were rather different from those of most Germans. On the other hand, he fit Duden's profile of the successful emigrant. There were quite a few others like him, university-trained young people of means who emigrated for political, philosophical, or personal reasons. Duden preached the need for collective action, and as early as the 1830s a group of politically active young men led by Paul Follenius and Friedrich Münch, who had read Duden's *Report,* formed the Giessen Society with the intent of recruiting like-minded emigrants to form a German community in Missouri. About five hundred members arrived in America in 1834, but they split up soon after reaching St. Louis. Few of the members were real farmers and they had neither the skills nor physical stamina to make a life in the wilderness. The lucky ones found other occupations, but a significant number died in abject poverty or committed suicide. Münch, who went through very difficult times on his 160 acres near Duden's old farmstead, finally succeeded and also became an influential journalist and spiritual and intellectual leader of the burgeoning German community. But none of these societies were successful as a group. In some ways, Theodor would recapitulate their experience.

In his letter, Lensing wrote, "You will see your friend Degenhardt in St. Louis working for the post office." Rather than serve time for involvement in the Bonn *Burschenschaft,* Lorenz Degenhardt fled Germany around 1836.

Before Theodor's departure, he and Anton settled accounts. Theodor signed over his inheritance from the Provost to Anton for a total of 46,000 thalers, payable over six years at 4 percent interest. Anton gave him 2000 thalers for the trip with the promise to send 10,000, the sum mentioned in Lensing's letter, "as soon as possible." In addition, Theodor retained first mortgage on the property. With these assurances, he felt confident of success.

Theodor turned his back on the fatherland and his father's land on 9 December 1844. Instead of sailing to New York, he and Wilhelm Noot, a boyhood friend who emigrated with him, decided to sail to New Orleans. The Mississippi, America's Rhine, would lead them to Lensing's homestead.

Theodor in America

The French Revolution and the Napoleonic Wars, which turned Germany on its head and gave the Provost the opportunity of a lifetime, also had profound repercussions in the New World. The land that Theodor attempted to settle in 1845 was marked by those events.

The Peace of Paris in 1783 ended hostilities between England and its rebellious colonies in the New World. By the terms of the treaty, the thirteen colonies became independent. The United States' western border was set at the Mississippi River and its southern border at the thirty-first parallel, Florida's northern boundary; the territory west of the Mississippi and south of the thirty-first was controlled by Spain.

Although the Mississippi River was a remote part of the United States at the time, farmers west of the Alleghenies shipped their produce down the river to the Spanish port of New Orleans. The Spanish agreed in 1795 to give Americans the "right of deposit" in the port, that is, the right to store export goods duty free. As a result, river traffic by flatboat, keelboat, and barge increased dramatically, promoting settlement in the interior of the continent.[1]

This arrangement was acceptable in part because Spain was a relatively weak and overextended country that had been at war with revolutionary France since 1793. In all probability, if Spain had closed the Mississippi to American ships, traders, and farmers, the United States would have had little difficulty seizing New Orleans. However, the United States was not yet prepared to take on more territory.

In 1801 newly elected President Thomas Jefferson got word that Spain was about to cede Louisiana to Napoleon and the French. La Nouvelle Orléans had been founded by the French in 1718, but it had already changed hands several times by the American Revolution. Although the Spanish had founded several settlements up the Mississippi in what was called Upper Louisiana, of which present-day Missouri is a part, they were unsuccessful in administering the territory. Because they were so overextended, they severely undercapitalized their projects. They also realized, after several attempts, that a land link between the Mississippi and their holdings in Mexico and New Mexico would be extremely difficult to maintain.

A French presence in North America would pose a threat to the United States, which was well aware of Napoleon's imperial ambitions and record as a general in the field. Fears arose that Napoleon would block access to the Mississippi or at the very least impose unacceptably high tariffs on goods flowing through the port. Worse than that, the new country feared it might not withstand a military assault. Jefferson hoped for an outbreak of war between France and England to distract France from its North American land deal with Spain. So intense was the fear in the United States that the young country planned to ally itself with its former colonial master against Napoleon, and this in spite of overwhelming sympathy for the French Revolution.[2]

In 1802 France planned to send troops to Louisiana to take possession of the territory. This occupation never took place because twenty-four thousand of the forty thousand French troops who first retook the island of Santo Domingo were killed by yellow fever.[3] This debacle and the prospect of war with England convinced Napoleon to sell France's Louisiana territories to the United States in 1803 for about $15 million.

Although small numbers settled west of the Appalachians before 1815, mass migration to these frontier areas began after the War of 1812 and particularly after 1815. Population figures tell the story in gross terms:

	1810	*1820*	*1830*
Ohio	231,000	581,000	938,000
Indiana	25,000	147,000	343,000
Illinois	12,000	55,000	157,000
Missouri	20,000	67,000	140,000[4]

Americans poured into the Northwest frontier, settling the land and homesteading farms. Within a very short period, a number of new territories quickly became states: Indiana in 1816, Mississippi in 1817, Illinois in 1818, Alabama in 1819, and Missouri in 1821.

Missouri had applied for admission to the Union in 1819 as a slave state, and the "Missouri Question" was passionately debated in Congress. At the time, the number of "slave" and "free" states was even at eleven each. Not wanting to allow the slave states an advantage in the Senate that would offset the free states' advantage in the House, Representative James Tallmadge of New York introduced an amendment to the statehood bill that "further introduction of slavery or involuntary servitude be prohibited . . . and that all children of slaves, born within the said state . . . shall be free." Southerners understood clearly that this amendment meant the eventual end of slavery in that state. The amendment was defeated and heated debate held up Missouri's petition for more than a year.[5] In the end, a compromise was reached. Maine, which had been a part of Massachusetts, was admitted as a free state in 1820, and shortly thereafter, Missouri as a slave state. In addition, although slavery was legal in Missouri, it would not be legal in any other territories of the Louisiana Purchase north of Missouri's southern boundary, 36°30′.[6]

The Missouri Compromise of 1820 resonated with many German immigrants who, like Theodor, left home in part because of social and political injustice. In one of his early letters, Theodor decried how badly whites treated blacks and Indians, and his nephew Bernhard's letters show that he was sympathetic to abolitionism. As Eduard Mühl, publisher of the *Hermanner Wochenblatt*, would write in 1852, "We hold ourselves as free men who did not escape slavery in our old home lands to support it here in America." Theodor would have agreed.[7]

Unfortunately Theodor's first letter home has been lost. Perhaps it passed through too many hands and never found its way back to the addressee. The mails were also very unreliable, and it is important to realize that letters often took two to three months to arrive. To get an answer to a question or a request could take four to six months. It is clear from the correspondence between Theodor and his family and friends that many letters simply never arrived. And because of the time lag, the correspondents seem to talk past each other; letters would be written before the reply to the previous one was received and were always out of phase.

Theodor's second letter was addressed to Anton:

> Loutre Island Montgomery (Missouri)
> 22 April 1845

Dear brother!

You are getting this letter because tomorrow is mail day, and mail only goes out once a week.

I heard that the Gertzen brothers want to leave Rees [a small town on the lower Rhine] in June and that their brother is waiting for them over here. He seems to think that they could bring a few things over for me, including my dachshund Advocat who was left behind against his will. I told Gertzen that the dog is old and spoiled and might not take well to the trip, so it wouldn't be such a good idea. Check the people out yourself and determine whether you think he could make the trip safely. Then give them the flintlock in a case that can be locked with the key. Paint my full address on it with oil paint, just to be careful. Then pour resin along the seams, and smear the iron parts with tallow and fat. Sea water is corrosive. Furthermore, give him a well-packed tin case of seeds of all sorts. For some reason we forgot sorrel, used to keep one from getting sick from too much meat and warm weather—horseradish—strawberries—seeds—woodruff—broom—jasmine (bush)—clove, and all species of pine, beeches (fagus), asparagus seed, etc., etc. Don't wait, because the people are going to be leaving soon. Ride out to Rees yourself and discuss the matter with your friend Disch.

Don't come to the conclusion that there is no flora here or that the above-mentioned don't grow here. About this, I will write you later, and I will return the favor with a collection of seeds from here. Finally, I ask you for chunks of cork for fishing and twine so that we can make nets ourselves.

On Sunday two weeks ago we wanted to go fishing for the first time, but during the night all the nets, which were hanging in Lensing's kitchen, burned. It was doubly annoying because we were looking forward to it and nets are not to be had around here. That's why the Gertzens' coming is doubly good. The region is not particularly advantageous for sailing because there is too much wood floating in the water. Lensing lost a lot of meat in the fire as well as two saddles; I lost mine as well. The technique of building with wood just is not fireproof. But more on this later. I promise a more detailed account, and will go on chronologically now.

The last time, I wrote about our arrival in New Orleans. This is a city that has grown extremely rapidly. They live and haggle and make deals; everything appears to revolve around making money. The moist climate makes it very unwholesome, which is why the wealthy leave this damp grave during the summer and head north. Those who are thirsty for money stay during the unwholesome months, especially August and September, and make a lot of money. Generally, these people come down with a fever if they aren't native, and then they are bled. Even so, they often die.

On board there were a number of Frenchmen with different professions; a few days after arrival they had all found work at good pay. Germans don't fare nearly as well because French is more common down there than English. One hears Spanish there as well. Life is much more diverse than I have found in other large cities. For example, a meal may cost either a dollar or five cents, the former in what is called a restaurant here, the latter in saloons. The saloons, which are extraordinarily abundant, are patronized heavily from early morning till late at night and are very profitable. From 10 to 12 in the morning and again from 4 to 7 they set out a great selection and quantity of cold and warm meats and vegetables. You order your drink and a special glass is set before you with the bottle and you take as much as you want. Or, the waiter can prepare a mixed drink, of which they know how to concoct an extraordinary number. These wines which have been mixed with herbs, ice, and liqueurs don't cost any more than a simple whiskey, which is generally chased with a good gulp of water. You can eat as much as you want, and the barkeeper likes it better if you eat a lot rather than just sampling this or that. Then you pay five cents, one-twentieth of a dollar. It is the same in the best as in the worst drinking establishments. There are only six to ten where you have to pay ten cents. Now you buy yourself a cigar in a cigar store and pay between five and ten cents for it in this land of tobacco. Then you go to the theater or a ballroom, and generally the admission comes to about a dollar. You can take a hotel room for 24 hours for between $3–4. However, we rented a decent room in a private house for $4 per week.

Before we reached New Orleans, we saw the St. Charles Hotel rising above the city. It is a building something like the Pantheon in Paris; however, it is only an inn. The drinks are served in the rotunda, and business people go there to meet. You will also find information about travel and business tacked on the board. For ten cents, a guest is well fed, and plantation owners and craftsmen go there to satisfy their appetites. The atmosphere is decent and quiet, even though there are no police around to enforce the peace. We walked around the environs of New Orleans for a few days with a rifle, accompanied by a Frenchman; he had an acquaintance in the area who grows vegetables for the city. It is a pleasure to see how things grow here, how the land produces one crop after another. That's why the land is leased on a monthly basis. Everything is flat; the highest and best-known hill near New Orleans, Cypress Hill, is six to ten feet high at most. Once we shot an eagle out of the air with pellets. This was the only game of any interest in the area. We shot a few birds for the feathers, but we ate them that evening. Everything, with the exception of vultures, is tasty. Even though there is hardly any game, one hears shooting throughout the day and night. One amuses oneself by shooting birds, but if the truth be told, we did nab a couple of woodcocks, which are smaller and redder than ours. We also went out several evenings without seeing any at all. When doing this, one person usually carries a plain frying pan and throws a bit of cypress wood on it from time to time. This wood burns very bright, and then the other person follows up closely with a rifle and shoots the woodcocks sleeping in the grass. Another time, we wanted to shoot ducks at dusk; they are abundant here, but they are easier to come by at home. In short, there's not much to hunt. The forest, which mainly consists of cypresses, started to green when we arrived, even though its main color was gray as a result of the moss which covers the trees. The moss is very fine, four to eight feet long and gray. It is used to fill mattresses and is good for encouraging milk production in cows. It is soft and dry, and hunters use it as a plug. It gives the forest a somber quality.

The cypresses were starting to grow; however, brown still dominated the green. I would love to see this forest again. The grasses came up so thick. I saw many new lilacs, but no old ones. I found a wonderful regularly formed magnolia with a diameter of about one and a half feet. Otherwise, the forest is comprised mainly of cypresses that can be four to five feet at their bases and are as swollen with water as trees at home that grow in damp areas. However, they develop strange vertical spikes at their roots measuring one-half to one foot in length, and they make it hard to walk through. My highest water boots came in very handy. Regards to everybody.

Your Theodor

Theodor knew that his letters would be read and reread by family members and friends. They would each follow the stages of the trip along with him and experience vicariously everything he saw. Detail was as important as length. He also had to be certain not to slight anyone, so each letter was addressed to a different person but was a chronological continuation of the previous one. These first letters went out in exactly one-week intervals; as he wrote Anton, "the mail only goes out once a week." His next letter was addressed to his sister Annette and her husband, Wenzel Höynck.

Loutre Island Montgomery, Missouri
30 April 1845

Dear sister and brother-in-law!

In my letter of eight days ago, I left Anton stranded in the swamp near New Orleans. You have probably read the letter, and so I will carry on from there. This flat swampy land did not appeal to me particularly although it was interesting to see. There is a form of fern (if I can call it that), whose botanical name I don't know. The locals call it "latennier" [palmetto], and it is very peculiar. One or more grow up out of the mud to a height of one to two feet. They form thick clumps about one-half to one foot in diameter. Four- to eight-foot sharp, ribbed stalks grow out of these clumps, and culminate in a "fan" consisting of a single leaf which is neatly folded in nature's workshop. Such a fan is in the shape of a half-circle and can have a diameter of three feet. Their stiffness creates an extraordinary murmuring and rushing in the slightest breeze. A single plant alone creates a beautiful green effect and makes up for the somberness of the Spanish moss. Since the livestock don't touch it, the plant always looks strong and healthy. Cows only eat it when its fresh asparagus-like shoots first break the surface of the ground. People use the leaves to make fans.

The cypress, this enormous and almost sole inhabitant of that humus-rich expanse, is a very valuable tree because it can be split so well. Over here every field that is under cultivation is fenced off in order to keep free-roaming cattle away. However, don't be tempted to think that these are fences like the ones surrounding our pastures. You would get a better idea if you think of pig farms, since these delicate little animals are hard to keep out and require dense fencing, which takes a lot of work. The way it is done here is to drive five- to six-foot stakes into the ground with ten-foot nogs thickly set from the bottom to a level of about three feet so that one's fist cannot go through it. Alternately, they set the nogs at the end on top of each other, without stakes, and create a zigzag wall to a height of five to six feet. Over here you see such fencing almost exclusively, especially where there is an abundance of wood. That is why wood that is easy to split is so valuable.

However, Louisiana doesn't possess nearly as much arable land as one would think just looking at a map. Only the land along the shores of the Mississippi, a half to an hour wide, is somewhat higher, and all land lying behind this area is two to three feet lower and therefore unsuitable for plantations because of its wetness.[8] The Dutch would be able to reclaim masses of land here more easily and quickly than at home, and there would be a general improvement in the health of the region as a result.

As I already wrote Anton, we spent a few days with a French farmer. This man, once as healthy as can be, has become sickly and no doubt won't last long. Money is the cause. He can earn his monthly rent in a single day. He goes into town every night at about 1 or 2 o'clock with his vegetable cart. During the day he hardly gets any rest because he has to check on his workers. No human can stand such a life for any length of time. Three times a day we had meat, and a bottle of whiskey stood on the table for all to drink from as they pleased. People often mixed it with water. It is absolutely unimaginable how things grow in gardens here; the richness of the soil and the warm moisture do wonders. But, but, the health problems! In July and August the water is covered with a green slime, and shortly thereafter fever breaks out. The farmer introduced us to a Creole he knew who showed us around.

This man lives a more philosophical life than his neighbors. He has few needs, and the few he has are satisfied by his fields. Instead of earning money, he goes hunting. It is necessary to have a leader, in part because of the bogs, in part because of the creeping, prickly undergrowth, which would all slow us down. Alligators, which are not nearly as terrifying as you might think, were taking their winter naps, and so I unfortunately didn't see any. I missed their hiding place because of an incomplete railroad embankment. This railroad was supposed to link Lake Pontchartrain via a canal with New Orleans. So, the line is laid out straight as an arrow through the bogs and puddles. Lake Pontchartrain is overgrown with reeds very much like those at the mouth of the Mississippi.

In New Orleans it took us a long time to air out the things still good and well preserved.

People are rather uninhibited in the theaters; in the orchestra many people seemed to act along, that is, talk or let their pleasure or displeasure at the goings-on on stage be known openly.

Before I leave New Orleans, I want to mention one more thing. There are beautiful orange hedges in the countryside around the estate houses. Below, there is a fence made of boards or laths, and the orange trees are planted inside and hang with their dense green crown of leaves over the fences so that they are almost invisible. Large full fruit hung down in abundance, and there was more fruit on the ground than is the case with our apple trees. I would love to see and smell them when they are in bloom.

The *Maria,* pronounced "Ma-rye-a" here in good English fashion, was supposed to take us up the Mississippi to St. Louis for $25, but because of low water couldn't get much past the mouth of the Ohio.[9] Then the captain announced that whoever wanted to remain on ship had to pay an extra dollar per day; those who wanted to get off would be refunded money on a pro rata basis. Food is always included in the steamer fare, except for steerage passengers. As luck would have it, we were on an island, and there were five steamers moored near us all with the same problem. Good advice was expensive. Camps, my dog, was happy to be on land again, and we walked through the woods and admired the large trees. The cypresses had disappeared somewhere below the Arkansas River. Sycamores and cottonwoods were the most common sight as well as creeping vines that reached the tops of these giants. The trees didn't have their leaves yet and so I couldn't identify many since different climates make trees grow differently, and their age makes them seem strange.

If a sand bank or island forms as a result of flooding in the previous year (which happens a great deal) then this new land will be covered with cottonwoods the next year. These are so similar to each other that one would almost think they were artificially planted. Such regular plantings along the shores are in contrast to the wild growth everywhere else.

It is about 1200 English miles from New Orleans to the mouth of the Ohio; from there to St. Louis about 200, and another 100 to here. All on the river. This distance took us about two weeks. We left New Orleans on Thursday evening. About 24 hours after passing the Ohio, we were on the island where a small boat took us on for $8. Sunday evening in St. Louis and under way again on

Monday evening for another $5 until we got close to Hermann. On Thursday evening we arrived at G. Lensing's.

The water was extremely low and could only be navigated by very small boats, which accounts for the relatively high price. This thing was so run-down and flimsy that it made the *Maria* look grand by comparison. At night we had to lie close together on the floor, sometimes frying because of the heat from the stove and alternately freezing because of the penetrating wind.

The thought that I might have missed winter this year disappeared completely. The spring coming north from Louisiana was no match for the harsher air of Kentucky, Illinois, and Missouri. One can get tired of traveling. The rest of the baggage cost another $30 from New Orleans. I saw my first hills near Vicksburg, Mississippi, which lies between the Red and Arkansas Rivers. Then they disappeared for a stretch; upriver it became hillier again. However, they are not nearly as impressive as I had thought they would be. There are some rather nice stretches, but the romantic wildness is missing. Our taste may be somewhat spoiled; I'm sure that some would like this region better if the mountains were stripped of their green and here and there the ruins of robbers' dens could be seen on the hilltops. It already looks a thousand times better here than the stretch between Cologne and Emmerich. It could be as nice as above Bingen if more people came and one saw little towns and fields more often, more variety. It will never be the way it is between Koblenz and Bingen, and supposedly there is nothing comparable to Switzerland anywhere in the United States. This is what one hears from people who have seen the east coast. In general, natural beauty is more an expectation than an actuality.

I'm tired of writing this letter, and my eyelids have slid over my eyes more than once. Don't let that annoy you into not writing. Postage here is reckoned by the number of pieces that a letter consists of which is why one uses large sheets of paper and no envelopes.

If the Gertzens have not yet left Rees, then get me a good shovel. Geveling, the smith in Elten, probably makes the best. Don't let him spare the steel, even if it costs three times as much. It doesn't have to be light either.

Regards,
Theodor

Annette had already written Theodor, knowing how important it would be for him to hear the news from home. Her letter also contained a special request:

Emmerich, 25 March 1845

Mr. Theodor van Dreveldt
c/o Mr. Gerhard Lensing
Post Office Loutre Island
County Montgomery
State of Missouri
in North America

Dear Theodor!

Last night the Rhine spilled its banks as far as Viehoff's and sexton van den Borg's house. Fellinger already had a team ready to empty his barn when it receded suddenly. Water has already been standing in his deep cellar for several days. We haven't been spared either; at the moment the waters are rising again. The little mill gate was completely destroyed by ice floes last night. The "Ütterdicksten" near Voorthuyzen was under water yesterday, and the Wätering and Wildbach were rivers today; Anton will let you know more details when he writes.

Just now a large group of people has congregated before our door, people who not an hour ago were sitting quietly in church. Now they cannot get home until long planks are laid out. Hinter dem Hirsch, a part of the market, and the Mühlenberg were clear, and still are, but I can see the Rhine rising quickly right now. We are going to have to clean out our kitchen cellar.

Anton is doing quite a job at Voorthuyzen. The grown trees have been cleared from the garden, and that is where your brother wants to put the nursery. He also wants to build a house on the Springkamp for the farmer since the buildings where Anton is are pretty dilapidated. They are also busy with the new road, as much as the winter would allow. As far as the house on the "Wild" is concerned, I believe the plans are also finished. Our attempts to sell went very badly; much too little was offered for the Eltenberg, for this house, and everything else. The grain prices are just too low, and people are not making a profit on their harvests.

P.S.: Theodor, could you please send me a lock of your hair as soon as possible. Make it as long a lock as possible. Dorchen wants

47

to make us a nice flower bouquet bound with the hair of all our dear family members. I'm sure you can send that in a letter.

Theodor's next letter was to his very good friend, Dr. Franz von Weise, in whom he would eventually confide his troubles and whom he would ask for help:

Montgomery, Missouri
6 May 1845

Dear Doctor!

I enjoyed your note, particularly because it was the first news that I had received about aging Europe from there since 10 December of last year.

You have probably been told of my accommodations here. I will assume that you already know and tell you about other things. So, to the point. In my last letter, I was on the Missouri River. In the Indian language, this is supposed to mean "Father of the Rivers," and so I imagined that in comparison the free, German Rhine would be no more than a newborn baby. The Father of the Rivers in its still state is not as full as our Rhine (or better, your Rhine). Its shores seen from the water are more pleasant to the eye than the flat pastures and low wetlands near Emmerich because it is hilly and therefore not monotonous or uninteresting. Of course, if one takes a longer trip, then it becomes so. But, if one were to spend say eight days or three weeks on the Rhine, wouldn't one become tired of its shores too? One can make the trip from Cologne to Emmerich on the Rhine often and with great interest, but if one were forced to look at cliffs and destroyed or ramshackle houses for three weeks, then one would get sick of this otherwise beautiful stretch.

What is so big about American rivers is not their breadth but their length. You can go hundreds of miles upstream and still not perceive any difference in breadth. I went through many cities whose names are greater than their size, e.g., Napoleon, Memphis, Cairo (pronounced Kee-ro in the English manner), Washington, etc. Generally, one is not prepared for what one will find given the fame of such names. One can hardly believe the size of these little towns until one realizes that only four or six years before, there was dense forest where there are now streets. So then, one no longer expects to see royal palaces and Belgrave Squares.

It's a bad sign that one doesn't see sailing ships on the Father of the Rivers. The reason is that there are parts of the river where the current is too strong. It is also too shallow in parts and a sailing boat just does not have the power of a fuel-driven steamer. The wood that is burned is much less dangerous than the trees that have fallen over and lie in the sand or mud hardly breaking the water line. They can be a real hindrance when going upstream and more than a few small boats have been wrecked on account of them.

We landed across from Hermann, i.e., the boat tentatively approached the shore. Then they put out a gang plank, carried our baggage to shore, and sailed on. We climbed up the steep 12- to 15-foot-high clay and sand bank, looked at the little boat receding, and stood alone in the forest with our bags at water's edge and my dog Camps at my side. I then went off to reconnoiter. Noot stayed with Camps and the baggage. It was about 3 o'clock in the afternoon. First I saw only trees, but then I made out a log cabin. The windows and doors were open, but there was nobody home, not even a dog. There was sand all over and the mud on the walls told me that water had chased away whoever had lived there. I walked farther and saw a taller log cabin in a fenced-in field. I climbed the fence, got to the house, but again found no signs of life. I came upon 4 or five more houses and finally thought that everything must be dead, until I heard a cock crow. Walking toward this sound, I finally came upon a young girl who was so shy that I could hardly get anything out of her about Lensing. I'm sure she was frightened by my beard. A young Negress of 16 to 18 seemed equally scared of me and called for a Negro. I asked him in vain for a cart to transport my baggage, even though I offered money. I promised a reward if he would at least go with me to show me the way, but he turned me down claiming that he was sick.

I was not in the best mood as I went my way. Finally, I heard chopping in the woods, went in that direction and came upon several Negresses who also backed away as I approached. I made up my mind then and there to shave my beard next day. Nearby there were several Negroes and a white man doing the same work. I had no better luck there getting a cart or directions. They pointed me toward another house. Luckily I found it. Here I was provided with a Negro and an oxcart and reached Lensing's in the dark at about 9 o'clock.

You will understand what it was like to meet an old university friend out here in the wilderness; I certainly can't describe it. L. Westhooven from Emmerich has bought a nice farm nearby. However, he is still sick and lives with Lensing. He is very weak and his condition is alarming in view of the fact that his sister died of tuberculosis. Yesterday he did travel to St. Louis to buy various equipment he needs for his land. However, in Hermann, which is about two hours from here on the other side of the river, he almost had a relapse of his fever.

The first night was spent in talk and the next few days were spent getting to know the area and local conditions. You may well wonder why I still don't have a rifle. You often saw me with an axe, a plow, or a shovel. The reason why I haven't been hunting is that there is no game here and secondly because I haven't had any time.

Since I want to get to know the local conditions thoroughly, I need to experience the land myself and get my hands dirty. Lensing didn't have much room, so I built my own house near his in the local style. It is made only of wood, has four walls and a center wall as well as an entry hall. The house is 22 feet long and 18 feet deep. The door is located in the middle of a long wall; the central wall is 8 feet from the east wall. The east side has a window and the northwest side has a six-foot-long fireplace. The lower wooden log on the ground is squared off; the next log is notched and on the upper side is squared off again. The third log is grooved and squared on the top and so on until the desired height is reached. My house has 11 or 12 logs up to the roof.

Many people hew the logs afterward so that they look better and dry out. Then the borers, which eat the wood from the inside, are less of a nuisance. But I think it is nicer and more American with the inner bark, but I don't think I'm going to live like that for long. Anyway, such a house has advantages in the summer if it is not completely tight because it is much cooler as a result of drafts. The chinks in the wood that occur naturally as a result of slight curvature of the wood are plugged with small wood chips and then sealed with mud or clay on the outside. In the hewn ones, this is done on the inside with lime and the whole wall is whitewashed. It then looks like one of your white walls. Many houses here have no windows but two doors on opposite ends. In the smaller room in my house, there are 4 poles along the wall running from north to south. This is where the 2 beds are. The poles are connected with a hickory-walnut raffia which is as tough as leather, and Noot and I place our beds on these. It's nice and airy. The roof is made of clapboard, which are boards about 4 feet long, 6 to 8 inches wide, and ½ to 1½ inches thick (as available). The better houses have shingles that are made more regular and produce a more regular roof. A house such as I have described could be built for $30–35. The floor is usually made of flattened logs, but these were too rough and so I used pine boards.

Over here a house is put up in a single day. Four men stand at the corners and hew the logs. This is no light work and requires a strong and practiced hand. There are not many who know how to do it. Neighbors help each other with such tasks at no charge. About 15 to 20 men are needed to frame a house. Doors, windows, and chimney are set in later. Such house construction is always half feast; when William of Hohenzollern appoints a mayor, there is always a big feast for the servants.

It took me a long time to plant, but I don't want to get into this now if this letter is to get off tomorrow. But, it was part of the reason I didn't write you earlier.

There are many grouse here, but they are no larger than our quail. Hares are larger than our rabbits. There are also a few deer, and riding around with three dogs (and also without) I saw one for the first time recently in the evening. It would take a good 6 weeks to bag one here. There are a few pheasants and many snipes and ducks. In short, there is not much of interest to hunt. But I accept this gladly. In exchange I am freed from a patronizing government, from bothersome police, from crawling spies, from creeping civil servants, from hypocritical pietists, etc., etc.

Your Theodor van Dreveldt

P.S. Everything I said about hunting pertains to an area 3 to 5 hours wide; in other places things are very different.

Loutre Island, Missouri, Montgomery
9 June 1845

Dear Brother, Sister, and Brother-in-Law,

From the various letters I have sent, you will have learned that I got to the above address about mid-February this year. I live with Noot near G. Lensing, who with his brother began to clear the land here in the forest to make it arable. His brother married an American. They and her parents first went up the Missouri and about two years ago went out to Texas. G. Lensing lives on the left bank of the Missouri a little above a small German town named Hermann that was founded five years ago. The river valley is about one to two hours wide in this region. Further up, it is supposed to be as much as four to six hours wide. The valley is surrounded by hills with bluffs that are heavily forested. The hills develop into high plains called prairies. In some areas the prairies come right up to the river; at other spots they are many hours distant. For example, here there are some spots where they are two hours away, at others, five hours, depending on where springs and small brooks arise. The prairies have a hard clayey substrate that doesn't allow rainwater to get through. The water collects, finds a way out, creates a bed for itself, and eventually becomes a branch or "creek" as it is called here. Creek banks are forested whereas the prairies are not. Why? This is a much-argued question, and I have heard all sorts of theories. I'm not in a position to judge because I don't know enough about the land and the weather patterns. Apparently, when it rains one has to wade through the water. Coarse grass grows there as well as a number of other plants; cattlemen from all around drive their herds there. You shouldn't think that the prairie is like your pasture land, however (more on that later). There is a particularly surprising transition from dense forests to these flat, open expanses. The transition is abrupt and is marked by wild apple trees. When they are in bloom, they form a 5- to 8-foot-high border of rosy flowers that is quite beautiful. Unfortunately, they don't last long. The fruit is not worth much, except perhaps as a preserve or in vinegar.

Grain of all sorts grows very well on the prairie, which is why a great number of settlements are to be found there. Making the land arable is also quite simple; one only has to plow. However, there are two things missing: wood and water. There is only rainwater; it would be almost impossible for an individual to dig a well. There aren't any even in small towns such as Daneville [Danville]. There are supposed to be springs there; however, they are little more than puddles. It seems to me that it shouldn't be too difficult to plant trees; the soil seems suitable for spruce. However, because of the lack of water, I wouldn't choose to settle here. I remember reading in Cooper's *The Prairie* that there are also hilly prairies with running springs. That would be something else. The Loutre is one of the largest creeks around here and gives the region its name. It forms islands that can hardly be reached even by horse when it rains.

Rain showers here are generally much heavier than yours. That goes for storms too. It can thunder and lightning for days. There are storms that last as long as 72 hours. I have yet to hear of lightning damage, and nobody has a big fit when it thunders as they do where you are. I'll write more about the prairies when I have seen them closer myself. They have enormous advantages for cattle ranging.

The hilly terrain between the prairie and the river valley is made up of limestone and is thickly wooded with tall trees. Nevertheless, one can ride through with little problem. There are settlements wherever the soil is rich, and there, people need a great deal of wood in order to fence their fields and also because of the uneconomical way they treat the wood. You know what good "foresters" herd animals are, especially sheep, which continually destroy saplings coming up. Unfortunately, there are too few sheep. I have not yet seen a forest in pristine condition, untrammeled by human activity. Ten to fifteen years ago, the bottom (that's how the Missouri valley is called) was so dense that a man could hardly get through it on foot. However, I would not deny that it has lost what in Europe is considered beautiful in the process of settlement. It now looks more like your parks. Unlike English parks, the region lacks nicely cambered and graveled paths. It doesn't have open fields and pastures either. The most giant cottonwoods, sycamores, oaks, and walnuts are spared the axe and elicit a sense of wonder and a somber feeling. And these forests are not to be thought of as virgin just because the French refer to them as "vièrge." Occasionally one sees a bald old-timer who seems to embrace his progeny for the last time with spindly arms. This is a less common sight in your forests. Only in gorges such as in the Sauerland, where transportation is difficult, did I see trees die a natural death. Although the forests have no conifers (except for a few cypresses at higher elevations) the forests are much more diverse than yours.

It would be a bore to list all the types of trees. When I know them better, I will give you a more detailed account and send you seeds. I would much rather tell you a little about agriculture as it is practiced here, even though you may have heard some things about it already. You said you wanted to hear it from me. So, I will describe how it is here. If that conflicts with other accounts you have heard, then the reason may well be regional differences. Trees less than 1 foot in diameter are generally chopped down; larger ones are killed, i.e., a strip of bark is cut off at a level of 2 feet. That is what is usually done to sycamores and hickories. Most trees treated in such a way die during the first summer; sycamores may leaf up for another 2–3 years. Brushwood is usually cut at ground level and not uprooted; the hoe then destroys it. This work is much more difficult because of the many hazelnut bushes. Their roots are hard to kill by plowing. The fallen wood is chopped just small enough so it can be easily handled and is then burned in dense piles. Time brings down the larger trees; first the wind breaks off dried twigs and branches, then the trunk. They all seem to rot more quickly in this climate than in yours. Occasionally they will burn a standing trunk sort of like a giant candle. This is sometimes done to elms in the third or fourth year after it has been killed. Sometimes dead trees are pulled down during spare time in the winter.

Almost every farmer who doesn't own a lot of slaves will try to enlist his neighbors in the spring to roll logs. It's not easy work. The logs are shortened, and it takes about 26 people to roll them together and pile them up. Then the field is generally only plowed once before seeding, with a colterless plow without a share beam but with two handles. The plowshare is often made of wood. There is not even a loop or plowfoot as there is on Belgian plows. And, the plows have to be short and light in order to be easily lifted from the ground when they get tangled in thick roots. Of course, trees are the main obstacle at first, especially when plowing, and it is often impossible to keep a nice straight furrow. However, once the land has been broken up, it is not particularly hard to work. Boys and Negresses are often seen doing it. The main plowing takes place once the land has been prepared. After plowing, the land is seeded; furrows are made with a plow at 3–4 foot intervals and then traversed the same way. Seeds or plants are placed in these transverse furrows and then the soil between the furrows is plowed across. This is often done with a colter plow that has neither a plowpoint nor a plowshare and is used to destroy weeds or loosen the soil. Or it is done with a shovel plow that only has a lancet-shaped share beam (plowpoint) and no plowshare; sometimes a garden-variety plow is used which is called a "kery," or "carry plow." At times, 1, 2, or 3 furrows are made in one plowing through a row, and the plantings may receive 3 or 4 such plowings before harvest.

As you know, maize (corn) and tobacco are the most profitable crops. The farmer's very existence is dependent on corn; tobacco allows him to purchase goods from stores. Flax, hemp, wheat, rye, barley, oats, and buckwheat are also grown, although somewhat less. Corn can yield a thousand-fold harvest since one stalk with 2–3 ears can yield 500 to 1000 kernels. It is a beautiful plant, but not the same as the one you call Turkish wheat. This plant we call "puffcorn" because the children place kernels in the ashes in the fireplace and they puff up like little flowers and serve as a snack. Otherwise, it must belong to the same family.

The local corn was supposed to reach 12 feet this year, but that probably won't happen because of the drought. Corn is the only feed here for horses, cows, and pigs as well as for poultry. It agrees with the animals, and they like it. Horses are given a little coarse fodder if they aren't going into the woods. Pigs fatten to a delicate plumpness. Their meat tastes nice and sweet; the raw bacon is almost oily like your smoked salmon and not too fat. The schmalz is liquid and tastes just as good as olive oil on salad as far as I'm concerned. As you know, I traveled to the south of France and had occasion to try out good oil. People eat it three times a day. The pigs generally weigh between 100 and 200 pounds at slaughter; they could easily be fattened longer, but people don't like it that way. Whoever has many Negroes also slaughters fatter pigs.

I liked cornbread right from the start. I ate lots of it on the steamship without knowing what it was. There was also another food made of corn meal which the captain gave me to try with a somewhat quizzical look. I liked it, somewhat to his surprise. Not all of my compatriots felt the same way about it. Many made an awful face at first, but in time everybody gets a taste for it. Wheat flour is excellent here; it is ground in steam-powered mills. People eat fresh cornbread at almost every meal. It is easy to bake, and it is made in special flat panlike pots with iron lids. The dough is loose and reminds me of your *ratlekoek*, depending on whether it contains a lot of milk and fat. Many a foreigner has eaten it thinking it was cake.

I will tell you about tobacco later. For now, just this: the crop prospects for this year are the worst. Because of the drought, almost nobody in Missouri has plants. Last year's tobacco is rising significantly in price as a result.

If you want me to write in the future, you will have to do the same. I will note each letter that I send out. Even things that you consider boring will interest me to read. Perhaps it is too much effort to write. Of course, I make the effort for you even at 25° Reaumur in the shade.[10]

I'm thinking of riding down to St. Louis in order to take a look at the land and visit compatriots on the way, among them a certain Eversmann [Ludwig Eversmann, a friend of Duden's], who lives not far from Duden. In St. Louis I generally stay with "the former pearl of Emmerich." She has a small *pension* in the English manner. Mainly Germans and Englishmen stay there. I don't think she's doing all that well.

Scholten's dog Bello bit me in the arm, which is why this letter laid around for so long. It's better now. Please pass along the regards that I forgot. Can I take that for granted?

Theodor

This was the last relatively unencumbered letter that Theodor would write for a long time. One can imagine that Theodor saw the land around Emmerich in the Missouri bottom, or flood plain, and hoped that here he could replicate Voorthuyzen. But anxiety about money and his recurring fevers began to creep into his letters. Annette became very alarmed about her brother's safety. She made it clear that she thought he was going through a youthful phase and that he would soon come to his senses:

Emmerich, 2 August 1845

Dear Theodor!

Anton brought us your letter of 9 June. We are always so happy when we get news from you. I am just very concerned that you have a fever again. We are all sorry that you are so far away.

We used the Salm garden during this time, but Höynck rented

the Salm house to an Amsterdammer for 80 thalers per year. The renter's name is de Vos; he's a writer who wrote a little too freely about the Dutch government, and so he has had to leave the country for a while. He chose to settle on the Eltenberg for a while. His family consists of himself, his wife, and five children.

After some time I would hope that your curiosity to learn about foreign countries and foreign nations will have been satisfied and that we will once again see you in our midst. An educated man must forego a great deal over there.

Theodor might have taken some amusement from the fact that Germans were not the only ones running afoul of their government, but by the end of July, his concerns were quite different. The tone of the letter was similar to the one he wrote Anton from Paris:

Dear Brother!

Even though I have not yet had the pleasure of reading a few lines from you here in America, although you promised me in December of last year that you would write immediately, I nevertheless do not wish to deny myself the satisfaction of a conversation with you in the hope that you might finally be moved to start writing. You have no lack of time and even less of material; every little thing that concerns you and every change in your circumstances, no matter how unimportant it may seem to you, whether in the bush or on the property, interests me. Just write off the top of your head. Nobody but me will see your letters so you don't have to feel embarrassed. Why do you want to deny me further the opportunity to communicate with you? Weren't we on good terms when we parted? Why shouldn't we still be? I'm sure that you would want it. But it won't work if you can't even summon up the desire to write. It is easier and more pleasant to read a letter than to write one; but if one has feelings for the person to whom one writes, then even the writing is not too bad. If I had done what you are doing, then you would know nothing about me, and I would disappear from your memory. If writing is really too burdensome, then just write short notes and I will see your desire to show friendship. Presently I am here, as you can see, trying to get rid of this fever and to recover, both of which I have succeeded in. I feel pretty much as I did before. As you know, I lived at G. Lensing's; since he didn't have room for me, I built a log cabin.

In this sensitive brotherly letter, Theodor once again touched the shame that ailed Anton. Being told by his younger brother, against whom he harbored unspoken resentments, that he should not be embarrassed probably just intensified his resentment.

Theodor then went on to talk about the nature of his ailments, which he alternately attributed to the bad air, as Duden did, or the ill effects of the sun:

I already wrote about this, so you are aware of the complicated construction. I left the chinks open to create a draft. However, this is rare in the bottom since there is hardly a breeze in the middle of this dense forest; one doesn't even feel storms much. The heat is terrible. Such a house is basically a cabin; whoever is not yet used to the climate will really suffer, especially if he gets sick. As long as one is healthy, one doesn't feel it that much, but one feels it all the more when one isn't. There is no protection against the night air, which is very unhealthy, in part because of the continual flooding this year. One hardly knows where to crawl. Most nights I slept in a hammock outside under the overhang in front of the house. Sometimes I slept on a board on the ground. I had such a fever. I probably spent too much time in the sun yanking weeds in my garden without a hat. Years ago, this didn't bother me, and so I am curious about how the effect works. This time it affected my stomach nerves and gave me a feeling like seasickness. Also, I couldn't turn my eyes without pain. My appetite was gone, and I decided to shake my stomach back in order by hard riding. But that didn't work this time. After eight days I thought I was better, during which time, as I now know, I had a high temperature. At that time I didn't believe it because I simply didn't want to have a fever. However, in the evening I really began to shake, so I realized it was time to take an emetic. Afterward I had shaking and high temperature on two consecutive days and decided to take quinine. They are much quicker to use it over here than in Germany. All the doctors follow this method here. The climate acts much more quickly and harmfully than where you are. I was in a bad way when I got on the steamship for St. Louis. All the rooms were taken and so I had to sleep on deck.

However, I got over the fever, and the change in food enabled me to just about get my old strength back. I've been here about two days now.

Just as Duden had, Theodor consistently wrote about mosquitoes when talking about his fevers:

I almost forgot to mention one more amenity that affected me greatly while I was sick, namely mosquitoes. These are much like yours, but we have a smaller type as well called "netts" [gnats] whose sting is just as nasty. They gather in damp places and around waterfalls in numbers that exceed a million to the millionth power. If one rides through the forests, they aren't bothersome, but as soon as one stands still even for an instant, for example if one's horse is drinking, they cover one all over. As soon as one rides again, they are gone. If one wanted to swim, one would be eaten alive.

On Loutre Island they told me that there are so many mosquitoes in St. Louis that I would soon be driven back, but I hardly feel these tormentors at all. Every bed has mosquito netting, and at night one hears them buzzing around. Last summer while I was sitting by the ditch at your place drawing the house in Voorthuyzen, they were plenty troublesome as well. In general, the mosquito problem is not as bad as one thinks it is in more northern regions. Also, this area is healthy again, and I could stand the inconveniences if I had a stone house. Then I'd be able to deal better with the heat and the night air.

There are ice cellars in better-built farmhouses. There is always ice in drinking water. A popular drink in the taverns is called a "mint julep" and is made of fresh peppermint. It reminds me of May wine: ice cubes, which eventually melt, sugar, and spirits such as brandy, Madeira, port, sherry, etc. Everything costs the same. Then they give you a straw that is about nine inches long, which allows you to enjoy your drink slowly. In any case, it would be hard to drink because the ice is so unpleasant on one's teeth. It is an absolute joy to suck on a straw.

Now, dear brother, I hope that you will do all in your power to get me some money so that I can start something here and get properly settled. This uncertainty, as you can imagine, is very unpleasant. I wrote a little while ago and asked you to send me $200 for a start. That won't be enough because I have already borrowed so much that you will have to send me that much again. I hope that the $200 is on the way. Don't let me down. I am far away from you and have to reckon months ahead in order not to spend months in dire need.

Annette sent me a lovely little letter that, in vain, whetted my appetite for news from you.

Greetings!

Your Theodor

P.S. The postal regulations have changed. From now on, ½ ounce will cost regular postage; no more numbers of pieces of paper.

By the summer of 1845, Theodor was becoming increasingly desperate. His repeated letters to Anton went unanswered, and he began to suspect that Anton was purposely holding back his funds. Not only was he without money, his fevers came and went, leaving him without the strength to work. In all probability, he had a type of malaria known as intermittent fever, which could take the form of three-day ague or four-day ague. His letter to Franz von Weise, in which he clearly laid out his agreement with Anton, attests to his anguish at his brother's behavior:

Loutre Island Montgomery, Mo.
11 March 1846

Dear Doctor!

Before I left, I made an agreement with Anton on 27 September 1844, which you know about. In it, Anton took over my inheritance from Provost Goossens's will of 22 October 1834, for 46,000 Berlin thalers. Of that, Anton was to pay me 10,000 thalers as soon as possible in order to facilitate my trip to America. The balance was to be paid in convenient sums within six years; interest was to be paid at 4%. Upon my departure, I received 2000 thalers, and in his letter dated 22 June 1845, the only letter I have received so far from him, Anton writes, "Day after tomorrow, the 24th, I will go to Emmerich in order to clear up the matter of the 10,000 thalers." Later he writes that I will "receive the monies through Minderop." He also mentions that my brother-in-law Wenzel would have dropped the division of the estate or perhaps would not have brought it before the court if he had not threatened legal action against Wenzel. This pains me greatly because I detest disunity between siblings. Nevertheless, one might well become incensed at the dereliction of duty on the part of conscientious Prussian jurists [i.e., Wenzel].

You may judge my mood from what I have written above. Almost nine months have passed since I received the last, and so far only, word from Anton. That is really not proper. He may be well-intentioned, but he has the maturity and the time and should not leave me in suspense for so long, especially since I wrote him that I had to borrow money ($200) and agreed to repay it on 1 January 1846. I made this promise at the beginning of July 1845 at a time when I had to leave here on account of fever, thinking that I would certainly have received the money by then. Because of this, I plead with you to follow up this matter for me. You have power of attorney, and please see to it that the contractual agreements are fulfilled. Earlier, I proposed to Anton that if he sent me more than 10,000 thalers now, I would back off from the six-year term. He didn't even answer me, and so I must now insist upon timely fulfillment of the contract.

Theodor did not receive an answer until November. Soon after he wrote the above letter, he realized that many of his letters were not getting through, probably intercepted by Prussian postal police. Their activities were hardly a secret; the 17 October 1845 edition of the *Hermanner Wochenblatt* carried an article, dateline Würzburg, which stated, "There is a great deal of discussion here about the ministerial decree that gives postal authorities the power to open letters and packages with a witness present if there is a grounded suspicion that they could contain banned newspapers. (!!!)"

Unable to work, unable to move, his ties to family tenuous, Theodor felt he was a virtual prisoner. His next letter also shows how fragile his alliances in America were:

21 April 1846

Dear Doctor!

I hope that you have received my two recent letters. One of them I sent via le Havre and the other via Bremen. This one I am sending via Rotterdam. At the moment, I have no idea where I stand or what I can expect.

I read in a letter that Hülkenberg brought that Annette is very worried and frightened that I do not write. What I have long suspected and what the newspapers here report, namely that Prussia has recently begun to violate the privacy of the mails, must be true.

The newspapers have presented the most conclusive details and damning proof. Even though I have heard hardly any news from home, I have written assiduously, now to Anton, now to Annette, and to both together. I am still waiting for my money.

I had to let good occasions for travel simply pass as well as advantageous opportunities for buying livestock. Of course, even if I get my money this summer, I would still have to buy fodder at great cost in the fall, which I could have grown myself during the summer. Perhaps I will only be able to leave by winter and will have to live through a winter like the last one for which I was not prepared. I want to leave here as soon as possible; it is too unhealthful here.

If someone had just written to me that I would not be getting the money, then I would have acted differently, would not have waited from one post day to the next for half a year, and would not have ridden each time like a fool to the post office, and all for nothing. Apart from the fact that the region and climate are not fit for me to settle, my immediate living situation doesn't appeal to me anymore either. I already wrote in detail about Noot. When I came back from my trip in October, Lensing told me that Noot bought the farm primarily with the help of Mönnig, Scholten, and Westhooven. Later I heard that this was not the case. For example, Westhooven knew nothing about it before Noot bought. Lensing takes the position that as many Germans as possible should settle here although he himself would not have built here if the flood of immigration to Missouri had occurred earlier. Settlement causes land prices to rise and there is good opportunity to sell. One can buy land, but not sell it and only seldom can one rent it out. That weakling Noot was convinced to serve these plans, and so he betrayed me.

It must be clear to you how ardent is my desire to get away from here. In a short amount of time, I have had sorrowful experience with humanity. Cleff rewarded me for helping him come over by stealing the chest that was entrusted to me and which I left in Lensing's care. Lensing, whom I always thought of as selfless and honest, disparages Noot, whom I always treated as a true friend.

Exactly what happened between Theodor, Wilhelm Noot, and Gerhard Lensing is unclear; we only have Theodor's all too cryptic account.

The pain that he felt and the bitterness at being, as he saw it, betrayed by his brother are evident in the next letter that has come down to us:

November 1846

Dear Dr.!

In my entire life I have never received a letter that was such balm to my spirits as that dated 21 August 1846. I haven't received any letters concerning my financial affairs since 22 June 1845. I felt I was dying physically and mentally. Though my fever was not too bad, I had to sit here at night without a lamp. One can't get oil here, and I can't burn fat in my lamp. So, I read and lie at night in front of the glow from my fireplace. I don't want to ask Lensing for help. Being alone, he has enough to get through during the day. I can't pay anyone since I haven't had work for a long time. A person who works hard all day can digest the food I have, but not a sick man consumed by fever. Please keep this to yourself; I don't want Lensing's family to know about it, especially since he contracts with his brother-in-law Disch in Rees, who is an agent who tries to lure people over here.

If Anton has had sleepless nights, then he has time to write and take this burden of uncertainty from me. He can make light at night; I can't. My nights are now more than 17 hours.

You know human beings well enough to know that a friendship that has been dissolved cannot become neutral. On my honor, I viewed Anton as my friend and treated him as such. But by his negligence he has tormented me as one can only be tormented by Jesuits. You know that a broken friendship leaves a deep wound and an ugly scar behind. That is how it is between Anton and me. These statements are not feverish rantings. Your lovely letter has cured me.

You write, dear friend, that I should come back and that I will always be sick here. I never wanted to remain in Missouri; Anton knew that, and even so he has kept me in this sickly place. I want to go to Wisconsin, about which not a word has come to me concerning illnesses. And, if I don't like it there, I'll go on to the older eastern states where sickness is unknown. You are confusing Missouri with America as a whole.

If my little brother hadn't kept me here, my body would not be so powerless, and I would have long ago been industriously at work in Wisconsin and probably married. Doctor, I did not come here in order to remain alone. I knew that over here, family life formed the basis of political life.

Then he accused Anton of "borrowing" money for his own use:

Anton built a house and two barns and acquired an inventory of animals and implements, and these hardly out of revenues. Therefore, he has in all probability broken the contract with me.

Franz von Weise defended Anton, who he felt had made every effort to procure the money:

Elten, 28 December 1846

My Dear Theodor!

It was with deep regret and great astonishment that I read in your letter dated 21 October to Hortmann that you have to date received neither news from me nor from Anton. I had already gathered from your earlier letters that my letters hadn't gotten to you, which is why I wrote several times about your financial affairs here. The last letter was dated 23 August, and I sent it from Rotterdam via le Havre. In July Anton sent you 3 letters of credit, each via a different route, le Havre, Liverpool, and Bremen. If I'm not mistaken, they were for 2060 thalers. The fact that you received the monies so late was really not Anton's fault. You have it on my word that he made every effort; no sooner was the bond settled than the Poor Commission in Münster where he was going to get the money called off their offer saying that because of the inheritance agreement by which you held first mortgage, their money was not secure enough. Even though Anton sent them your and his specially concluded agreement and in spite of my notarized assurance that the money was to be used to pay off your share of the assets, neither that administration nor any other was willing to put up the capital. So, I managed to get Anton 2000 thalers from the church foundation, which he sent you as a letter of credit via Rotterdam. That this tardiness has caused you great hardship is something I feel acutely bad about, and you can be assured that it has caused Anton no less embarrassment and grief, especially because it was not his fault.

Von Weise states that the lending institutions refused to advance money to Anton because he did not hold first mortgage on the Voorthuyzen property; if there was a default, they could not get their money from Theodor because he was physically beyond their reach. Whether Anton actually sent letters of credit is unknown. Although letters frequently disappeared, it was less often the case with letters of credit, upon which commerce between nations depended. That three letters of credit sent through three different ports were lost is possible, but not probable. Anton once again found a way to humiliate himself; other people had to procure money for him that he should have been able to get himself. Finally, Anton felt moved to write:

Voorthuyzen, 7 February 1847

Dear Brother!

First, I give you my hand and trust in your sense of justice and that you may become convinced that it is not my fault that the monies that were extended, a letter of exchange for 3500 liquid through Treek in Emmerich on a New York bank, have not reached you. I received 3 letters of credit, of which I sent the first off in June, the second in August, and the third you will receive now. I hope that this one gets to the right address. Other monies, besides this 2200 thalers which comes from the Eltenberg church, have not been extended. In my last two letters, I asked you to change your power of attorney because I couldn't get any money with the power of attorney as it is. Enclosed you will find two replies from the Münster Poor Commission, which originally had agreed to a capital of 13,000 thalers. The obligation was made out to Carp in Emmerich and the capital was already recorded in the mortgage book. The other reply I got from Wesel, where I was also supposed to get 13,000 thalers; to save postage, I won't send you that reply. Dear brother, at this moment, I'm not in the mood to write, but I promise that within the next three days I will write in more detail and send you the receipts from the Emmerich postal authorities that I in fact sent you those letters in June and August.

With tears I embrace you in my thoughts, dear Theodor, when I think of your constrained situation. Please write soon to your loving brother,

Anton

Theodor might be excused if he was less than impressed by Anton's short note and suspected that the promised receipts would never arrive—which, as it happened, they never did. Even if everything else he wrote was factually correct, Theodor would see Anton as a man who could not be trusted with important matters and simply did not take care in the discharge of his obligations, familial or otherwise. Anton's effusive greetings would probably have sickened this very direct and forthright man.

This letter seems to define Anton's flaws: uncommunicative and furtive, but overcompensating with an absurd effusiveness; untrustworthy even when he was telling the truth. He was an alcoholic, ashamed of who he was and unable to be, or appear to be, straight with any other person. In early 1847, Annette wrote Theodor:

> I haven't seen Anton for a long time, which pains me bitterly; he doesn't even listen to my most earnest pleas. First thing on New Year's, I sent your letter over to him with the urgent request that he take care of this matter if he had not done so already. I asked him to write me a few lines letting me know where things stood; I would much rather that he came here himself. He replied that he was going to town next day and would come by. I was very happy at the prospect; I waited longingly all day, but in vain.

What Was Going On in Germany

Theodor may have been hasty in leaving Germany for greater political freedom. Although censorship was practiced by the post office, the Prussian and some other German governments, realizing that social unrest was boiling up, began to allow limited self-government in certain areas and even loosened up the censorship laws that came in with the Carlbad Decrees as a way of containing rebellion. Yet when one looks at local newspapers from the era, one is struck by how little news there was. Archival copies of the Emmerich newspapers were destroyed during World War II, but the nearby Rees newspaper, *Kreisblatt für Kreis Rees,* has survived. It consisted primarily of serialized light fiction and adventure, ads for local business (including solicitations by emigration agents), and a few news stories.

Because political views could not be directly expressed, stories and poems often had double meanings or were couched in such a way that they would be considered clever rather than dangerous. Even these were often unsigned or carried a pseudonym. For example, an unattributed May 1846 poem titled "Der beste Censor" (The best censor) makes the point in lilting rhyme that God is the best censor because He lets us say anything and is embarrassed by nothing.[1] It makes a deft swipe at earthly censors by pointing out that even with this permissiveness, His power remains intact. An obviously topical poem published on 1 January 1848 by a certain "G. Pfarrius" is titled "Warte Raabenpack!" (Just wait, you raven pack!).[2] In it the king goes out on fall maneuvers and comes across a fish pond that has turned into a muddy swamp populated by ugly frogs. According to Prime Minister "Raven," who seems to have a snuff habit, this denial of rights has occurred because the fish are represented by frogs in the parliament (*Reichstag*). When the prime minister suggests that a dam be built to restore the pond, the frogs croak, "Just wait! You raven pack! We'll get you back!" Then the king silences them and says that he himself will represent them. Both of these rhymes were clever and gave little offense; in no way did they confront power directly. This constituted political journalism in much of Germany.

In October 1846 Franz von Weise excitedly wrote Theodor about a new system of local government in Emmerich, although it is unclear at this remove exactly what von Weise was talking about. Again, the records have been destroyed. What he wrote was certainly tantalizing:

> However, in spite of many shortcomings, our municipal codes do give the town representatives the right to control the actions of the mayor. They also have the right to call a town meeting regarding community matters, and I think we must work to assure that there is unity among the members. It seems that the right-thinking people are gradually gaining the upper hand here.

Town meetings were not opened up to the public until 1848, but von Weise hoped that Theodor would want to return so that he could participate. He wrote again in June 1847:

> I'm sure that you have read more in your excellent newspapers about political matters here than I can tell you about. There's just one thing that I would like to mention, namely that all members of the state parliament [*Reichstände*] are infused with such a liberal and good spirit that I really expect the best in the future. At the last session, a majority voted for the emancipation of the Jews. The debates are altogether so interesting that if you haven't read them already in your newspapers, I will send them as soon as they are published, which is the intention.

Von Weise knew very well that these developments would interest Theodor.

The newspapers that Theodor in all likelihood read were indeed quite good—and opinionated and confrontative. As von Weise noted, Theodor could read about political debates taking place in Germany. The papers also tackled the major social, political, and economic issues facing America head on; they were not narrow or parochial in their focus. German-language newspapers abounded, and not just in major cities like New York and Philadelphia. West of the Mississippi, the largest-circulation daily was the *Anzeiger des Westens,* published in St. Louis since 1835. The *Westliche Post,* a rival paper founded in 1857, also published a weekly magazine supplement called *Mississippi Blätter.* Hermann had a very influential newspaper as well; the *Hermanner Wochenblatt* was published weekly beginning in 1845.[3] Because there was nothing like a wire service, newspaper editors freely reprinted articles from both German and German-American newspapers as well as translated English-language articles. In this way readers became familiar with a cross section of opinion.

In spite of his political interest and the free journalism practiced by Germans in America, there is no evidence that Theodor ever involved himself in the lively debates that swirled around him. He never mentioned the *Hermanner Wochenblatt,* nor its free-thinking editor, Eduard Mühl. Nor, with one exception (nativism), did he ever comment on politics in America. It is possible that he was too ill and preoccupied.

The Revolution of 1848 and Theodor's Return

At last, in May 1847, after living in the United States for two full years, Theodor received the money that was due him (possibly the entire 10,000 thalers). Shortly thereafter he wrote his friend Franz von Weise, but every topic he touched spoke of his loneliness. Despite his evident disappointment in Germany, one is left with the feeling that if he felt he could, he would more than gladly return home:

> Since I last wrote you, I have thought a great deal about returning to Europe. In my opinion, the purpose of life is to enjoy it. A stay in Paris, Italy, and Vienna seemed attractive, but I'm already 36, and after 4 or 5 years, I'd have had my fill of that unstable life. I remember how much I yearned for my own hearth after I left for here. And what then? Maybe come back here? By then I'd certainly be too old and gray for family life; now I'm really anxious about it. . . .
>
> You know the daughter of the Czech who was murdered by William the Previous in Berlin? It seems to me that it would be a noble deed to bring this unhappy creature over here, and perhaps she would not be averse to sharing her life with a man who approves of her departed father's actions.

Then he confided a secret, a recapitulation of his own history:

> In Paris I lived with a working girl, as is the custom there. She was not infertile, and when I was gone she bore a son. Since then, I have sent her money. Anton was the only person I shared this with, and I made him swear to send Adele Legumille, Rue Jaques 176, Paris, money from time to time. I doubt whether he has actually done it. Can you give him a kick?

Finally, his thoughts went in a different direction:

> America's free institutions are the main reason why I decided to live here, and I am convinced that no other country would satisfy me in the long run more than this one. Despotism angers me; that's just how I am. I'm angry at the situation in Prussia, and in particular that there are so many educated people there who are politically indifferent. Take Wenzel: if he can make money, he is satisfied and pacified. . . .

I can't write Anton yet. I'm not in the mood since getting his last letter in which he lied to me. I haven't received the letter yet which he promised he would send me "in three days," and I probably never will. . . .

Even if Anton wasn't writing, Theodor now had some capital. With it he set out for Wisconsin to "observe the Indians." In a long letter to Franz von Weise written in stages and postmarked early March 1848, Theodor told of his adventures:

Indian territory on the right bank of the Mississippi stretches about as far as Prairie du Chien; on the left bank, to about 100 miles north of St. Peter. The Winnebagos who live down there have sold their land, and will move this year to their new site up on the Mississippi. Next to them live the Sioux, and above them the Chippewas.

There were a number of reasons why I decided to spend the winter here. For one thing, I wanted to see and get to know the Indians, about whom I had read and heard. Hunting, which I saw in August and September, was also a factor, as was the sheer prospect of a winter here. When I was in Missouri, people told fearsome stories about the winters. My nearest neighbor is 2–3 miles down the Mississippi at the confluence with the Rum River, 30 miles north of St. Paul and 27 miles from the St. Anthony Falls [now in the middle of Minneapolis]. There are no whites to the north, the south, or on the opposite bank from me. To the north for 70 to 200–300 miles there are only so-called "trading posts," single houses where trading is done with the Indians. The Sioux live opposite me, and the Chippewas to the north; both tribes have permission to hunt on this side and below on the other side. However, each tribe is afraid of the other because even though they have smoked the peace pipe, they continue to look for opportunities to nab each other. I had counted on a more comfortable winter than I ended up sampling.

I took a trip to the Rum River with an Englishman named Smith and an American, J. John. We found much game there: pheasants, ducks, geese, swans, carrier pigeons, bear, deer, wolves. All you had to do was load and shoot; in a short time you had enough meat (namely carrier pigeons) to keep you going. After a few days, there was no fun in it anymore. In any case, here we hit upon the idea of spending the winter together. I went down to St. Louis to get my horse, which I had left at Westhooven's, who had moved there, as well as to get my other things, my dogs, and food supplies, which are much more expensive up here. In the meantime, the other two were supposed to build me a hut.

By the time I returned, John was long gone; he had gotten sick of it and hadn't informed me, even though he had placed orders for goods. Smith was still there, but there was no hut. It was the middle of November, cold and damned bitter, not the best time to build a shelter. I could have spent the winter with my neighbor on the Rum River, Mr. Holms; however, his hut is small and so smoky that I feared I would go blind if I spent an entire winter in that smoke pit. Even the few days I did spend there hurt my eyes.

Mr. Smith, who wanted to help in the beginning, was more hindrance than help. So, I was pleased when he decided to live with Holms and leave me to fend for myself. He let me make the fires, cook, etc. In short, he wanted to be served rather than share the labors. He was what I would call an egoist, an honest and good-hearted one (if those things are compatible), and an educated man. What bothered me the most was his constant complaining, which made me even more aware of the miserable circumstances. When he was gone, I actually saved time. Except for one-pots with flour and water and a little fat, I didn't cook. The dogs and I survived on that, and there were no more plates, knives, and forks to wash. Then, after I was more comfortably situated, i.e., I have a window and lie on the ground with my back and feet by the fire as I write this on a trunk, I have begun to cook again. This damned way of living has really gotten to me.

You know how building is done here: one lays logs on top of each other and fills in the chinks with mud and dirt. It was too late in the winter for me to do this because everything was frozen solid, and if I had with great effort filled a few chinks with warm water during the day, the frost at night would have dislodged it again. I tried to fill the chinks with reeds and grass; I think you will quickly see that this does not make a tight wall. The wind blows through from all sides, and the worst thing is that I didn't build myself a fireplace but am relying on a small stove. When it is cold and windy, the best I can do is lie on the ground and use the oven as protection and for a little warmth. Sometimes, the only way to stay warm is to lie in bed. Once, I couldn't even get warm there, and it was only by placing a puppy at my feet that I was able to avoid the pain.

It was at that time that I lived badly and worked too hard. At 10 in the morning, when I crawled out of bed, the temperature stood at 28° below zero Reaumur [−31° Fahrenheit]. On top of that, I had a slight fever, and I began to conceive an idea which I will tell you about later. Then I realized that I could not continue like this, and I started to look after my stomach a little better. I ordered provisions and lard, of which I had a supply in St. Paul. Initially, I thought I might pick them up myself. I started cooking again, and thereafter only had a fever three times. In the meantime, I have gotten much stronger.

Don't let the −28° give you a false picture of the climate here. That was an exceptional day; the usual is between 12–16°. Then the sun is stronger than in Europe and can be very pleasant. And the sun shines most of the time; there are few overcast days. My frozen feet were the main reason I suffered so from the cold.

Recently, when I came back from St. Paul, I harnessed my horse Charley to the cart. He never used to work and is about 9 years old; I've had him going on 3 years. The load was a light one, since I didn't want to strain him the first time. A Frenchman, or as they say here, a French-Canadian or "half-breed," accompanied me with his ox cart. (The white population is mainly Canadian, descendants of Frenchmen and Indian women.) The first thing that happened on this trip was that I broke a shaft on the cart coming down a hill. Luckily, nothing happened to the horse. I spent the night with the Canadians, whose 20 families live near the St. Anthony Falls. They are good-natured people who speak French and Indian; they understand little English. I like them better than the Anglo-Americans. The next day, we had to cross many small brooks, some of them knee deep. There are no regular paths or fords so that I had to wade across them while leading the horse in order not to magnify the load in the worst spots and increase the chance of tipping over.

Then my companion's ox cart got stuck in the mud, and we had to unload it. We had to do that again later because his ox couldn't get up the hill. As a result, we didn't make it to Mr. Holms's place, but had to camp out in the snow. It was late by the time we got a fire started, and it took me a half hour to get my shoes off because my feet were frozen to the shoes. As a result, I have suffered terribly from cold feet all winter. They are so tender now that the slightest cold is a torture.

I have no problems in dry weather when I can wear moccasins, Indian shoes made of deerskin with a piece of blanket wrapped around my feet. But when it is wet, and I have to wear boots, then it is very hard on me. I'm sure you are saying that it serves me right and why wasn't I wearing boots on that trip in the first place. Well, there's a reason for that too. I had sprained my right foot and could only limp about in shoes. I sprained that foot when I jumped from a flatboat onto our sunken steamboat; I collapsed like a Goliath.

I have to tell you about a little adventure. I had lost too much time at the lower falls of the Mississippi between Keokuk and the Mormon city (more on their temple later) to get to Galena where I could wait for a better steamboat than the one I was forced to take. It starts to freeze hard so early here that shipping generally ceases at the end of October.

In St. Louis I had taken a boat that connected with another one just above the falls, and I was obliged to wait for it. It had been expected for 8 days, and it turned out that because of the wind conditions, it had been unable to get past the upper falls in Davenport. When the water is high, namely in June and July, the boats can go right through, otherwise their cargo has to be loaded at great cost onto flatboats pulled by horses. Sometimes this can cost a steamboat $300–1500 because wages are so high here. The lower falls are the worst; they are about 12 miles wide. I got to Galena about the end of October, and so I had to take the *Argo*, a tiny old boat that was ready to sail when I arrived. The little crate got us to within 30 miles of Lake Pepin when, at 2 in the morning, I was awakened with the news that we had sunk. I immediately jumped out of bed, thinking only of my horse and dogs. You know how steamboats are set up here; I already wrote about that. The horse was on the foredeck out of the water. In order to go aft, where the dogs were, I had to wade. They lay right at water level, and it was then that I learned that we were wedged into a solid bank and could neither sink further nor get free.

I am convinced that the old crate was driven into the bank on purpose. We waited, more or less, hoping for another steamboat that was supposed to come upriver. It didn't come, and our provisions ran out. A compatriot, namely a Swiss, and some others live a few miles upstream and trade with the Indians. Another person, who chops wood for the boats, lives downstream. A few days later, they came and brought some bread and fish. The machines were brought to shore, which consisted here of an island. Since I had no more fodder, Charley was pushed into the water, about 3–4 feet deep, to graze on the island. One morning, my dear Charley was not on the island anymore. I assume that the deck hounds, as they call the stokers and sailors, had used him to get to land after they were put off.

The captain had held these people without food until they had brought the machines ashore and then let them off on the island. One, who was trying to steal blankets, waded about half way to shore and then stood still and screamed because of leg cramps so severe he thought he was going to drown. The others were merciful enough that they dragged him into the boat. About 6–8 of these people were quite drunk because the captain had given them a barrel of whiskey before. I have no idea what happened to these people. There has been no word, and I assume they died in the woods. When I felt my way ashore, I found footprints where these unfortunates had waded through.

It isn't so terrible to get wet in November up here, but not to have dry clothes and a fire is a matter of concern. I also found Charley's tracks; he was on another island, taking care of his needs. The dogs were chained by the shore. Tilla is a strong, 3-year-old untrained bitch, of a breed much favored in Missouri as a farm dog and even as a quasi tracking dog. She is a pretty yellowish brown. Then there is Castor, an ill-tempered, ash-gray, table-high dog with black stripes along his back and deep-set little eyes. He is Tilla's son and had to be put away because of his meanness. I thought, now that is the sort of dog I need here.

I wanted to take Charley from the island to the Swiss's [place] 3–4 miles away and was told that there was an Indian path along the shore. You cannot possibly imagine what an Indian path is like. I first saw one near St. Paul when I visited an Indian camp and got lost. In short, they are made in such a way that a white man who isn't familiar with them doesn't see a path at all. I got through the first water just fine. Getting out of the stream on the other side, the banks were steep and muddy, yet, when a horse gets out of the water, it is generally able to do so easily. But then we came to a second stream with steep banks. Since I couldn't find a suitable place to ford and because it was getting late, I thought that it would be better to go back and try again next day.

But then I came to the spot where I had crossed the first stream and couldn't get across even though I forced the horse into the water several times. He got his front legs into the mud so that the water was up to his shoulder blades but his hind legs were still high and dry. As a result of these exertions, a strap tore. I finally managed to tie the horse to a thick tree stump and came up to put on the saddle and buffalo hide (which I brought along in case I had to sleep outdoors). He shied away and I fell backwards and one of my pant loops got caught on a branch. There I lay, on my back with my legs up in the air and I saw Charley take a leap over the tree, his front hooves heading directly for my chest. I thought, "*Adieu, mon plaisir.*" But I was lucky and he only grazed my jacket; the muddy hoof prints were there. So, I got up none the worse for wear and found another spot where the horse got in more easily but was soon swimming. We got back to the steamboat and by that time it was a bit on the cool side.

These little adventures don't have much charm if you have to endure them alone. They are good for a laugh when you tell them to friends, but I do think that they are best avoided. Finally a steamboat arrived, but unfortunately it was going downstream and not up. The captain left the boat with the cook and everything as well as two of the deck hounds. A man from St. Paul, a young person who absolutely had to go upstream, and the man who gave us the fish stayed on board. The captain had given the boat to the latter since he knew that the ice would soon carry the boat away. Our party stayed with the intention of waiting overnight for the next boat and then continuing our journey by land.

The wreck had been completely stripped. There were no beds, no chairs, no tables. Fortunately the man from St. Paul had bought the stove, but it was still unimaginably cold in the middle of the water. And that wasn't all. We didn't have anything to eat or to drink. The other people, except for the man from St. Paul and myself, got into a fight and started to smash all the windows that were still intact. Then the present owner got the idea to set the boat on fire and yelled that everyone who still had things on board should save them and himself. He began to make a fire in front of the stove. I lay nearby, pretending to sleep, ready to grab him by the throat if it came to that. But Jason, who knew the man, got there before me and bit him until he stopped.

The next day the Swiss came with canoes made of hollow trees along with a flotilla of Indians. Their intention was to plunder the boat and break it up. They showed me where the horse could ford the two streams and where to find their house. Even so, I had to get through some very swampy terrain. Charley got stuck once, and I had to jump down so that he could get himself loose. Exhausted, we finally arrived at several huts where the people spoke German. We had hardly arrived when news came that the other boat had come and that my baggage was on the way. Luckily the boat had to take on wood, and it was so dark that it had to stay the night. I finally got my two suitcases, but I had to pay $8 to get them transferred from one boat to the other. On November 11th I arrived in St. Paul without further mishap.

I celebrated St. Hubert's day with perhaps a little less enthusiasm than you.[1] I hope you haven't sworn off this saint. The Americans don't know him at all; all poetry gets lost here.

Now, you are probably thinking that I was wrong not to hire people to help with the work. One reason for that is the uncomfortable relationship (for Europeans) that exists when one has to live with such people. They see themselves as the complete equals of those who hire them and think nothing of eating at the same table. They are always in your rooms and act much the way an intimate friend would in Europe; they allow themselves every imaginable liberty. This is made somewhat bearable by the fact that even the most average American is at a much higher stage of civilization than any of our compatriots of the same class. When they come here, ours suddenly become arrogant idiots. As a result, I would rather work alone than be subject to such unpleasant company. In addition, nobody can be had here for under $20 per month or $200 per year. In this regard, there is almost no choice but to hire blacks who are much like our farm hands. But this also has its drawbacks and can be costly.

Another reason for my going it alone is that I was told that I could easily hire Indian women to do all household chores. As is well known, Indian men do nothing but hunt; all work is beneath their dignity. Indian women are real slaves. I was told that they like to live with whites because they are better treated and the way of life is better. But, as I said before, a tribe lives in this area that puts fear into everyone else and nobody dares do anything. It is true that one can buy a woman cheaply enough, i.e., for presents costing about $25 which one gives to relatives. But this is variable, and sometimes several hundred dollars are required. In any case, no sooner have you bought one and clothed her decently than she runs away. This happened to a neighbor this winter; the woman ran away the next day. If I had found it practical, I would have done it as well in order to learn the Indian language and to prepare myself for a trip to the Rocky Mountains and California.

Now I have a completely new plan, however, which I don't think you will disapprove of. I talk to you from my heart. You may well imagine what a pleasure it is in my solitude to converse openly with an old friend. You will also realize that there are things that I have divulged to you that are not appropriate for third parties who, not knowing me as well as you, could easily misunderstand and spread bad rumors about me. As I said, not a soul, not even Anton. If he hadn't initially read others' letters, he might have felt more of a need to write me directly.

As I said before, I did not have the opportunity to answer your letters earlier. I was in St. Louis only a few days before going up the Missouri where I unknowingly passed by Louis Westhooven's, who was storing my things. I stayed a few days with W. Noot, who went down with me to Washington, Missouri, to pick up a small package that happened to contain letters for me. Then I spent a few more days in St. Louis in order to buy articles I needed for up here. I also made time to write out a will in case I am scalped or otherwise mutilated. I also took the liberty of naming you and Degenhardt, who is a notary in St. Louis, as executors. Degenhardt comes from Eversberg, Westphalia, and I remember him from Arnsberg and Bonn as a demagogue [here a neutral term meaning "leader" and "orator"]. He fled and has been living here for 10–12 years. I trust that you will accept. I have one copy of the will among my papers; another is in a safe at Angelrodt, Eggers & Barth in St. Louis.

And now it is time for the business part of this letter. I read your letter of 29 October with a certain apprehension since I was almost at the point of wanting to return. I have been thinking about it for quite some time. The twenty-fourth of January, which was both my birthday and the date I arrived in the land of freedom, decided the issue for me. I was sitting alone in my hut and had received a small basket of Rhine wine from St. Paul just a few days earlier. Dr. Engelmann in St. Louis had recommended that I eat meat three times a day and drink a glass of Rhine wine, and this regimen had cured me. I was drinking alone for the first time (I had two bottles of Geisenheimer) and I realized that I had purchased many privations for a great deal of money. Freedom is a good thing and worthy of a man, and yet over here it comes at a damned high price.

The first thing that confirmed me against life in the United States was nativism. Germans are hated here, or better stated, despised; they are called "Dutchmen," although educated people know the difference between them and Germans. It is true that I have never suffered as a result. In fact, I could tote up numerous cases in which I was treated preferentially and with special care. Nevertheless, all native-born Americans have a certain xenophobia. I don't want to speculate how things would be in Germany if so many foreigners arrived as here, especially poor and uneducated ones who tend, by their competition in the work force, to lower wages.

In short, it is very uncomfortable to hear one's compatriots spoken of so badly. In addition, there were problems with the language. I always hated English. If French were spoken, I would find it easier to live here. But the country has many advantages, and you can't accuse me of being a weather vane if I put this letter away several times in order to think the matter over some more. Finally, I have come to the following decision:

I am going to go to Switzerland and buy a few acres of land there, enough to support a household. I plan to earn my living growing vegetables and fruit. If it should prove impossible to live there, I will not have burned any bridges and could still return here. Of course, the religious squabbles over there are unpleasant, but religion has its mean sides here as well. Over here, in order to get away from it, you have to move to an unpopulated region. But as soon as more people start to arrive, that species known as the clergy insinuates itself and churches are built on top of churches.

Neighbors who once lived together harmoniously begin to quarrel
and become enemies. Instead of getting together to savor Sunday,
they hide and secretly nourish a hypocritical religiosity. Unfortunately, in order to escape this dreadful state of affairs one would
have to escape all culture as well. It is sad that these two seem to
be an inseparable pair. In this regard it is somewhat better in the
large cities, but I need to live in the country and have physical ex-
ertion. Given this plan, I don't need my entire inheritance here;
please send me 2000 thalers as soon as possible.

Xenophobia formed a sort of negative counterweight to the democratic ideal that Theodor so admired. Nativism was real and widespread. Native-born Americans often had little sympathy for the hardships endured by recent immigrants and did not like the fact that
Germans kept up their language and wore different styles of clothing.
To some, the worst offense was drinking beer in beer gardens on Sunday. Germans in particular were also suspected of importing foreign
and radical political ideas to the United States and in some places secret
societies were organized to keep Germans out of elected office and deny
them civil rights.[2] One of these societies, the Order of the Star Spangled
Banner, organized in 1849, came to be called the Know Nothings because when they were asked about their organization, they replied that
they knew nothing about it.

During the period leading up to the Civil War, the Know Nothings, who had been melded into the American Party, attempted to
divert people's attention from domestic problems by whipping up anti-
immigrant sentiment. This was particularly true for the election of
1856, but their candidate, Millard Fillmore, received only eight electoral
votes. That was the end of the Know Nothings as an organized party,
although xenophobia continued. The election of 1856 was also notable
for the clear and ominous sectionalism of its outcome. Democrat James
Buchanan won the election by carrying the South. The Republican candidate, John Frémont, took most of the Northern states. Frémont, an
abolitionist, would later become an icon of the Germans.

It is clear from his last letter just how alone Theodor felt. Although
there are no hard numbers, it is known that a substantial number
of immigrants returned home because they were unable to deal with
the social isolation — including the lack of female companionship — the
language, and the backbreaking work. Those immigrants who joined

clubs such as singing circles or the quasi-political gymnastic clubs known as *Turnvereine* were far less likely to be returnees.[3] Theodor was an individualist who tended to do things himself or in ad hoc alliances.

Theodor could not have known when he sent his letter dated 6 March that open revolt was taking place in Prussia. Once again, the winds of revolution came from France. In February King Louis Philippe, who had come to power in 1830, was deposed, in large part because he refused to reform election laws. As might be expected, the first German reactions came in the neighboring Rhineland. On 3 March a largely middle-class crowd stormed into city hall in Cologne demanding civil rights, suffrage, labor protection, a minimum guaranteed standard of living, and state education. A week later, political meetings in Berlin gave way to barricades, strikes, and open insurrection. On 17 March King Frederick William IV lifted press censorship.[4]

The reforms that Franz von Weise had described evidently were not enough or just whetted people's appetites. Baden in southwestern Germany was a particularly intense hotbed of radical activity. At first King Frederick William IV and many of the other ruling princes appeared to move toward an accommodation with the demonstrators. However, weaknesses in the movement soon became apparent that enabled the king to renege. For example, middle-class liberals felt economically threatened by an organized working class, which was trying to gain equal political and social rights.

An assembly convened in Frankfurt attempted to hammer out a constitution that would satisfy all the competing political interests. Delegates came from all over the German-speaking lands and included monarchists, constitutional monarchists, democrats of various stripes, and socialists. In spite of their best efforts, their disunity and political inexperience (there were no political parties at the time) doomed them to failure. In addition, the nationalism of many of the leaders played into the militarism of the Prussian and Austrian aristocracy; that summer Austrian forces under General Windisch-Graetz bombarded Prague after the Czechs declined inclusion in a united Germany. The Frankfurt Assembly hailed this "victory of German weapons." Conservative monarchists reasserted themselves throughout the German states and with military might regained full control. A brief uprising in Prussia in 1849 was crushed militarily.[5]

Many of this failed revolution's leaders, often referred to as '48ers, went to jail; some were executed. However, by a strange historical quirk, quite a few of them ended up in Missouri. They brought their democratic, and in some cases radical, ideals with them. People like Franz Sigel and Friedrich Hecker who made names for themselves during the revolution went on to play important roles in the Union cause in Missouri. German immigration spiraled after the '48 Revolution, fueled by hopelessness, poverty, and discontent. In the 1840s 385,000 Germans emigrated to America; in the next decade that figure swelled to 976,000.[6]

Theodor heard news of the revolution while in St. Paul. On 23 May 1848 he wrote his friend the doctor, and he left no doubt as to his sympathies:

> I would gladly have been there to add my voice to topple all the thrones of the world, and I would have spoken and written now in Europe as much as my strength would have allowed. For the moment, I am too late to give my physical support to the cause of human rights and against brutal power. My breath stopped for joy when I heard that the Hausvogtei [Berlin prison for political prisoners] had been stormed and the martyrs set free, and that it was my old infantry battalion that was the first to go over to the side of the people. They showed Willy in his palace that the people are not just there for his benefit. Why don't you just lock him up in an iron cage like Knipperdolling? But, of course, the Devil's black police won't leave their brother in the lurch. And in your region and Westphalia, in whichever districts come under their religious and political shadow, they will use their poisoned tongues in the service of obscurantism and Prussiandom.

The depth of Theodor's hatred for the monarchy is summed up in the image of the iron cage. Bernhard Knipperdolling was a leader in Münster of the Anabaptists, a sixteenth-century communistic Christian sect. He was elected mayor of Münster in 1533. The regional Protestant princes and the Catholic bishop of the city united to crush the movement, and after Knipperdolling was captured he was brutally tortured. His headless body was placed in an iron cage and put on public display in 1536.[7] The "Devil's black police" refers to the Catholic Church, particularly the Jesuits, which Theodor and many other democrats, like the French revolutionaries before them, saw as a reactionary prop of the monarchy.

In Emmerich the revolution looked nothing like it did in Berlin and other hot spots. Certainly, many people wanted a constitution and relief from some particularly onerous taxes, but in all probability the majority wanted a continuation of the monarchy with constitutional guarantees rather than a republic. Emmerich had a few local leaders, Eugen and Emil de Witt, Jan van Nooy, and a merchant named Custodis, who were particularly vocal about needed changes and gave impassioned speeches. And there were occasional broken windows. However, there was no general uprising in Emmerich, population 6636, nor were there in most other small towns.

At the first People's Assembly (*Volksversammelung*) on 26 March 1848, Eugen de Witt read a petition to be sent to the United Representative Assembly. A wonderful eyewitness account of the "hubbub" in Emmerich is contained in a 4 April 1848 letter written by August Hortmann to his cousin Heinrich von Gimborn, who was away from home at the time:

> A few citizens started to light lamps in the evening in the old market, especially Lensing, Nollen, Wolters, and others. They were joined by more people, and soon many were gathered in the street. When they were a crowd, they marched through town singing. There were a large number of *Turners,* and soon the lower classes had united together. First they went to the houses of several teachers (Klein, Dederich, Hottenrott, Bach, Montigny) and sang. Then they continued marching through the streets.
>
> Soon the upper classes joined them and we had a lively evening until about 10. Later, when I went to your house, I found a large crowd busy imbibing punch. Present were: J. van Eyck, J. Haas, Karl van Eyck, K. Romen, and H. Bleckmann as well as Grandmother, Uncle Eduard, Uncle Pit and Aunt Mieke, Paß, and many more. It was a motley crew!
>
> Next day the *Turners* joined us and we all got German cockades and fashioned a German flag. We wanted to get together that evening again and march through town, which was supposed to be lit. However, Dederich advised against it, and so we didn't.
>
> In the evening, the lamps were lit (the entire front of your house was lit with little lamps), and people were out in the street celebrating, just like the day before. Two large troops of people marched through the town and sang a little ditty to the director, the mayor, etc. You could see the apprehension on the face of the latter, who

had been serenaded by students the evening before. He came forward and told the crowd to have a good time but also to maintain order. Which we pretty much did, except a few of the mayor's windows and those belonging to several others got smashed.

A few days later a citizen's watch was organized because people were concerned about order. Arndt was made commandant. Uncle Pit is first lieutenant; Uncle Eduard, officer; and your father, private. The watch marches through town after 8 in the evening. Some of the guards are armed with guns, others with sabers and pikes.

Emmerichers also make use of the right of free association. They have organized a People's Assembly. The second gathering took place last Sunday. I attended, and so I want to try to describe this Polish parliament for you.

Custodis, who has become the man of the people around here, was elected president at the first assembly. De Witt, the postal secretary, was elected secretary. The president climbed the podium and opened the assembly, which took place at the Kronprinzen (the first was at Wolter's). The president and secretary sat near the podium, surrounded by Emmerich's nobility (Barbus and company).

The town councilor stood in the next room. Custodis stepped down from the podium, and de Witt began to speak. He demanded that the slaughter and flour taxes be turned into a class tax. The mayor tried to tell him that the former was actually more advantageous to Emmerich. Then de Witt spoke again, and when he asked the assembly if they were satisfied with his proposals, they all yelled "Yes!" and "Hurrah!"

Then Custodis took the podium again and made numerous proposals. He was constantly interrupted with yells of "That's right!" "Bravo!" "Long live Custodis!" Well, he's the hero of the people, and everything he proposes goes right through.

During his speech, when he made his proposals about transforming the slaughter and flour taxes, he said, "After superficial calculations..." Bartwijk called out, "That doesn't count!" Thereupon, the entire crowd turned to him and yelled, "Out with him!" "Throw him out the door!" And in fact, people started to move in his direction. But he just stood his ground quietly, while several of the town councilors jumped out of the windows, fearing fisticuffs.

Perhaps because the People's Assembly attracted all Emmerichers, including those of the presumably more radical and violence-prone lower classes, a Constitutional Union was founded in July by members of the civic organizations the *Bürgerverein* and the *Societät*. The Constitutional Union saw itself as a "union for the safeguarding of the constitutional system along democratic lines" and was open to all voting citizens. Its political base was much more middle class, and after its founding, the People's Assembly no longer met.

Despite disbanding quickly, there were some early victories for the People's Assembly. In April the council meetings, which had hitherto been closed, were opened to the public. This came on top of the royal proclamation of freedom of the press on 18 March. Flogging was also abolished, even in the army.

On 14 December 1848 the Constitutional Union in Emmerich agreed to send the following letter to His Majesty the King:

> It is with deep regret that the Constitutional Union recognizes that insurmountable obstacles have arisen, making agreement on a legal framework impossible. The Crown, finding itself forced to protect the fatherland from unforeseen dangers and sacrifices and put an end to the pernicious legal uncertainties, has therefore promulgated a unilateral constitution. We declare ourselves satisfied with the spirit of this granted constitution, and venture to expect that any imperfections and gaps in it will be remedied by the two chambers that will meet soon.[8]

Back in America, Theodor's plans had to be altered because an investment company in which he had money went bankrupt. Theodor felt himself torn between alternatives:

> Since I have had to alter my plan to buy a small plot of land in Switzerland and live there independently, I think it best to stay here for the time being. I await further news from you. I have decided to take part in a buffalo hunt for two months this summer in July and August. In the meantime, I will fill my time by visiting among the Indians. By that time I hope that travel money will have arrived so that I can see the east on my way back to Europe. Failing that, I will settle here and take up cattle raising. Then, if I have one or two teams, I will be able to earn the money I need by driving for Indian traders.

I hope to get detailed news from you soon about political events. Tell my sister Annette about my changed travel plans and tell her that I am well and can't remember when I was as contented and peaceful as I am now.

In early 1849 Theodor returned to Europe. Theodor was, in effect, never more than a tourist in America, suffering malaria in Missouri, spending a hard winter in Wisconsin to observe the Indians, taking part in a buffalo hunt, waiting for his money to arrive. In his short hand-written autobiography, Wilhelm Noot wrote of Theodor that he "traveled for several years for pleasure and knowledge."[9] He never struck roots. He never possessed a clear plan and, and unlike his brother, who was trained in agriculture, perhaps lacked some crucial skills to carry one out. In this he would have been like some other German immigrant intellectuals, such as the "Latin" farmers of Missouri and western Illinois, so called because they knew more Latin than farming, who attempted to wrest a living from the land.

Yet taken alone, such a judgment would be much too harsh. We cannot overestimate the hardships and the loneliness. Without a wife, without stable support from home, and subject to new diseases, life in America could be very difficult. Nevertheless, he learned a great deal about the country and it affected him deeply. Later, when his nephew Bernhard was a settled American, Theodor seriously considered bringing his family back over; when his own boys came of age, he sent them to America, wanting them to experience a free country, as he saw it. And back in Voorthuyzen he built a new house, called Neu (new) Voorthuyzen, in what he considered an American style, attached to a German barn. He even erected a silo. If he could not live in America, he would build a piece of America in Germany.

No sooner was Theodor back in Voorthuyzen than he set about finding a wife. At Franz von Weise's home in Elten, Theodor met Franz's young niece Caroline (Lina), then seventeen, and they fell in love. Lina's father, Carl von Weise, the Cologne magistrate whose family had recently been elevated to nobility, was not pleased. Theodor at age thirty-eight was too old for Lina, from an "illegitimate" family, and a wild man from America with an apparently insane sister-in-law. If he had read his daughter's love letters, some of which she signed "Lina v. Weise, Directress of the Kissing Institute," he would probably not have been amused. In time Franz's gentle prodding and Theodor's patience and good sense overcame the elder von Weise's resistance, and Theodor and Lina were married on 5 June 1849. Their first child, Maria, was born on 10 March the next year but died a few months after birth.

Judging from the letters that have survived from Carl von Weise to Theodor, the men appear to have developed an extraordinarily close and confidential relationship.

Anton in America

The speed with which Theodor went about finding a bride was matched by his moves to gain stewardship of Voorthuyzen. Theodor arrived in early February; Anton and his sons Bernhard and Hubert, aged thirteen and ten, put to sea a mere two and a half months later. Anton now allowed himself to be moved about like a chess piece by his dominant brother. Anton kept his ownership of Voorthuyzen, and Theodor pledged to send him money in a timely fashion, a pledge that Anton had not kept for him.

Before he could leave, Anton had to deal with his wife, Naatje Reygers. There was occasional mention of the "poor woman" in letters from Emmerich to Theodor. It is clear that she was having some sort of emotional difficulties, but whether she was insane, as claimed by many who knew her, or reacting to Anton's erratic and drunken behavior is unknown. Her records were destroyed during the Second World War; they probably would have raised more questions than they answered.[1] Regardless of the source of her difficulties, Anton had no place for her in his new life, his "new start," so he had her committed to an asylum in Holland. How Bernhard and Hubert were affected by their father's actions can only be surmised from later diary entries and letters by Bernhard. Hubert, who was intellectually slow, wrote very few letters as far as we can tell.

After a brief delay in London, father and sons boarded the packet boat *Hendrik Hudson* on 1 May 1849. They arrived in New York on 7 June (two days after Theodor's wedding) and were entered on the ship's manifest as follows:

Aaron Van Derveldt	45	Farmer	Germany
Brown	ditto	13	"	"
Henry	ditto	10	"	"

By whatever name, they had made it.

Atlantic passage aboard a packet boat was not a pleasure cruise. Packet boats were full-rigged ships usually with three masts and square sails. The American ships, of which the *Hendrik Hudson* was one, were generally built for the emigration trade and had large bulging hulls to carry as many passengers as possible in steerage. The *Hendrik Hudson* was considered a first-class ship for insurance purposes, having a very sturdy hull and being built with excellent materials. It weighed a modest 829 tons and carried 350 passengers when Anton came over: 46 in first-class cabins, including 2 infants; 22 in second-class cabins; and 282 in steerage, including 15 infants.

Anton and sons went first class and shared a cabin. They were well treated and well fed. For this privilege they would have paid some 50 pounds. However, in spite of packet ship advertisements stating that "the second cabins and steerage are lofty and airy, and are in every way adapted to promote the comfort and health of the passengers," the poor who traveled in steerage for about 3 pounds were usually subjected to conditions that can hardly be imagined.

In the 1840s and 1850s, two hundred to three hundred steerage passengers — although there are reports of as many as a thousand — were routinely crowded in the 'tween decks into rows of bunk beds. Often four people shared a bunk, unrelated men and women together. The entire area was poorly lit in order to prevent fires, and if the ship leaked, the floor was covered with filthy, sloshing water. Often there were no privies, rarely more than one per one hundred passengers, and people had to relieve themselves wherever they could. Whether the passengers were fed or not was up to the captain, and the food was hardly edible. Often the captain would extort whatever money or possessions the passengers had in exchange for food. Water was severely rationed and as the voyage went on had to be doctored with vinegar to hide the foul taste. No one could wash or clean because there was no water for it, and the stench was terrific.

In these cramped and filthy conditions illnesses such as cholera and typhus, which some passengers brought on board, flourished. Although dozens of fatalities were not uncommon, on one voyage more than five hundred of the eleven hundred Germans aboard the packet *April* were reported to have died of disease en route. The mortality rate for the crossing has been estimated as high as 10 percent, although some research places the overall death rate at just over 1 percent.[2] Controversy over mortality rates at sea aside, it is known that cholera epidemics all over the United States were caused by immigrants who were ill when they arrived. St. Louis was very hard hit by recurring epidemics.

Disease was not the only hazard. From 1847 to 1853, fifty-nine boats loaded with immigrants were lost at sea. In some cases, passengers were rescued by other ships; more often, all passengers drowned. The summer of 1849 was a particularly bad season for ship wrecks.[3]

Given the many hazards of the voyage, it is a shame that neither Theodor's nor Anton's first letters home have survived because they might have provided a first-hand account of the Atlantic passage. The first letter we have from Anton was written from St. Paul. The St. Louis fire that Anton mentioned was the Great Fire of 17 May 1849, which destroyed a large part of the city. In addition, during that summer as many as one hundred people died each day of cholera. St. Louis suffered 8423 registered deaths from the disease. That alone would have convinced him to move on to St. Paul.

St. Paul
25 September 1849

Dear Brother Theodor!

On the assumption that you received my letter from St. Louis, I will tell you about my trip from there. After a 5-day stay in St. Louis, we left the city on 26 June on the steamboat *Franklin II*. This year, St. Louis has been visited by a terrible fire and cholera outbreaks. After a 6-day trip, we arrived without mishap in St. Paul on 3 July. We stayed in Galena for a day and purchased all the items that Noot wanted. When we arrived in St. Paul, we finally met Le Roche, who sends his best regards. He told me where Noot lives. My meeting with Noot, his wife, and son Louis was felicitous; our reception was heartfelt and friendly.

St. Paul, the capital of Minnesota Territory, is growing by leaps and bounds; buildings are going up day and night. The number of inhabitants is estimated at 2000 souls. The governor is of German extraction; he moved here just last year from Pennsylvania and seems to be a sociable yet thorough man. The day after my arrival, i.e., 4 July, which is the anniversary date of America's liberation, Noot and I went into town to watch the celebration. The governor came up and welcomed us. We then fell into a conversation that lasted a half hour, and as we went our separate ways, he offered his support and advice should situations arise. This in contrast to the crowd of bureaucrats who suck out the people's marrow.

As far as region, climate, and way of life are concerned, one has to get used to everything. The soil contains an admixture of clay and is light and also contains sand with much humus. In my opinion, with a little work, it will be far preferable to the best marl.

The weather seems to be subject to far greater variability than in our region of Europe. This is primarily because of the frequent storms, although, in the summer after a storm, it can be uncomfortably frosty for several days. Nevertheless, because the soil has such a high humus content, it seems to hold the warmth better than any other kind of soil. Every farmer here tries to grow his melons, cucumbers, etc., without dung, in cold ground, and with only moderate preparation of the soil.

However, because of superficial and careless cultivation as well as poor choice when ordering seeds, these crops often fail, and so, I have seen the plowing up of the prairies. The sod is plowed in 16–18 inch furrows that are at most 3 inches deep. Once the land has been tilled, it is left for a year so it can be sown with oats or potatoes. I have seen numerous fields prepared this way that were not even worth mowing. Potato farming here is also poor. Potatoes are simply pressed into superficially prepared fields so that their success is left to chance and the elements. They are hardly tended at all. It isn't hard to understand why potato fields are completely obscured by weeds, given this cultivation.

Corn is also grown. However, it isn't worth growing here because it doesn't reach the necessary maturity. The proper cultivation of wheat appears unknown here. I have seen several wheat fields that failed. They sow wheat twice in succession here. In my opinion, the prairies in this region are particularly well-suited to sheep farming. In terms of plants, rye, oats, buckwheat, peas, beans, and potatoes should all do well.

Last week we went with Noot up the Rum River to where you had your claim. The house that you built, including additional outbuildings, are in the same state in which you left them. Last spring Noot planted potatoes in a few spots which the Indians seem to have harvested. We stayed there for three days. I was looking forward to finally shooting a deer, but all I saw was a few tracks. The damned Indians had been fighting there for five weeks and had either killed everything or driven it off. We didn't even see a single prairie chicken and so our hunting was confined to about 150 pigeons. I would like the claim if the damned Indians didn't live there and the area were more settled. However, the nearest neighbor is the ferryman who lives 3 miles away where the Rum River empties into the Mississippi. In your next letter, please tell me what I should do if I take over these claims. Noot apparently was offered $80 for it; on the other hand, I have heard from another person that he would sell it if he were offered $100.

This winter I will be forced to camp with Bernhard and Hubert at Noot's. You know about Noot's house: there isn't a single place where one can stand, lie, or sit dry. Our crates have been sitting outside for more than 6 weeks. We too have been subject to the weather; we haven't changed clothes for 6 weeks. Right when I arrived, I decided to build a small house, 20 feet long and 18 feet wide, adjacent to Noot's log cabin. We hired a carpenter for a few days; Bernhard and I did the rest of the work. We got the wood at St. Anthony's Falls using Noot's ox team. On that occasion, I received letters addressed to you that had arrived there the previous year.

Completely bereft of guldens, I and my two sons are now forced to stay with Noot and study English so that in the spring, should the opportunity present itself, I will be able to stake a claim and work it. Today I will write to the banker Angelrodt and ask him for a credit of 300 thalers. One can't make it without money here, and there are things that need to be bought before winter. Noot doesn't have a red cent either.

Bernhard and Hubert are doing well and send their best regards to you and your family. Give Lina my regards and a kiss.

Your loving brother,
Anton

How Things Go Wrong

The next few letters have been lost, but we get an idea of what happened from later letters—not just Anton's, but also those from Wilhelm Noot, Lorenz Degenhardt, Robert Barth, and Anton's young son Bernhard. It is impossible at this remove to reconstruct exactly what occurred and who did what to whom. One can only say with certainty that this was an immigration attempt that was coming apart. Like Theodor, Anton spoke little English and perhaps never really learned. Because of the language barrier, he did not realize that the seventy-five acres he bought had title problems. But, unlike his brother, Anton came into conflict with almost everyone. All of these letters coupled with what he had himself experienced of his brother would have told Theodor to protect himself and the family fortune as best he could—even if it meant cutting Anton off.

St. Louis

24 December 1850

Dear Brother!

From your letter dated 2 October, I take it that my letters have not been arriving, and I assume that they have been seized at the Prussian border.

I will use the days around Christmas to describe to you in detail how I was cheated and lied to by W. Noot. I'll write you a short note now because mail is going out to New York today. I left St. Paul at the end of May 1850 and arrived in St. Louis the beginning of June. I have already told you from St. Paul about my plans to come here or to go to Cincinnati.

When I got to St. Louis, I found the $200 account you had opened for me with Angelrodt, Eggers & Barth. Then I boarded with Westhooven, and at the beginning of August I rented a 20-acre farm from the previous renter about 6 miles from St. Louis for $50. I also bought his entire inventory, consisting of cattle, pigs, a horse, and his entire harvest for $450. We moved there with Westhooven and his brother-in-law Scholten. We didn't get along, and I used the first best opportunity to get rid of this family.

For $2000 I bought a property of about 75 acres of uncleared woods a mile from my farm on the land route to St. Louis. The land is of the best quality, and I apparently got it under ideal conditions: $200 down payment with the final payment due 1 January 1852.

Your brother Anton

Wilhelm Noot also wrote Theodor about his altercation with Anton, and in a separate letter about Anton's quarrel with Westhooven and Scholten. Even if one assumes that his account was self-serving, Noot's letters must have confirmed what Theodor already suspected. It showed a man completely out of control and leaving behind him a humiliating reputation. It should be remembered that these events, if we credit them, took place in very cramped quarters and that two young boys had to watch them unfold:

12 September 1850

Dear Theodor!

In case Anton has written you, I'm sure he will have tried to prettify his behavior toward me with lies. For now, I will relate to you what I consider my duty. I am very indebted to you, and I think that it is therefore necessary that you understand what Anton thinks and says about you. While in a particularly angry and drunk condition and in the presence of Bernhard and Hubert, Anton tried to paint you as a great egoist. He accused you of having the entire fortune in your hands and sending him here to Siberia, and he cursed you repeatedly. You may be able to cure him of this crazed opinion as you see fit.

Fourteen days before his departure, after I had reminded him repeatedly of the $100 debt that he knew very well he had incurred for boots, bedding, flannel, shirts, whiskey, etc. for himself and his sons, and after telling him that I would like compensation as soon as he arrived in St. Louis, he answered, "Make a more exact accounting so that you don't come up short." This I did. Having arrived in St. Louis, he sends me a bill for $125 for his help building the house as well as $200 for your old claim on the Rum River. Anton knows very well that I had to sell the claim for $100 specifically to help him. Many times I offered it to him so that he could live there, the last time just a few days before the sale. And, I have nothing against crediting him with this $100, although he says that I appropriated the claim illegally. He knows perfectly well that you gave it to me before I came here from Mishanni. Furthermore, he demands $25 for his sons' work. I charged Anton $3.50 per week per person. Anton had $30 when he arrived as well as bacon and flour valued at about $26.90 and a goat worth $5. Later he had Angelrodt, Eggers & Barth pay me two installments of $100.

When Anton arrived I already had two boarders. They gladly paid $3 per week and didn't drink a gallon per week the way Anton does. This winter a gallon cost $1. Also, Anton cooked for himself for quite a while because he could drink more and because he was embarrassed to appear at the table in front of my wife in a drunken state. His sons ate with us. But enough.

In December I am expecting another addition to the family. Your acquaintances in St. Paul inquire frequently about you. Jackson wanted to write you one of these days. Please give my best to your wife. My wife also sends greetings.

Your W. Noot

Matters seem to have gone from bad to worse, as this letter from Noot demonstrates:

Ramsey, 2 November 1850

Dear Theodor!

I hope that you are in possession of my letter dated 15 September in answer to yours of 9 January, which I received on 12 February. Since then, I received your letter of 12 September on 26 October.

It is irresponsible of Anton not to write you; if he had any sense and feeling, he would see it as his duty to write you frequently and in detail about his circumstances, which have become so muddled as a result of his debts. When he was here, I did everything in my power to get him to write. At the beginning of the year he actually started a letter to you. I gave him a few items to send along, but of course the letter was never completed, let alone sent off. He lied to me, saying that he had sent it off, but I know his ways only too well; he's tried this maneuver on me twice. Later, as I wrote in my letter of 12 September, when he accused you of being the greatest egoist and swore never to write you again, all my efforts were for naught. Because you have asked me to, I will write very openly about Anton. I would just like to say—perhaps it's superfluous— that you shouldn't think that I am exaggerating a bit because Anton mistreated me. What I wrote and am writing is the absolute truth. I owe you too much to forget my debt of duty to you.

Day before yesterday I received a letter from Westhooven—the first in a year—and I'm afraid it contains nothing good about Anton. The following are Louis's own words:

"Anton van Dreveldt and sons came to board at my place for a while last summer. Since he thought that he wanted to farm near St. Louis, he bought a farm 8 miles from St. Louis and convinced me and my family as well as Scholten to move to the farm with him. I gave up my business in town to do so. We moved to the farm on 27 August, and on 7 October we moved out again, Scholten with his 2 children and I with my wife and child. On Saturday van Dreveldt had gone to the city and returned befogged. Words were exchanged, and one thing led to another and we moved out on Monday after he treated us shabbily. I am in a hurry right now, but I will write you about it in more detail later and write up a bill so that I can either settle accounts with him or take him to court. While we were together he bad-mouthed you and your wife and child as well. If I get wind that he is doing the same to us, we'll teach him a lesson. Send us your bill against him so that you can take him to court as well. We will be pleased to help you. . . ."

But that was not the end of what Theodor got to hear about Anton. In 1851 his old university friend Lorenz Degenhardt confirmed what Noot and Westhooven had to say and then added details about the seventy-five acres that Anton had bought:

Westhooven talked him into buying a piece of land, and he [Anton] lost his initial down payment of $200. You see, Westhooven wanted to go into partnership with your brother, but your brother was to pay everything. The title to the land wasn't good. A payment on the land of $900 was due on 1 January 1851, and the land was sold because of nonpayment. The seller ended up re-buying it. I wish that I could give you more pleasant news about your brother. I consider it my duty not to cover anything up. Wherever I can help, I will do so.

How could Anton get himself into such a situation? Disclosures such as this could do nothing but confirm Theodor's resolve to hold his brother on a tight financial leash and let him stand or fall on his own.

Robert Barth of the St. Louis banking firm Angelrodt, Eggers & Barth also corresponded with Theodor. His assessment was sober and objective. Among other things he mentioned Anton's "quarterly money," the

$100 Barth was to pay Anton every three months. This was the tight financial leash Theodor imposed on Anton, exactly the sort of humiliating supervision that the Provost had exercised when Anton was a young man.

With his capital and property gone, Anton was reduced to renting a farm. During this period, several writers commented on how Anton and his children were living. And at about this time, Robert Barth mentioned that Anton was once again frequenting low saloons. Still, he tried to do the best he knew how. In October 1852 Degenhardt wrote:

> The farm on which he now lives must be miserable. Without having actually seen it, I can easily imagine how it might look. Miserable old log cabin with one room, as primitive as the one you built in Minnesota; rotting fences that allow the animals to roam the fields; in general everything in disorder and disrepair. The farm belongs to the estate of a local businessman, and the administrator doesn't want to spend any money on improvements. You can imagine how your brother and his two sons live and work there, without a woman or other person to help. I don't have to describe it.

Robert Barth raised other concerns:

> As far as the children are concerned, things are not good. They are growing up completely without an education, and I fear that your brother is making no efforts in this regard. It is just too delicate a matter to broach with him, and so we will have to let the matter take its course and hope for the best.

By 1854 Theodor and Anton were on the verge of an actual break. In response to what must have been an accusatory letter from Theodor, Anton responded in desperation:

St. Louis, 16 March 1854

Theodor!

I received your letters dated January and February on Monday from Herr Barth. By their provocative, insulting, and suspicious contents they are suited for repelling conciliatory souls. You have really achieved a horrible level of insult and suspiciousness in your last letter that verges on virtuosity. Your request for a rendering of accounts is as incomprehensible as everything that went before. In your letters, you keep talking about Noot. He can tell you better than I what he is about; I didn't make him a scoundrel, and I didn't make any claims against him. While I was in Minnesota, I paid him two and three times more than I owed. By way of thanks, he intercepted letters and money addressed to me. Don't think I only say this behind his back. Four years ago I wrote an account, yes, black on white, of his misappropriations and stated that if he did not cease and desist with his diabolical and egoistical intentions, sooner or later he would be punished for his diabolical and egoistic behavior.

Never, ever, was it my intention to anger you because you had recommended that I travel to St. Paul and Noot. It was my free will. If there had not been such bad cholera in St. Louis when I came here five years ago, I never would have gone to St. Paul. But enough of Noot; I don't want to hear or know anything of him.

I sent you a letter dated 15 December along with a few lines in English from Bernhard, which I gave to Herr Barth on 18 December 1853. Perhaps you have not received it, or perhaps you are denying receipt because I asked for advice on a matter that was unpleasant. Whichever; please change your opinion and answer the above-mentioned letter. Whatever your answer may be, I am prepared for it. If you feel anything for your brother, place yourself in the unpleasant situation and write me something reasonable. I don't want to keep you in an unpleasant situation any longer and bore you with this letter. I will make it short and to the point: I have left the farm. Bernhard will probably start a job in the next few days in a store. Hubert remains in the country for the time being with a former neighbor. I'm in the boring position of playing the retiree. It would be good to buy land, but it would have to be discussed. Send travel money as soon as possible; Anton is coming in order to cement brotherly love and fidelity with Theodor. Give my regards to whoever wants them.

Your brother, Anton

It was probably at this point that Anton conceived the idea of selling Voorthuyzen to Theodor so that he would again have the capital to buy a farm. Bernhard was to learn accounting and bookkeeping and become Anton's liaison to the American world. This plan does show a great deal of strategizing on Anton's part. The question was whether he could convince Theodor.

Unfortunately, the December letter that Anton referred to would have put Theodor in a very uncomfortable position. His plea for advice was of course designed to shake loose money, but more than that, Anton told him that he had kicked out of his house a man from Emmerich after the man had asked for help. Theodor would have to deal with the small-town repercussions of Anton's actions. This would have been the last straw for Theodor.

Bernhard's letter, dated 15 December 1853 when he was eighteen, was written in English. We only have a German translation, which has been retranslated. The contents were probably dictated by Anton:

Dear Uncle!

From your letter to Father, which arrived yesterday, I can see that you have sympathy for our plight. And so, I will fulfill my promise to you to write you a letter from America in English. I would be very pleased to get a reply from you, and I would very much want to write you about our adventures at least every other month.

At first we were well received by Noot, so it seemed. Our first priority was to get a house for ourselves because a few days after our arrival there was such a downpour that we were forced to take shelter under our umbrella in Noot's cabin, which only has a bark roof. Father built a frame house near Noot's log cabin. The wood cost almost $200. Father gave Noot our last money but hesitated to give him the supplies and money that had come up the river from St. Louis on the last boat before winter. However, then we had nothing, and Noot's behavior toward us changed. At first it was only little things, but gradually he became ruthless and mean-spirited. I will include a few examples since it would be too much to mention them all.

The first thing that happened was that Noot came and said that he had sold your claim near the island for $400 to an employee of Mr. Steele, which he didn't have the right to do. He said, "You wouldn't have wanted to live there anyway."

Then one day in the middle of winter when the average temperature was 30° Reaumur [below zero], he got it into his head to take away an elbow pipe that sticks out of our cabin. So, we were forced to put out the fire because of the smoke. The cold was so bad that Father's leg froze, and he was tied to his bed for 14 days.

We were forced to pawn our silver watch for $2 in St. Paul. This enabled me to buy some mustard for a plaster for his foot. As if that wasn't mean enough, Noot had the shameless audacity to tell Father that the pain would go away if he hiked a few miles in the snow. This after visiting us and seeing Father writhing on the bed.

In the mean time, we forced him to reinstall the pipe, which he had already tossed on a scrap heap.

I'm sure that after reading this you will say that it can't be true. Still, when we left him in the spring, he had the shameless gall to present a bill for $500 for room and board, which was a bit hard to take since we almost always made our own food. After Father got to St. Louis, he sent Noot a bill for a considerable sum of money. Then Noot shamelessly sent Father a letter through Angelrodt & Barth in which he threatened to make the entire matter public in the newspapers. Since he was apparently more afraid of such an airing than we, we looked in vain for it in the papers. I assure you that what I have written above is the absolute truth.

Later in his letter, Bernhard came to talk about his education: "If you do not send money, I will be forced to grow up like one of those people who only know how to do things half well, and I will be of no use to human society. It is in your power to send money. I beg you to do so, and I give you my most sacred promise that it will not be lost." Apparently, Theodor did send money for that purpose, and on 28 May 1854, Bernhard wrote that he was studying "double entry bookkeeping and arithmetic" at Jones' Commercial College.

Johann Anton Goossens (1765–1834),
Provost of the Foundation, St. Martin's
Church, Emmerich. A priest during
the Napoleonic Wars, Goossens was
influenced by the liberal sentiments of
the time. He fathered Anton, Theodor, and their sister Annette and profited from Napoleon's secularization of
the churches.

Left: Emmerich with Beurtschiffe and
St. Martin's Church, nineteenth century.

Above: "Before we reached New Orleans,
we saw the St. Charles Hotel rising above
the city. It is a building something like
the Pantheon in Paris; however, it is only
an inn." New Orleans (1840s). Courtesy
The Historic New Orleans Collection.

Above: Burschenschafter Theodor van Dreveldt (1831–32). Theodor joined the political fraternity at the University of Bonn. As a result of this activity, he spent time in prison. This experience led to his emigration in 1844. The window overlooks the Rhine.

Top right: "In St. Louis, I had taken a boat that connected with another one just above the falls, and I was obliged to wait for it." St. Louis Levee. Daguerreotype by Thomas Easterly, 1848. Missouri Historical Society, St. Louis.

Bottom right: Neu Voorthuyzen, built by Theodor upon his return in 1849. The style of the house is completely foreign to Germany and is thought to represent his idea of an American home. Theodor also built a silo near the house, another non-German touch. Photo ca. 1925.

Left: Theodor (1811–80), date unknown. Theodor was the younger of
the two van Dreveldt brothers.
A sunny personality, he was the first
to emigrate.

Right: Anton van Dreveldt (1804–
59), date unknown. The older
brother, Anton appears to have been
an irresponsible alcoholic who got
along with no one. Nonetheless,
with money from his sale of Voorthuyzen and help from his son
Bernhard, he was able to make a go
of it in America.

Left: Bernhard van Dreveldt (1835–66), date unknown. A troubled young man, ever ready to see a slight. Most of his letters from America show a preoccupation with dollars and cents. Bernhard came into conflict with almost everyone, except for his loyal wife, Maria.

Right: Maria von Weise (1839–1931), date unknown. Maria and Bernhard married over the initial objections of her father, and she gamely set about making a new life on the Illinois plains. She returned to Germany with her children three years after her husband's untimely death.

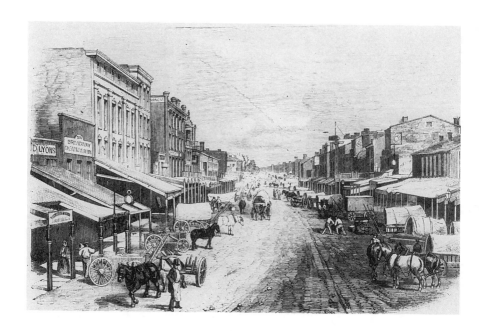

"I had a great deal to buy in St. Louis because a store such as ours has to carry just about everything, so it was no small task. Goods are very expensive, but I buy in the expectation that the prices will go even higher. Cotton goods are insanely high, e.g., calico goes for 16–17 cents per yard, plain unbleached cotton cloth is 25 cents, etc." The Broadway, St. Louis, the business district where Bernhard and Hubert bought supplies. Wood engraving from the *Illustrated London News*, 1858. Missouri Historical Society, St. Louis.

Bernhard: From Voorthuyzen to New Voorthuyzen

As Anton mentioned in his 16 March letter, he had decided to settle matters with his brother, and in the spring of 1855 he and Bernhard arrived at Voorthuyzen, Hubert having been placed in a school run by Wilhelm Krech, a free-thinker in Hermann, Missouri. The brothers renegotiated their agreement concerning the property, and Anton sold a portion of it to Theodor outright. With capital in their pockets, father and son returned to America. We may gauge the tenor of the negotiations by the fact that Anton and Theodor never wrote each other again; from then on, Bernhard handled all correspondence on behalf of his father.

After searching for suitable farmland through the summer, Anton decided on cleared acreage in Prairie du Long near Hecker and some fourteen miles east of Waterloo, Illinois, a flat and fertile expanse with a farmhouse and several stands of trees. The deed, entered into the deed book at the Waterloo courthouse on 3 October 1855, delineated the property:

1. Part of Claim 2071 two thousand Seventy one Survey 605 six hundred and five bounded and described as follows to wit: commencing on the south side of said Survey, on the west bank of Richland Creek, thence up the creek sixty poles to a corner, thence in a westerly direction to the end of said survey, so as to cut one hundred and seventy acres off the south side of said survey; also

2. The east four acres and a quarter more or less of the south east fractional quarter of Section three, in Township three south of Range eight west and commencing on the southwest corner of Claim 2071 Survey 605, down to the section line; also

3. Forty-seven and $^{14}/_{100}$ acres, more or less, being the northern part of the east fractional half of Section Ten in Township three south of range eight west. The said tract of land as measured and marked by Thomas Singleton County Surveyor on the 18th of December 1840 also,

4. Lot thirty seven part of claim 1262 twelve hundred sixty-two Survey 606 six hundred six containing forty (40) acres, also

5. Lot forty-five (45) containing thirty-eight (38) acres, it being the north west thirty-eight acres of Claim 1262, Survey 606, also

6. Lots forty-one (41) and forty-two (42) of Claim 1262 twelve

hundred sixty-two Survey 606 six hundred six containing forty (40) acres each.

For these 380 acres (more or less), Anton paid Christian Hermann Kettler $7500. Anton had learned from his earlier experience; the title to the farm was not clear at the time of sale so a trust was set up for the express purpose of protecting Anton in case Kettler could not prove ownership. According to the trust deed, Robert Barth was a trustee.

The first letter we have from Bernhard after the purchase is dated 7 November 1856, and the family may not have moved in much before then. Bernhard called the farm "New Voorthuyzen," a name that would soon be abandoned, probably at Anton's insistence. In that first letter to his uncle, Bernhard revealed that he had absorbed some of his father's diplomacy and tact. While reading this next letter, keep in mind that Robert Barth had been Anton's banker since he arrived in America and Theodor's banker and friend before that; he was also a trustee of the farm:

I can't avoid mentioning an unpleasant experience we had with Barth. Just so that you don't believe a distorted version, I must tell you that this is what happened:

When I went to Barth's office and showed him the two letters of credit for $2250, Barth told me that I would do well to sell it at a $1/10$% discount. I told him that I would certainly try to get the highest possible price for it and that I would be returning to the city in 5–6 days. Once I had Father's signature, he could buy it, assuming that he paid as much for it as everyone else. However, I wanted to draw $850 on it (an overdraft) since the first installment of $500 to Kettler was due next day, 3 October. At the same time, we also wanted to pay Kettler the interest that had accumulated over the previous year. Barth had no problem with that. Since you are familiar with banking practices here, you know that this is nothing unusual. Any American banker who has had a relationship with a client such as ours would advance him $2000 or more at the same rate as one's deposits. We expected the same allowances as we gave when Barth held our $6000 for more than 4 months at 6%. We would have liked to get 12%. From what I have written so far, you will see that we did not commit ourselves to selling him the letter at whatever price he wanted.

And we didn't. As soon as I left Barth, I went to a few other banks to find out how much the letter was worth to them. The first bank I went into (Blocke & Evers) offered to exchange the letter at par value, and the second bank (Weil & Bros.) even offered ¼% premium if I could get the letter back to them in 2–3 days with Father's signature. This was already $28.12 more than Barth offered, so I didn't even consider it necessary to visit the gentleman again, since a man such as Barth is not ignorant of the value of a letter of credit. So, I sold the letter to Blocke & Evers; I couldn't get it back in time for the other bank.

Well, Barth was very upset about this when I came by a few days later to deposit the money and repay my debt to him. He addressed me in a tone of voice more befitting a Prussian civil servant than a businessman in St. Louis. He seems to have gotten it into his head that dealing with another bank is tantamount to lèse majesté. Naturally, we closed our account immediately, and whether we do business with him again depends solely on him.

That is the twenty-year-old Bernhard, as prickly as his father and willing to overturn a long-term relationship over $28.12 without so much as an attempt at negotiation. His quick-trigger temper appeared in later situations as well and with little indication that he was hearing his own words.

How did he see himself? Unlike his father, who seemed never able to look clearly at himself, Bernhard made several attempts at self-assessment. In November 1860 he started a diary, which he quickly abandoned. In his first entry, dated 25 November, Bernhard wrote:

I also want [to use my diary] to think about the past as time and mood allow. The past — and my *very, very* unhappy youth. Should not this past serve as guarantor of a happier future? Have I not earned a holy right to a happy future as a result of suffering and my longing for an education of the intellect which I could not have? . . . But what is the point of all this: Man is the creator of his own fate.

Two weeks later, Bernhard gave voice to his basic insecurity and shame around people:

How anxious I become when I have to appear in public, even when, as was the case this afternoon, I had business before a simple justice of the peace. I sued John Emmerson for breach of contract regarding the digging of a ditch. I'm sure we will win, so why the anxiety! All I have to do is say a few words to the jury, which seems such a ticklish thing for me.

It's the same feeling I had in Germany last summer when I was not even able to respond to a toast offered me and Maria. Before and after I had no trouble talking. Shame on this dumb . . .

The toast was raised on his wedding day; one may imagine that the guests were amused by the young man's inarticulateness on his big day, but to Bernhard it was a sign of basic, abysmal inadequacy. A year later in a letter to Theodor, whom he respected and needed but who would also served as a goad and irritant, he wrote:

In one of your letters, you said that in my youth I had many advantages over other young people. Honestly, Theodor, you can't be serious! If there was ever a person who had to bury his youthful dreams in an early grave, it was I. I did it in desperation and with intense hatred for all humankind. Who knows what would have become of me had it not been for Maria!

Here is a young man seething with resentments, ashamed of where he came from and who he was. His mother was taken from him at thirteen and "put away." He had to live with an alcoholic father under miserable conditions and watch him fall out with every acquaintance he made. He wanted to become an engineer, but had to settle for a short course in double-entry bookkeeping and arithmetic. No wonder he was subject to rage. In fact, one might wonder that he functioned as well as he did. And how did he do it? " Man is the creator of his own fate." He "stuffed" it, lost himself in the daily struggle to make money. Bernhard also developed into something of a loner, falling out with several partners, always thrown back on his own resources. Still, he clung to family, even when they disappointed him. We should not be surprised to see rage in his letters squirting out under stress and at questionable targets.

Maria, his wife, occasionally played the role of peacemaker when Bernhard was angry at his uncle. She deeply loved Bernhard, who died at age thirty. Until her death in 1931 at age ninety-two, Maria always referred to him as "mein Bernhard"; her second husband was merely "der Dobbelmann."

Despite Bernhard's emotional undertow, Anton, Bernhard, and Hubert settled into farm life on their own farm. Bernhard's letters were full of activity. Even early on, he showed tremendous ambition and hardheadedness. Bernhard's moods and judgment are also evident in the following letters:

New Voorthuyzen
9 April 1857

Dear Uncle!

First, thank you ever so much for the good will you showed in procuring $5476.50 for us. I'm sure it cost a great deal of effort on your part to get it to me before our due date, even though it can no longer help me enter into the partnership with Hunersdorf and Grupe that I described to you. The day after I sent you our too-hastily-printed business cards, the entire project crashed. I found out that instead of being able to put up $2500, Grupe came to the table with $5000 — in debt to his former company in New York, Maschmeier & Grupe. He thought nothing of drawing me and Hunersdorf into his hopeless situation, a mean trick. Under those circumstances, I had no choice but to pull out while I still could, which I had to do carefully because I was almost too committed. I had, after all, agreed to have business cards printed up that bound my name to Grupe's. He might have been able to prove that a partnership existed because of it. In any case, I pulled back and consider myself lucky. Grupe has disappeared. I am in the same position I was in four months ago, except that I am down $200. Cheap enough, as it goes, for a lesson that my friend Bennert tried to teach me in theory, namely never to go into business with friends. Apart from that, I've lost time, which can never be made up.

24 May 1857. That is as far as I got, partly because of my depressed mood, partly because I was overwhelmed with business. I have recently had to wage some hard fights, but I am now again at peace with myself. That is the main thing, even if people's good opinion of me, which I used to enjoy, has lessened considerably. I have promised Father that I will stay with him until after the harvest. After that, I will seek further employment. Hubert is well and sends his regards. He has become a real farmer and can hold his own with anybody else.

One would think that having fallen out with Grupe, who tried to manipulate him into a bad deal, Bernhard would want nothing to do with him. But on 31 July 1858 Bernhard wrote Theodor a self-serving letter that contained an educational fable for the elder "greenhorn," delivered with Bernhard's usual high-handed arrogance. It finished with a little surprise, but no real explanation:

> I assume that when you stayed in this country, you had more than occasional opportunity to notice that young people never go very far as clerks. Often they even ruin their health in the process of benefiting their company. Customers from afar may come to the city only once or twice a year, and they get it in their minds to have a good time at the expense of the company where they buy. Then it falls to the clerk to accompany them all night long, sometimes for an entire week, as they go from one entertainment spot to another.
>
> No, the only way he will get ahead is if he opens some sort of business himself. That often requires good luck as well as the usual industriousness and perseverance. Then, in a few years, he may hoist himself into independence. I'm sure that you will have seen this often enough. Since such an opportunity now presents itself with advantages that stand out more clearly day by day, I hope that you will do everything in your power to make my desires a reality. In exchange, I pledge my services to you in whatever needs you may have in the future.
>
> In my last letter, I don't think I mentioned that I've known Grupe for years and that he is my only tested friend; he's almost like a brother. I mention this in order to forestall the spread of all the usual gossip about irresponsible partnerships and second marriages, etc., which are often on the tongues of people who haven't the faintest idea how business is conducted in America. You will get to know Hunersdorf personally when he visits, and if you are interested, he will fill you in on the details of our projected business.

The main subject of almost all of Bernhard's letters to Theodor was money. Bernhard buried himself in the making of money, in getting ahead, in escaping his past. We have no record of how Theodor felt being treated like a pump by his young nephew or how he reacted to the news about Grupe. Everything that Bernhard asked for was in accordance with Theodor's agreement with Anton, and Theodor almost always complied.

> Dear Uncle, I must once again knock on your door and remind you that America is a country where nobody rests and everybody

needs money. Yesterday, on Papa's 54th birthday, he gave the entire farm to me and Hubert to run on our own. He wants nothing more than a free roof and loving care from us. At the same time, Papa promised to lend us all of his monies which are currently in your possession and which you are to send over, at 8% interest. And so I have given up my idea of living in the city and will put all my effort and energies into making the farm more valuable and also make Freedom, about a mile from here, into a thriving small town.

And this is why I must now again make use of your ability to pay. By 15 November I absolutely need $1200, and I have every confidence in you that you will be able to procure the 2000 thalers that are due by then. Please see to it that the 2000 thalers in question are in my possession soon. Since I have been a partner in the store in Freedom for a year now, I need the money badly. You can imagine how unpleasant it would be to have to borrow money here at the usual high interest rate when we already have the money in Europe at 5%.

By the end of April, there was no more talk of his "most tested friend." Grupe had disappeared, never to be mentioned again. And again there was no explanation; perhaps Grupe was not willing to sleep in the store to keep guard. Bernhard introduced his new partner, Johan Bernard Jansen, in an off-handed way:

Freedom

28 April 1859

Dear Uncle!

I would have written long ago if I weren't constantly interrupted by one sort of business or another. Today, however, the opportunity is presenting itself to me. It is unusually cold for the season, and the weather is inclement. As a result, few customers are coming to our store, and Jansen and I, after having pretty much exhausted all means of entertaining ourselves, fell into the grips of boredom. He is dealing with it by reading and I by writing letters.

I don't think I have introduced you to Jansen yet. He is the son of a well-to-do farmer from the area around Wittmund in East Friesland. Kettler knows him well. He has been in America and this region for 6–7 years. At home, his father was unhappy with his altogether too cavalier conduct while attending a business school in Osnabrück; later he ended up as a clerk at his uncle Mainz's in Carolinensiel in East Friesland. There, he seems not to have allowed the experience to go to waste, and he bettered himself to the point that about two years ago, his father sent him $1000. He used that money to found our present store. He is very active and frugal, and his goal is to return to Friesland a rich man or not at all. Now you have something of a picture of him. I must add that, to this point in any case, I am quite satisfied with our partnership, all the more so since I would not otherwise have been able to participate in such a store because of my farm duties. It is only possible because I return home every evening while Jansen stays in Freedom and sleeps in the store. When I come in in the morning, he has generally swept the place and gotten it ready for the day. In exchange, I have taken over the bookkeeping chores.

I am quite satisfied with our profits from the business. Since February 1st of this year, we have sold $3800 worth of merchandise, which means that our sales for the year should come to $16,000. That is satisfactory for a start. If we had $2–3000 more capital, we could almost certainly count on sales of $25,000. Our inventory fluctuates between $3–5000, and our profit is on average 19%.

In fact, between 15 July 1859 and 4 December 1865, the commercial reporting agency R. G. Dun & Co. audited Bernhard's creditworthiness a total of 13 times. The first entry, with Jansen as co-proprietor, reads, "5123 July 15/59 Firm has no R. E. personal abt 25c$. 'D' out of the partnership is rich tho other is not. I think cr can be given to this firm to some amt with care."[1] Each subsequent report gave him and his company a clean bill of health as well.

It would be unfair to Bernhard to say that his letters were only about money. He also filled in Theodor about the problems encountered by a farmer and the daily routine of a store keeper:

> The only trouble we are having is with housekeepers. As you know, female help is at a premium here and there is quite a market, so it is hard to keep one for any length of time. It generally falls to me to find another one, even when I am in St. Louis. I can assure you that this is no easy task, and even though we now have a very good housekeeper, I would give God knows what if Aunt Lenchen were here and kept house for us.

> Each month we take turns going to St. Louis on buying trips. We get our goods as far as Belleville by train, and then from

there farmers bring it here by return freight when the opportunity arises. The Belleville & Red Bud Hack arrived at 4:00 this afternoon. It brought the mail, and we have to check the bags and take out the news for the Hecker P.O. As a result, things have livened up here, and I won't be able to finish this letter before tomorrow.

In late June, the daily routine on the farm and in the store was broken:

Prairie du Long, Ill.

2 July 1859

5 A.M.

Dear Uncle Theodor!

Returned home from St. Louis last night. Now that I have collected myself somewhat, I must discharge my sad duty and tell you that our dear good father has parted from life. Papa is dead and lost to us forever. The thought of it is terrible, but unfortunately true: I must tell you this fact as quickly as the news reached us since I am not able to write a long introduction, and you must be as strong and composed in the face of it as my brother and I.

Papa left us last Monday morning, 27 June, in good spirits with the intention of taking a trip up the Mississippi to St. Paul. We had just begun the wheat harvest, and since he never much liked the noise and doings of the workers, he decided to get away. He could also get away from the unbearable heat for 2–3 weeks. It was supposed to be a pleasure trip. He arrived in St. Louis on Monday evening in good condition and even accompanied a friend of his, Herr Rudolf Bockhoff, our housekeeper's brother, to one of the summer garden theaters that have become so popular in St. Louis. He stayed until 10 o'clock and then returned to his hotel to go to bed. Bockhoff accompanied him to the hotel. They said good night, and Papa told him that he would come by at noon the next day and have lunch with him. Next morning, Tuesday, Papa was still well, had his breakfast as usual, and then went to see Herr Barth to get some traveling money. He stayed at the bank for about an hour and left at 10:30 with the remark that he wanted to look at the steamboat schedules so he could get out of St. Louis and the heat as fast as possible. Instead, he walked up Market St. as far as 3rd, got on a tram, and returned to Hotel Ecke at 3rd and Green St. Arriving there at about 11:00, he went up to his room, which he never left again alive. At about 3 o'clock, Bockhoff, who had waited for Papa to show up for lunch, went to the hotel and sent the hotel keeper up to find out whether father was in his room and ask how he was. He came back down with the news that the door was locked from the inside and the old man was probably taking a nap. Reassured, Bockhoff left. However, when at 5:30 the door was still locked, the hotel keeper became suspicious and began to knock loudly on the door. Because there was no answer, they broke the door down and found — O horror! Papa lay dead on the floor.

Papa's death must have been sudden and must have come while he was changing his pants, which he did frequently during the summer because he always sweat so much. His watch and wallet were lying on the nightstand next to his satchel where he had put them.

Dear Uncle, don't ask me for details. The cause of death was stroke, according to the doctors and the jury that examined the corpse.

You may well imagine how upset Hubert and I have been since Wednesday at 3 A.M. when we received the news. We immediately drove to St. Louis and arrived in time to make preparations for a decent burial, which several of our friends helped us to do. Father is buried in Bellefontaine cemetery, perhaps the most beautiful cemetery in the United States. We have bought a family plot there under a huge green oak. I've ordered an iron gate which will enclose the entire plot, about 20'×20', and we will have a gravestone placed there. The burial was solemn and respectable and took place on Wednesday 29 June at 5 P.M. More friends and acquaintances attended than we had dared to hope given the short notice. Barth, the dignified old gentleman, was there with his wife and daughter-in-law, and he spoke a few fitting and friendly words of remembrance at father's open grave.

Dear Uncle, I have now filled you in, as well as I could, with the details of this sad event. I hope I will never have to write a similar long letter again. Of course, I will write a note to all our relatives, but I cannot bring myself to write down all these details again. I ask you to tell those who are interested, particularly Aunt Annette and Grandmother, exactly what happened. Please give my regards to your family and write soon. Remember your orphaned nephews

Bernhard and Hubert

With that, the book on Anton was closed. It is possible to see his as a quintessentially modern American death, alone and in a hotel room. Although he seems to have found a modicum of peace on the farm in Prairie du Long, it is unlikely that his demons left him. Alone, without a wife, given to drink and confrontation, his must have been a difficult life with few deep pleasures or rewards. Still, it can be said of him that he did make the right decision to sell Voorthuyzen to Theodor and buy his own piece of land. With this act, he destroyed his umbilical cord to the Old World and made a completely new start. Anton also managed to bring up a competent, if troubled, son. Unfortunately, Bernhard's younger brother Hubert's judgment remained childlike, though he proved to be a good worker.

We have no idea how Theodor felt or reacted when news of his brother's death reached him. Because Anton was his older and only brother, with whom he shared a family secret and a family burden, we can assume that Theodor felt some sadness. However, I suspect that the sadness was leavened with some relief as well since he no longer had to worry about what Anton would do.

Bernhard and Maria

As a result of his father's death, Bernhard at twenty-four became responsible for the success or failure of the family enterprise. In his next letters, we may see the burden, but also that he was not completely overwhelmed by it.

Still, the loss of his father put Bernhard's essential aloneness into relief, and it was then that he began to feel the lack of a helpmate. Marriageable women were a rather scarce "commodity" out on the prairie, and Germans, like other immigrants, tended to want to marry within their group. This lack of companionship and help had weighed heavily on both Theodor and Anton. Theodor married almost immediately upon returning to Voorthuyzen; Anton apparently never managed to form another relationship after having his wife committed. Barth had put his finger on that problem when he wrote Theodor, "If your brother had a wife who could run the house and supervise the children things might go better. You yourself know how things are on a farm where there is no female help except for domestic servants." Theodor had written Barth that he was thinking of giving America another try, with Lina. Barth gave his realistic opinion of why many middle-class women might not find America particularly tempting: "I'm sure that the idea is a troubling one for your wife, and I can't blame her if she doesn't want to hear about it. For women it is certainly a poor tradeoff; there are many things they must do without and deny themselves."

As Bernhard's next letters indicate, he had a pressing financial reason to return to Europe. Although he did not mention it, he also had a notion of seeing Maria von Weise, Theodor's sister-in-law, whom he had met when he and Anton were at Voorthuyzen in 1855 when she was fifteen.

> Prairie du Long
> 26 August 1859

Dear Uncle!

I received your letter of 31 July evening before last. Both Hubert and I are heartened to see that you are all deeply affected by our heavy loss. We are certainly deserving of that. As a result of this new circumstance, I often have such an oppressive feeling of loneliness and aloneness that I doubt I will be able to make my way. Only time, which makes one forget all, will allow me to get used to it.

Hubert is a loving and generous brother in every respect. He is industrious, but as you can well imagine, I almost have to act like a father when it comes to business matters, which makes things doubly difficult for me.

At the Probate Court in Waterloo, I had to apply for letters of administration. The law here states that if a close relative of a deceased person fails to demand administration of his estate within 90 days, then any unrelated person may do so after posting the usual security. I went to Waterloo right away in order to avoid this. Even if we don't assume that some stranger is going to try to mind our business, it is still better for us to administer the estate for the period of two years prescribed by law. In our case, there are few if any debts. The only thing I am required to do is place a notice in the Waterloo newspapers every 6 months for 2 years telling possible creditors to invoice us. Thereafter, we may consider all claims against the estate to be null and void. An estate that is not handled in this manner remains open to claims.

Since your last letter familiarized me completely with your financial situation, I see no reason to keep ours a secret. What follows is an accounting of our assets and debts as they stand at present:

380-acre claim in Prairie du Long now valued at $30–35 per acre; total value of the farm		$12000
Share tied up as of Feb. 1, 1859 in Jansen & van Dreveldt, the store in Freedom	$ 1150	
Our half of the profits after ½ year	$ 490	$ 1640
van Treek in Emmerich owes us 250 Prussian Thalers @ .72		$ 180
Theodor van Dreveldt owes 10,000 Thalers @ .72		$ 7200
4 outstanding invoices in Freedom		$ 345
Value of livestock on the farm	$ 1724	
Value of farm machines and tools	$ 1445	$ 3169
		$24534
In addition, the products currently on the farm are worth at least		$ 1000
		$25534

Our debts are as follows:

Bernhard and Hubert van Dreveldt still owe the store in Freedom	$	150
Bernhard and Hubert van Dreveldt owe Jansen and Dreveldt for goods	$	250
Outstanding wages and fees to farm hands, cobbler, and smith.....................	$	125
Salary for Miss Bockhoff, the housekeeper ...	$	75
Angelrodt & Barth burial costs	$	90
20′×20′ family plot # 870 in the Bellefontaine cemetery	$	93
For an iron fence in the cemetery	$	193
Total assets........	$	976
		$24558

That comes to 34,108.10 Prussian thalers.

As you can see, we haven't made any progress in 4 years; in fact we have lost ground. First, there was the expensive voyage in 1855 and then the first year on the farm, during which we had to live off of our money until we began to earn. Then we have to consider the unfavorable conditions under which we suffered, and still do, namely that we had to pay expensive American prices while only receiving German interest on our money; 4% instead of 12%. Still, I suppose we shouldn't complain.

As you can see from the accounting, we badly need money, and as soon as possible. The $376 that we owe Angelrodt & Barth is, of course, overdue; we should have paid it long ago. In addition, we want to buy a marble grave stone for Papa, which will cost another $150–175. And you can well imagine that the $1640 that we invested in the store is not half enough.

If it would shorten the inheritance procedure and if I could pick up the 10,000 thalers, then I would be prepared to make the voyage to Europe even though I would incur considerable business losses here at the store. In that case, it would be reasonable for you to pay half my fare, which would probably come to $500 round trip. Again, if my presence would shorten the procedure, please let me know immediately after receipt of this letter.

We are currently racking our brains trying to figure out what to do with the farm. We don't want to sell it, and in any case, that would go against Papa's wishes. And, as I'm sure you know, renting out a farm such as ours is a bad deal, considering that renters generally wreck more in one year than is covered by two years of rent. It would be a shame if the farm were to fall into such hands.

The farm is now set up very nicely. Even though the house isn't elegant, it is nevertheless well and comfortably furnished. The shade trees around the house are wonderful; some of them are already tall enough to shade the house. The fruit trees are always heavy with fruit. We have 13 horses, among them 2 of the best breeding mares around. There is also a 3-year-old stallion and a fast buggy horse named Hector. He has often done a mile in 3 minutes with me at a trot. We also have 8 dairy cows, 25 head of young stock and steers, and 30 pigs, etc. Then we have a mower, a sower, an apple mill besides the cider press, a chaff cutter with 40 blades, and generally every other kind of machine that a well outfitted Illinois farm should have.

If we had female relatives, the farm would make a wonderful homestead. However, as things stand now, where we have to use hired help to get the work done, everything costs too much and is too much trouble. So, this fall we will probably decide to auction off our personal property and then rent out at least part of the farm.

I think I will be able to get a declaration of right of inheritance for me and Hubert; I just don't know in what form. In any case, nobody here knows that Mama is still alive. Write and let me know whether you think it is absolutely necessary to mention her in the declaration.

Your nephew,
Bernhard van Dreveldt

Prairie du Long
10 November 1859
Hecker Post Office

Dear Uncle Theodor!

. . . With regard to renting out the farm, you misunderstood me completely. I never intended to rent the entire farm, but rather let out individual fields to neighbors for ⅓ of the produce. In the future, e.g., next winter, we would build a log cabin for a renter in a far corner of the fields about a half mile from the main house. He would then work those fields that we did not intend to work ourselves, again for ⅓ of the produce. If you understood the local conditions better, the practicality of this plan would be clear to you.

We could, for example, get much more from our fruit gardens. When Hubert and the farm hand are not too swamped with work, as has been the case, we would not lose a single apple. Furthermore, we can spend more time tending the fruit trees and planting hedges, etc. In this way, the actual productivity of the farm would remain pretty much the same as if we worked it ourselves. Last Friday, 4 November, we sold off $1200 worth of expendable cattle and farm equipment, which comes to about $120 in interest annually.

I don't see why you think that this step is the first on the way to selling the farm. Let me repeat, a sale is the furthest thing from our minds since we have had too many bitter experiences and have bummed around the world too much without a home. We know the value of a homestead. I appreciate your concern and suggestions about my partner. However, I think you are overdoing it because, as you correctly noted, anyone who has had as much bad luck with partners as I have will know how to protect himself unless he is a complete greenhorn. Jansen is not without means, as you seem to think. His parents must be fairly well-off. I also wish that I could stand on my own feet and be responsible for my own affairs. However, given the situation over here, that is rarely possible. The things you can use loyal servants for in Europe you need a partner for over here, otherwise you will be cheated in most cases or the business will be neglected if you can't be there to supervise.

Dear Uncle, with regard to the monument on Papa's grave site, it certainly would have been more practical if we had waited until we had money. However, we could not rest satisfied until we did everything that our filial duty required, and so the monument will be ready in 5–6 weeks. It cost $200, and when it is completed I will send you a sketch of it. Also, since the Bellefontaine cemetery is a fairly aristocratic cemetery, it would stand out if a grave site didn't have some sort of ornamentation. As far as my coming over is concerned and your suggestions regarding a wife are concerned, you would have little trouble convincing me after the year of mourning. Even though I hardly expect much joy from life, I have come to the conclusion that a man without a family in America is like a homeless pilgrim who can never set down roots. Hubert's condition also serves to underscore the wisdom of such a move.

However, as things stand right now, I could not, with the best of intentions, leave here, and so these matters will have to remain wishful thinking for the time being.

Hubert sends his regards.

> Your nephew,
> Bernh. van Dreveldt

Despite the difficulties that Bernhard felt would keep him from going to Europe to complete the financial transactions involving his father's interest in Voorthuyzen, he made his way to Germany in early 1860. The letters from that trip are candid and revealing:

> Cologne
> 6 April 1860

Dear Uncle Theodor!

I feel the urgent need to confide in someone, and you are the person in whom I have the most trust. You are the ideal person to give me advice. I am in a state of almost fevered excitement. Since my arrival in Europe my life has been given a particular goal, and for me there is only one further purpose. I now know that if all goes well (I don't even want to contemplate the alternative) I will partake of such joy as I have never been worthy of, nor ever will be. I am very clear that if it should not work out, I will be as un-utterably miserable as ever a human being can be. All of this talk has but one object. All of my thoughts are filled with your sister-in-law Maria. I know now that I not only love Maria, which has always been the case, but that I worship her. Without Maria, there will never be joy in life for me.

There can be no question of a relationship between me and Maria's sister Agathe, which I could have told you when I was at Voorthuyzen recently. Only Maria is in a position to make me happy. Without Maria I will be nothing and completely incapable of working, since the business would have no purpose without her. But at her side, work would be a high pleasure, even if I had no rest from morning to night. If only to know that she took some use or comfort from my letters. Dear Uncle, I now understand what a joy it is to be able to work for such a noble and loved being. You will consider me empty-headed and my feelings fleeting, but I tell you that my love for Maria didn't start the day before yesterday. I have loved her from the moment I laid eyes on her, and sometimes, in my very eventful life, the thought of her was all that kept me going.

Otherwise, I might have perished. Papa must have known this, because sometimes, when we confided in each other, he would say, "Bernhard, if you want to make me happy, you should marry. Go to Cologne and fetch Maria; I know that you love her." — If only the fetching were so easy. Although I am independent and can venture to offer her a secure, if modest, life — still, will she accept it?

I don't know if you can understand my feelings, but place yourself for a moment in the position of a man who has staked his entire happiness and fortune on a single card and who is still uncertain whether he will win or lose. I don't dare make the decisive move, even though when it comes to business, I'm generally quick to seize an opportunity. I find now that I'm not suited to high-stakes games. I'm generally not bashful or monosyllabic around ladies and have no trouble forming short-lived relationships, to the extent I have wanted them. But now, when it is a matter of "to be or not to be," I can't bring myself to utter the word.

And on top of it, there's the disfavor caused by my relationship with Agathe, with whom I started a little something. As a result, they all seem to think that I'm stuck on Agathe, and Maria will probably be even more reserved. Even though I thought about nothing but her for the past five years, she knows nothing of that. Your in-laws are very dear people and have received me with open arms; how much I would like to call them Father and Mother. The old man is still very weak, though.

Theodor, I have tried to give you as true a picture of my feelings as I can. If you are in a position to give advice or help me, I ask, as a friend and relative, that you do so and answer immediately. Even though the affairs of lovers are uninteresting to third parties, for me it is a question of life and death. — Don't forget my regards to my aunt and the children.

Your nephew Bernhard

Evidently Bernhard found his courage, because next day Maria wrote to her brother-in-law Theodor and Bernhard added a few words of his own:

Cologne
7 April 1860

My dear Theodor!

If you can put in a good word for Bernhard, please do it soon, better by word than in writing. Our situation is unhappy. Father is angry and doesn't want to hear of it. Come to our rescue soon. We are depending on you for a good outcome.

Maria

Theodor, there is nothing that I can add to what is written above. You may draw your own conclusions. I am in the process of moving out of their house. If you can do anything for us, please come and as soon as possible.

(written at 6:30 in the evening)

Bernhard

Another letter soon followed:

Cologne
9 April 1860
7 A.M.

Dear Theodor!

If these lines should still find you at Voorthuyzen, don't delay, leave immediately. Your presence here is absolutely crucial. My and Maria's hopes for happiness depend on you alone. If you can't convince her father, then all is lost. Maria loves me completely, and I have also gotten her mother's wholehearted consent. The other family members are also in favor of the union, especially Maria's brother Adolph.

However, her father reacted so differently when I asked for Maria's hand. First he brought up my poverty, and when I tried to present evidence to him that I was capable of providing for a wife, i.e., one with expectations that weren't too high, he stated that evidence wasn't necessary. He already knew all about my circumstances, having discussed them with Theodor, who agreed with him completely. To come to the point, nothing would come of it. Never, ever. Then there was the matter of America: the word alone was enough to make him say "No." In addition, I was still too young and Maria was a flighty girl, etc. Well, enough. He made up all sorts of excuses for denying his consent that really had no substance. The real reason is neither here nor there, but is probably egotism.

You can imagine that the scene that I and later Maria had with him upset him greatly, especially given his condition. I am sorry about that. He also said that if he had known about all of this, he would have forbidden my visit, and he commanded Maria, in

119

the harshest terms, to leave the house and stay with Aunt Canetta until I was gone. I had no choice but to tell him that I would leave the house immediately, which caused a stir, but which I then did. If only I had checked into a hotel when I first arrived. Poor Maria; I'm almost sorry that I came to Europe. Perhaps Maria could have forgotten me.

I am now staying in the Hotel du Nord, room 29. We expected you this morning; Adolph and I will be waiting at the train station this afternoon. If you can't come today, come tomorrow in any case. Don't delay, I ask you as a friend and relative.

Best wishes to you, Theodor, until we see you today or tomorrow. Give my regards to Lina and the children,

Your Bernhard

The reasons von Weise gave Bernhard for his refusal may have covered his real concerns. Naturally he did not want his daughter to leave the family circle. In addition, his family had recently been elevated to nobility, and like all "newcomers" he was particularly sensitive to what was considered socially proper. He knew that Bernhard's mother was in an insane asylum in Holland, that Anton had been a drunk, and that the entire family was of illegitimate lineage. Given the ideas then current about the heritability of family traits, his reaction is understandable. He knew all of the family secrets because after his daughter Caroline's marriage to Theodor, he and his son-in-law had become close friends and confidantes. This made Theodor the ideal person to lobby the distraught and very ill father. Still, the elder von Weise might have wondered why the van Dreveldt men kept raiding his family. We do not know whether or not Theodor intervened with Maria's father, but less than a month later, the picture was completely changed:

Cologne
Wed., 2 May 1860
8 A.M.

Dear Uncle Theodor!

We received your kind message yesterday morning. I say we because, as you have correctly guessed, we have been together. I'm rushing to reply, but not as you wanted, in rhyme, but in ordinary prose. I also have some good news for you: we have set our marriage date for the 19th of this month—the sooner the better, that is if nothing else gets in the way. Father and Mother are completely in agreement. The former will not have to postpone his planned trip to Voorthuyzen on our account. Father is still quite weak, but yesterday when we told him our plan, he said he thought it is good that we are in a hurry, since he doesn't think he will live much longer. Also, we won't have to go back to America right away but can spend a few weeks in Voorthuyzen and Cologne after the honeymoon.

Yesterday evening we asked Father whether we, i.e., Maria, Franz, and I could take a trip to Laacher See. Much to our disappointment he felt it would not be fitting. So, we have to stay home today as Mother can't go out and Frau Rath isn't coming. I wish that this period of having to think about what's "fitting" and "unfitting" were over.

You complained that Lina is making the children vain, especially the girls. That really can't hurt; it gives the girls self-confidence. And anyway, Barbara and Tonia are beautiful children you can be proud of. On Saturday you took a terribly long walk again. I think that given your condition it isn't advisable. You should use the chaise more often, then you would digest your food less thoroughly and wouldn't get so fat.

Franz, who just came in to visit, thinks this letter is long enough, and I do too. Maria, Father, Mother, and Franz send their regards, and Wolter wants me to thank you for your special attention. Give my regards to Lina and Agathe as well as the children, and give Barbara and Tonia a kiss for me.

Your Bernhard

But Maria and Bernhard were not home free yet. As the following letter makes clear, the issue of Bernhard's grandparents, the fictitious Antonius Gosuinus van Dreveldt and Gerarda Julia de Beautxant, was going to be troublesome:

Cologne
14 May 1860
7:30 P.M.

Dear Theodor,

I just received your message of this morning and am replying this evening. Father thinks that your declaration concerning the grandparents won't be sufficient. But, if there is any way that you can get away, please come, especially on Father's account. You have no idea how upset the poor man became when I opened the letter in his presence. Since it came special delivery he asked what it contained, and I had to tell him that you wouldn't be coming.

He said that if you don't come, he would not be able to enjoy himself. He threatened not to attend since he couldn't get used to the idea that the man who is making his older daughter happy would not be present at his Maria's marriage and stand by his side. The poor man cried like a child and made me promise to write you immediately that if Lina's delicate condition doesn't worsen, which he almost has to assume, that you will make every effort to come.

If Lina's condition allows it, come on his account. You can't imagine how much Father is looking forward to the wedding meal and especially your presence. He even had the idea of seating you next to him, among other things. If you absolutely feel that you can't come, then please write a note to Father, which will calm him. But if there is any way that you can come, then do; I think that the farewell to Maria will really affect him, and then you will be the one person who can talk to him.

But now to a different matter. I don't particularly like the fact that you entrusted the letter to Pastor van Roggen to the post office; I just hope it arrived. If you can't come, please make sure we have the following: 1. grandfather's death certificate, 2. grandmother's notarized consent, and 3. the pronouncement from Aalten [regarding Bernhard's mother]. Theodor, please keep in mind how important these documents are. If we don't have them and can't get married—half of Cologne, at least our acquaintances, know that we are getting married on Friday and Saturday—it would be fatal if we didn't have them. Please get to this quickly and do it with American speed. I am almost becoming concerned at this point. With all the other bad news, you can't blame me. First Johanna Höynck says she isn't coming right away but later with Agathe, and then Friedrich Höynck begs out, and finally you as well, which I suspected even though I hoped the opposite.

Please give my and Maria's greetings to Lina and Agathe, and I hope that Lina's condition will still allow you to attend.

Your Bernhard

In the end, Theodor must have produced documentation that satisfied the authorities. The wedding would go ahead. Unfortunately, Theodor felt he could not attend because Lina had just given birth and the doctor had prescribed complete rest for her, as was the custom of the times. Under these circumstances, Theodor could not very well leave her alone, and this was understood. Maria very much wanted to include her sister in her prenuptial joy:

Cologne

14 May 1860

My dear Lina,

The happy day on which Bernhard and I will be united forever is fast approaching. As a result, I am becoming ever closer to you and become more like you. And so, I feel the need to pour my heart out to you and tell you about my happiness. I regret that you won't be able to be here on the 19th, but we will see each other soon at Voorthuyzen, perhaps in two weeks. And then, Lina, we will have to say farewell for a long, long time. I will be very sad, but not unhappy, the way I used to feel when it was time to leave Voorthuyzen. I yearn for my new homeland, and I think that Bernhard feels the need to return.

Father has pretty much gotten used to not seeing me as such a part of the household anymore. Still, he is fearful about my departure and definitely does not want to be in Cologne when we get back from our honeymoon and set out on our long journey. How I wish that you could be at our wedding, but even so, I will love little Agathe, who now makes this impossible. I wish that you will have great joy with her, and am very happy that it wasn't another boy. Three of them are quite enough. From what I have heard, she is a lovable little baby, as pretty as Barbara. Agathe writes me that little Ernst doesn't want to walk yet. I hope there's nothing the matter with him; he was such a magnificent boy last year.

Bernhard wants to send his letter today; if it isn't uncomfortable for you, please advise Theodor to come, if only for Father's sake. Father is still very upset by the news. I had certainly expected Johanna Höynck; we sent more than a few invitations.

Jenny Herwegen has already had a silk dress made for the wedding, and we haven't even invited her yet. Frau Herwegen made me a friendly invitation to come to her house for a farewell coffee. I had told her that I intended to, but now that Johanna isn't coming, it is too much effort. Farewell, dear Lina. I will see you again soon, but under much different circumstances than I had imagined. Here's a kiss from

Your sister Maria

After a stay at Voorthuyzen and a honeymoon in Friesland and the East Frisian island of Spiekerooge, Bernhard and Maria van Dreveldt set off for America.

Southampton docks
18 July 1860
on board the steamer
Saxonia

My dear Theodor,

I'm going to use this opportunity to write some more about us. We arrived here yesterday morning at 6:00 after a very pleasant trip, during which we got to know the captain, the ship, and passengers. We were very satisfied and look forward to a pleasant trip. Apart from occasional nausea, Maria has not been seasick yet. The ocean is as flat as a mirror. The *Saxonia* is a beautiful and large ship, 367 feet in length, the best and most beautiful ship belonging to the Hamburg Line. We will remain here in Southampton until 12:00 noon today, when we will begin the actual ocean voyage to America. I don't know yet how many passengers will be joining us in first class; there were 19 from Hamburg, a small and pleasant group. Captain Ehlers is a pleasant man and an able captain. We are seated at the table with him, and Maria never lets the table conversation falter. In all, there are about 360 passengers on board and more than 100 crew, a total of almost 500 persons. As Carl probably already wrote you, he was on board almost until we got to open sea opposite Cuxhaven, where he had to say farewell and go back to Hamburg on the little steamer with which we all came. He was very sad at the farewell, as was Maria, but only for a short time.

Because of the stay in port here yesterday, we had the opportunity to see the Southampton races. A young Havanan, a young businessman from New York, Maria, and I rented an elegant open coach and rode about. Later the two of us coached around the entire town by ourselves. In the evening we went to the theater, where we saw *Lucia di Lammermoor* in English. Yesterday was a very pleasurable day.

The captain hopes to be in New York in 11 days; he told Maria at lunch today that she would probably be seasick by this evening. At the moment, 12:30, we are being tugged out of the harbor, and in an hour we will have reached the Isle of Wight, where the pilot, who will take this message ashore, will leave us. So, I have to end the letter.

Give my best regards to Father, Lina, Agathe, the children, Aunt Annette, Johanna and Höynck, the doctors in Elten. Maria wrote to her mother, and our letters will be posted together. Of course, Maria sends her regards. I look forward to letters from you when I get home. The best to all of you from your

Bernhard

After arriving in America and visiting Niagara Falls, the couple stayed a few days in St. Louis until they were picked up by Hubert and Jansen. At home they found the news of Carl von Weise's death. Very ill, he lived only a few months after his youngest daughter's marriage. After her departure he had gone to Voorthuyzen, at Theodor's invitation, to recover. A few days later, he passed away in the place he had come to love. His grave is next to the church wall in Hochelten, outside Emmerich.

This news was not unexpected, and Maria wrote her sister Lina:

Father's death was a real deliverance from long suffering, and I had said farewell to him forever in my thoughts. Mother was also prepared. Certainly, she was the one who was most pessimistic when the illness began, and her judgment was correct. She will really feel the loss when she returns to Cologne, but time will heal that. You must have had upsetting times in the last few weeks and during the burial. Mother writes that all the children attended the burial, so even Agathe and the little boys came. It must have been a full house.

Politics in Black and White

In his letters home, Theodor had frequently talked about his love for America's free institutions, nativism notwithstanding: "I have always loved freedom, and the republican form of government as it exists here has become so dear to me in the time I have lived here that even with the comparatively minute abuses, I could not again live over there under an absolute monarchy. I would find it easier to live in Austria. At least there, people know where they stand. But where you are, the nation is mocked, and freedom is brought down by buffoons." There was nothing like American freedom in Europe.

As the United States had expanded westward, agitation for political inclusion had made the system more open. Thus, for example, by 1832 presidential electors ceased being elected by the state legislatures and were chosen by popular vote, except in South Carolina. By midcentury, almost all property qualifications had disappeared. Increasing numbers of white men felt able to participate in the governing of the country at all levels and make their views known freely.

But the leftover business from the Constitutional Convention, namely what to do with slavery, had never been brought to a conclusion. Because the economy of the South was agrarian and based largely on slavery, it developed very different social structures and ideologies from those of the free-labor North. As Northern industry expanded westward with the railroads, the conflict between the two systems intensified. Each came to see the other as inimical to its own existence. It was clear to Southern defenders of slavery that Northern capitalists wanted to invade and destroy their comfortable way of life. To "free-soilers" in the North, the expansion of slavery would plunge the nation into medieval feudalism, destroying free labor and political freedom.

The South saw the Missouri Compromise as just another tool to destroy its institutions, and as more free states entered the Union, the South would be increasingly isolated and outvoted in Congress. The Southern political establishment felt trapped. The Mexican War of 1846 can be seen as a Southern attempt to create more slave territory south of 36°30', thereby circumventing the terms of the Missouri Compromise.

That compromise became void in 1854 with the enactment of the Kansas-Nebraska Act sponsored by Democratic Senator Stephen A. Douglas of Illinois. By the terms of that act, popular sovereignty, a plebiscite, would determine whether these territories (both north of 36°30') would enter the Union as slave or free-soil states. The result was a bloodbath in Kansas in 1855–56 as pro-slavers rushed across the border from Missouri to make it theirs, capturing the territorial legislature and legalizing slavery. By the summer of 1856, Kansas was in a virtual state of civil war.

The region around St. Louis and western Illinois is a useful place to look briefly at the conflict that was developing and would soon engulf the entire country. St. Louis, lying as it does at the confluence of the Missouri and Mississippi rivers, had very strong geographic, historic, and economic ties with New Orleans and the South. On the other hand, the railroads coming from the East bringing large amounts of investment capital forged increasingly close ties between St. Louis and the Northeast. By the 1850s, despite Missouri's status as a slave state, many Missourians, such as B. Gratz Brown, a founder of the *Missouri Democrat,* realized that slavery could not be an engine for economic progress. In addition, as more and more Germans immigrated to that region to escape political repression, they developed into a potent force in opposition to slavery. These factors created an interesting blend of conflicting political and social influences as well.

Eduard Mühl, the publisher of the *Hermanner Wochenblatt,* was the first journalist in Missouri to come out four-square against slavery. The 29 October 1852 edition of the newspaper contained the following statement: "We hold ourselves as free men who did not escape slavery in our old home lands to support it here in America." He was not alone; very few Germans held slaves, and a huge majority of them opposed the institution. Even as early as 1845, Mühl reprinted articles such as this one from another German newspaper that might have reminded many of his readers, Theodor included, of humiliations suffered in Germany. Mühl and other editors of German-language newspapers like him knew their readership well.

The Punishment of Slaves — We may get an idea of how the South punishes its slaves from the following example:

Victorine, the female slave of a master in New Orleans was recently convicted of theft and sentenced to 20 lashes of the whip and the pillory. She served the latter part of her sentence between 11 and 12 in the morning in front of the recorder's office. A big blue paper cap was set on her head with the word "THIEF" printed in large letters on it. A sign hung on her chest gave her name, crime, and punishment. After she had stood for an hour in the public pillory, she was taken back to jail, where the 20 lashes were administered.

This in eighteen-hundred and forty-five!

St. Louis was the center of German life in the Midwest. In one of his letters to Theodor, Robert Barth wrote about Heinrich Börnstein. Börnstein was undoubtedly one of the most colorful characters in St. Louis politics, an unclassifiable original, who, in Steven Rowan's words, "is at the bottom of almost every story worth telling about St. Louis Germans from the day of his arrival in 1850 until his final departure in 1862."[1] He certainly generated a great deal of heat.

Börnstein had left Germany for Paris in 1842, primarily because he felt constricted by German culture and society. Something of a jack-of-all-trades, he became an actor, translator, and publisher of socialist writers banned in Germany, including Karl Marx and Friedrich Engels. The poet Heinrich Heine first published his well-known political poem, "Germany, A Winter's Tale" in Börnstein's *Forward!* In response to Prussian pressure, the French government closed him down, and Börnstein and family ended up in St. Louis. In 1850 he took over the German-language newspaper *Anzeiger des Westens* (Western advertiser) and immediately became embroiled in local politics and the issue of nativism. Here is Barth's take on the man in an 1852 letter:

A certain Heinrich Börnstein, a rather infamous individual over there, has become editor of the *Anzeiger,* and since then he has created more disunity among the Germans and more difficulties with the Americans than one would wish. Just imagine, this man was shameless enough to state that Americans did not understand what real freedom and republicanism was and would have to learn it from the Germans! He even initiated a German platform. What do you have to say to such presumption? He and several of his ilk, who three years ago tore things up with their nonsensical sloganeering and created such a fiasco, want to preach republicanism to people! Isn't that too much? Of course, he realized pretty soon that he had landed in a hornet's nest and dropped his platform. Nevertheless, he goes on spouting the most miserable nonsense, speaking to Germans' prejudices and passions in an attempt to incite them against their American neighbors. Unfortunately, he has succeeded only too well. During last April's elections, we had an uproar in the first precinct in which people were shot and houses demolished or burned. This has opened more than a few eyes, and several older citizens have gotten together to found a new newspaper to counter him. Naturally, he doesn't like it one bit, and so he attacks them in the meanest fashion. He particularly goes after Angelrodt [Barth's partner] and Dr. Engelmann [who treated Theodor for the effects of malaria] and tears them apart daily in his paper. As you see, my friend, things could be better here as well. The only advantage we have is that, in time, things are able to balance out. The worst thing is that in the meantime, nationalism is given oxygen and things are made worse for the poor Germans.

The *Anzeiger* developed into a radical abolitionist newspaper, and Börnstein eventually became involved in the radical wing of the Republican Party. In 1861, as a general, he even led a contingent of mainly German volunteers that overthrew the pro-Confederacy Democratic governor and installed a Republican, thereby averting Missouri's secession.

Of course, Barth was not far off the mark when he accused Börnstein of making life more difficult for the Germans because the radicalism with which he and many Germans became associated was fair game for the newspapers supporting the pro-slavery Democratic Party. They often twisted the words of the German press to whip up nativist sentiments and called the Germans "black Dutch," among other things.

But none of this is to say that because many Germans were abolitionists or that abolitionists in general were anti-slavery, that their motivations were completely idealistic or that they transcended the racism of the day.[2] There were several reasons in the late 1850s to oppose slavery. Many free-soilers, who opposed the extension of slavery into new states, did so because they realized that free white labor could not compete with cheap slave labor, not because they thought slavery was inherently an inhumane system. In fact, the prevailing notion in the North was that blacks should stay where they were, namely in the South. If the South became free, then free blacks in the North might even be induced to return there. Even many abolitionists felt ambivalent about having blacks in their midst, and the German press was not immune from such ambivalence. A letter from an Illinois Republican to his Congressman is illustrative of the widespread ambivalence:

The people of the North will never consent to come in contact with the institution of slavery in the territories. To work side by side with negro slaves . . . will leave [them in a] condition little above slaves themselves. [Southerners] keep their niggers if they will, but they must not bring them in contact with us. No matter whether we are opposed to the extension of slavery from our humanity and love of right and justice, or from hatred of niggers (of the latter are many Illinois Republicans) we are terribly in earnest in our opposition to the extension of that institution.[3]

The Republican Party, which had been organized in 1855, was a heterogeneous group. Many Germans belonged to the liberal and even radical wings of the party, which contained abolitionist lions like Charles Sumner and William Lloyd Garrison as well as openly white-supremacist free-soilers like Illinois Senator Lyman Trumbull. Trumbull, who was Bernhard's senator and liked to send his constituents packets of tobacco seeds (which Bernhard dutifully forwarded to Theodor), was very clear on the issue: "We, the Republican Party, are the white man's party. We are for the free white man and for making white labor acceptable and honorable, which it can never be when negro slave labor is brought into competition with it."[4]

A Republican like Trumbull could never conceive of giving blacks equal rights, and in all probability, neither could most of his constituents. As Trumbull explained, "When we say that all men are created equal, we do not mean that every man in organized society has the same rights. We don't tolerate that in Illinois."[5] Nevertheless, the Republican Party would have seemed like a progressive alternative to the Democrats, who were firmly entrenched in the South and largely represented Southern interests. The Republican Party was struggling with the issue of slavery; there appears to have been no comparable "liberal" wing of the Democratic Party.[6]

This is the social and political soup in which a stressed young man, his success with Maria notwithstanding, found himself. Buffeted by anti-German nativist sentiments, German radicalism, open and veiled racism, and a feeling that the country was careering toward some unnamed denouement, Bernhard might well have been tempted to lash out at easy targets.

Bernhard and Maria in America

Among Bernhard's first acts upon returning to Freedom was to buy out Jansen, with whom he had apparently become disenchanted. Jansen then proceeded to open up a store in Waterloo, about eleven miles away.

> I am now running the store in Hecker by myself with my clerk Cunitz. He worked for us before, and I pay him $20 per month plus room and board. As you may imagine, I have my hands full, but I enjoy it more and look forward to doing business. I leave for work in an open buggy at 7:00 in the morning right after breakfast and don't come home before evening. When the weather is good, Maria sometimes walks toward Hecker in the evening, meeting me half way. Then, I give her Hector's reins and we ride back home pleased and happy.

On another occasion he wrote:

> I am all alone here [i.e., without a business partner], but at least I am making a good start at a thriving business. I just need patience and perseverance. At the moment there is nothing to be done, and I am just happy to get by. For one thing, I have two competitors in Red Bud, only 7 miles away. One of them is a Yankee, and he is better set up than I am. Then again, Hecker is still much too unimportant a town for people to come to just for a store. I have to sell cheaply, and, what is more important, have to have a reputation. If we had a mill, things would be very different. And then, of course, the bad times. But why complain? I'm not going to lose my courage because of these problems. Things are bound to improve; I think that Freedom will become quite a little city one of these days, and then business will improve all by itself.

However, his hopes were tempered by matters out of his control. On 24 August 1860 Bernhard wrote:

> In general, things look pretty sad here, worse times than I have ever experienced in America. All the crops are dried out. The corn crop, which Hubert talked about so enthusiastically and was so promising, will only yield ⅓; wheat, barely ¼. Nevertheless, what

there is, is first rate; nice full round kernels. The apples are shriveling on the trees. Oats and hay were very good, though.

It hasn't rained here for 7 weeks, and the temperature is more than 100° Fahrenheit almost every day. Recently it got up to 107° in the shade for several days running. You can imagine what things look like.

On 27 September he reported about the crops again:

Around here the wheat and corn failed completely, which has had a terrible effect on our store. I am really careful not to buy too much; I would rather make several short trips to St. Louis to buy items in short supply. I got back this afternoon from my second trip there. All week long there has been a fair in St. Louis, the annual agricultural, trade, and art exhibition. Unfortunately, I had no time for it; yesterday I was there a total of 2 hours. The business has to come first, and this is the reason I didn't take Maria to St. Louis this time.

She will come along early next month, but will probably have to stay at home for a good year after that. This morning at 3:00, Hubert and Cunitz set off for the fair. Hubert is very interested in it. You would also like the agricultural machinery, etc. Exhibitions like this cannot fail to make an impression on Europeans. Yesterday when I went by the fair grounds, there were at least 35,000 people in attendance, and there will probably be more today because the Prince of Wales, who arrived in St. Louis yesterday, will attend. No Yankee will want to pass up the opportunity to shake hands with the prince. I'm sure that by this evening, the poor man's hand will be aching from all the republican handshakes he will have to endure.

As you can imagine, there is no end to politics this close to the election. For my part, I believe that the Republican party will win and LINCOLN will be our next president.

Even with all the problems he was having, Bernhard could write, "Maria has made me a completely new man, and I go to work each morning with joy. I now know what I'm working for."

For his part, Theodor was beginning to think about selling Voorthuyzen and moving back to America. His father-in-law was dead. So was Anton. The political situation in Germany had hardened to a pre-

1848 state, and Theodor might well have felt out of place there. A date was even set for the sale of Voorthuyzen: 29 November 1860. On 27 September Bernhard wrote:

> You can well imagine how happy we are at the prospect of seeing you all here with us. I am most concerned about whether Lina will want to live here long term. It would be just wonderful for us, particularly for Maria, if you settled close by. Consider everything well, and press on with the sale of the property. The rest is of secondary importance.

Then a few days later, on 1 October, he wrote more soberly:

> We think a lot about you, and Maria and I have already settled all of you in various places in our discussions. I just hope it doesn't fall through. When you arrive, you must certainly be prepared to live with us for a considerable period of time. We want to avoid a headlong rush to buy a home. The best thing for me would be if you bought the neighbor's farm and could stay in the area. We could then be "a very strong family in every respect," as they say here. Up to now, I haven't spoken a word about your plan to anybody because I constantly fear that it could come to naught. Sometimes, when I think about you while I am working in the store, I take the uninvited liberty of making plans for your future. For example, the following plan is currently my favorite; I think that it is what I would do if I were in your place. You will get 50,000 thalers, which comes to $36,000. You will need $1500 for the voyage, etc., $5000 for an appropriate homestead — a small farm — for you and your family. That would leave about $30,000 left over, which, if you don't speculate but simply lend out, should bring you at least $3000 per year. Since you would live here in the country for next to nothing, and given the income from the farm, you could almost certainly keep half. In addition, you will be free and unconstrained and can use a few hundred dollars to make deals on the side. For example, in Kansas and Nebraska (as in Minnesota in the past) one can sometimes make thousands with an outlay of only $500–600 if one buys at the right time, pays the taxes, and knows when to sell.

And on 24 October:

> Maria was deeply affected by your latest letter, particularly after she saw the announcement in the Cologne newspaper. She didn't

believe that you would act in earnest so soon. Women are much more attached to their neighborhoods and homes than we are, and it is more difficult for them to leave a place to which they have grown accustomed. Lina, too, will find leaving Voorthuyzen difficult, at least that is what Maria thinks, who herself is so attached to Voorthuyzen and had such pleasurable experiences there. Things were not any easier for me and my dear departed father. I have to admit that if I had 120,000 thalers, I would be tempted to buy the property myself. But the heart has nothing to do with an issue that only dollars and cents can settle.

Of course, I don't have to tell you that your present life in Voorthuyzen *"en grand seigneur du moyen age"* [in medieval knightly splendor], as you describe it, is a real life of luxury compared to what you will find here. When you come, just let us know early enough. If we can, Hubert and I will pick you up in New York. Above all, make certain that as much of your assets as possible can be made fluid immediately; as you know, time is money. Send me 1000 of your posters and plans, unstamped. As postmaster, I get 60% of all postage paid, so it would cost me much less than you.

As Bernhard mentioned, Maria could hardly believe that Theodor was going through with his plans so quickly. She wrote her sister:

Theodor's detailed plans for your voyage here have really surprised me; I don't yet completely believe it. I would love it if you came. I will never find a woman friend here, and Bernhard is elated at the idea of having your entire family in the area. Of course, we should be your last consideration. I have not been here long enough to know whether you will like it here; however, I think there is a world of difference between your emigration and mine. A girl begins a new life when she marries, no matter where, and her happiness is least dependent on country and people or house and garden. I think it is very different for a woman who has already lived for 11 years in one place and has experienced life's joys and sorrows there. In any case, I would like to advise you not to sell those things that you love and take pleasure in; bring them with you, large and small. Whatever you leave behind, you will not find here. Everything has a different fashion here, and your stay will seem foreign enough that you will only feel comfortable for the first year if you bring familiar things.

134

And in the same letter she wrote:

> Today I was thinking about how we would put you up here when you and Theodor arrive with your children and maid servants. It will work out. I think that you can have three rooms, which will be enough to sleep in. Schooling is already taken care of. This week a new school will be finished and available for use on Bernhard's land. The children can go there to elementary school in English. It will be wonderful when we are so close that we can drop by to visit.

Theodor and Lina were not the only members of the extended family who were contemplating relocation. On 29 November Bernhard answered Theodor's query about Maria's brothers:

> Hubert and Franz shouldn't come until they are good and ready for it. Hubert would find it easy enough to find a suitable position, if he has the courage and perseverance to stick it out and a certain dumb pride did not keep him from seeing things as they are. One could easily imagine, for example, that "Baron" Hubert v. Weise would be called on to deliver a package or even pick up an instrument known as a broom, etc., without anyone thinking that this might be an inappropriate occupation for the young man. The same would apply to Franz, though in a somewhat different way. If only he can find the energy to rise above unpleasant circumstances which are unavoidable when one starts out in a subordinate position. If so, then Franz may expect to take what he has learned and now must come to understand, and look with equanimity toward his future in America. Adolph, on the other hand, should stay in Europe, where a better future beckons him than here. He should not totally reject his father's wish that he take the state exams.

Hubert, Franz, and younger brother Wolter all eventually joined the family in Freedom, remaining there for a time before striking out on their own. Adolph also emigrated in 1866.

The date set for the sale, 29 November, arrived. Because of the distances involved, it would be weeks before Bernhard and Maria learned about the outcome of the sale. No matter how much Bernhard wanted to become a real American, it is clear that at a basic level he felt himself to be European. The fact that the sale would "rend our last connection to Europe" evidently tormented him:

I have been in a very strange mood all day. It is the day of the sale in Voorthuyzen, and even though I have no material interest in it anymore, it seems to me that something important is happening that affects all of us. Have you really sold it? Or have you kept the property? These are the questions that I ask myself almost hourly; I am awaiting your next letter with almost fearful anxiety. I often hope that you kept Voorthuyzen; it is as if the sale rends our last connection to Europe. However, these are useless fantasies. But it is true that if I had an independent fortune, even if it were only $40,000, I would be a thousand times happier in Europe than here. But, what for? The solution is patience and perseverance.

The long-awaited news did not arrive at the farm until 26 December 1860, almost a month later. Voorthuyzen was not sold. The exact reasons why Theodor decided to remain in Europe are not known. Most probably they are complicated. It is possible that he could not get what he thought the property was worth. Then again, he and his wife lived a gracious life filled with guests and travel, a life that could not be duplicated on the plains of Illinois. And at forty-nine he would have been a little old for a new beginning.

Bernhard's response to the news was both honest and typical. His motives for having wanted Theodor to come ran to fantasy business deals and monetary speculation:

Prairie du Long
29 December 1860

Dear Theodor!

Your long-awaited letter dated the 2nd of this month finally arrived three days ago. The letter had very different effects. Maria said, "Thank God. At least Lina can stay at Voorthuyzen"; Hubert said that that meant you weren't coming, and I said nothing. I had gotten so used to the idea of seeing you here that your decision not to sell has really hit me hard. Even if I didn't expect to see all of you here at once, I did think that after the sale, you might come out alone. And if you then decided to return to Europe after all and rejoin your family, I figured that you would find it advantageous to invest part of your fortune here to take advantage of the high interest rates. I had already worked out a business relationship in my mind, charging interest, expediting money, etc. And, too, I would have been only too happy to see you here, probably more for my sake than yours. You have no idea how I miss having a close friend here with whom I could talk openly about business matters. I can't very well talk to Maria about these matters all the time, particularly since they are occasionally unpleasant, which is unavoidable. I have no one to turn to here, not anybody I would trust. Hubert is satisfied with everything that I do and doesn't oppose me. Maria seems to like it here, at least that's what she keeps telling me. I feel that way too, and I love her more every day, if that is possible.

So, since you are not going to come, my most fervent wish is that I will one day succeed in increasing our fortune (in 10–15 years) to the point that we can return to the Rhine as gentlemen of private means. Maria doesn't want to hear of it. She says she's happy and satisfied, etc. Nevertheless, I have my plans, and that is my goal which I intend to work toward.

These are bad times, however, and nobody could take it amiss if one did not only give up one's plans, but one's hopes as well. Because of the failed harvest, none of the farmers have money. Add to that the revolution in South Carolina and the probability of war once our next president is inaugurated. Who knows where things are headed. I had planned to build a new store by next spring, but I now think it would be better to wait until the times are better. Everything is in ruins, and we are in the middle of a terrible crisis — even worse than in 1857.

Gold now fetches 7–8% premium in bankable funds in St. Louis. A while back, I sold ours at 1%. What a difference. If you had come, you would have made money.

The South has broken off almost all its trade with the North, and everything is in ruins. Not long ago, several steamer shipments of flour had to return to St. Louis because they didn't want to receive them in New Orleans. What stupidity! If the South allows itself to be guided by such stubbornness, I fear the worst. Here in the North, a pro-Union movement is being organized, and the Southern fire eaters are being criticized for reacting before they even have cause for complaint.

Yesterday, the murderer Alter was hanged in Waterloo, and I attended this gruesome spectacle of execution for the first time. In order to comply with the law mandating a non-public execution, a 16-foot high wooden fence was erected around the gallows scaffolding. Nevertheless, this "sovereign" people tore it down so as not to miss a moment of the spectacle. Much to their shame, it must be said that most of the participants were Germans. The whole thing repulsed me.

Bernhard's letter mentioned two news items that are of interest. Before examining the more important item, the break in trade with the South, consider the local news of the execution. Violence was not uncommon on the prairie; people were armed and sometimes settled disputes with bullets. Bernhard discussed the Alter case in a previous letter dated 27 November 1860. His description of the courthouse will do nothing to improve the image of the legal profession:

The first death sentence was pronounced last week during a special session of the circuit court meeting in this county. The accused, a German named Henry Alter, lived only two miles from us last summer when he committed the crime. The murdered man, Heinrich Hentze, also lived close by. It seems that the two neighbors had been feuding for some time. Alter had a poorly built fence, and Hentze's and other neighbors' animals often took advantage of this. Finally one day Hentze's pigs broke into Alter's corn fields, ruining them. Alter, a very rageful and vicious man, began to shoot his neighbor's pigs. Hentze, seeing this from his house, ran out to Alter to try to talk to him, but after a short discussion, Alter told Hentze that he was going to shoot him. Hentze then tried to get away and was just about to climb over the fence when Alter shot him in the back. Some of the shots exited his chest, and Hentze died instantly.

After a half-hour deliberation, the jury pronounced him guilty, and the judge set the date of execution for 28 December. Voilà, a dark side of American life. One more thing. Last week when I was in Waterloo because of the trial, I had occasion to observe the behavior of the lawyers and judges, which is quite an eye opener if one has just returned from a trip to Europe. Just imagine, several lawyers in a row leaning back on their stools, their feet propped up on a heap of law books and papers on the table while another lawyer delivers a long-winded speech or the clerk swears in a witness. Most of the lawyers, jurors, witnesses, and observers are smoking cigars or chewing tobacco. What a sight for European eyes! There are a lot of problems, and more than a few things will strike you as very American, given that you have been here.

Of course, the more important news concerned the South. In late November Bernhard had written to Theodor about politics, something he knew would interest his uncle. Carl Schurz (1829–1906) was one of the most influential German immigrants of the last century, certainly the most influential veteran of the 1848 Revolution. Schurz became heavily involved in Republican Party politics after arriving in Wisconsin in 1855 and served as a general in the Civil War. He settled in St. Louis in 1867, where he became the editor of the *Westliche Post*. Schurz was elected to the Senate from Missouri the next year. His lengthy speech, the one Bernard sent, was given at the Cooper Institute in New York and printed over two issues by the *Missouri Democrat* on 19–20 September 1860. Like Theodor, Schurz had studied at the University of Bonn, but in 1847.

I made a special point of packing Carl Schurz's speech this way. I figured that if it were actually opened, the censors would see that its contents are harmless and put it back in. If it arrives, I will send you newspapers from time to time. It doesn't cost much. I hope you didn't have to pay postage due. I put a 3-cent stamp on it.

Politically, things are quieting down again. Abraham LINCOLN, the rail splitter, will be our next president, and that is all right. (Lincoln is supposed to have split fence rails on a farm.) Everyone did their best to push his name through, and now that the elections are successfully over, people are getting back to business. Only the hot-blooded Southerners aren't cooling off so fast. They are not at all resigned, and recently, South Carolina ran up the palmetto flag; they want to separate from the Union. Of course, the whole thing will end up like a bad joke. The South reminds me sometimes of the way we used to play ball as school children in Elten. They take part in the presidential election, and when it doesn't turn out the way they want, they say that they won't play anymore. I don't think there will be a split though; the South would harm itself most of all.

In fact, the Lincoln victory was mainly a sectional affair. In addition, of the approximately 4,682,000 votes cast, Lincoln only took about 1,866,000, or just under 40 percent. Stephen A. Douglas, the Democrat, polled about 1,377,000 votes, and John C. Breckinridge, the States' Rights candidate won the South with a mere 850,000 votes. Another candidate, John Bell, polled about 690,000 votes.[1] The country as a whole was clearly more conservative than liberal Republicans and German anti-slavers would have wanted to admit. On the other hand, the fact that Breckinridge, who won the South, was for states' rights but not for secession indicates that the South was not particularly united.

But Southern interests now realized that the differences between the North and the South were irreconcilable and that Northern industry would crush them and dismantle the social system that had worked so well for wealthy whites and commanded the loyalty of Southerners in general. On 17 December 1860 a convention was convened in Charleston, South Carolina, to consider what to do. On the twentieth the convention approved an ordinance of secession, and within six weeks Mississippi, Florida, Alabama, Georgia, Louisiana, and Texas had followed suit.[2]

On 13 February Bernhard reported on some of the effects that the secession was having on business in the St. Louis area and in New Orleans; however, he did not fully appreciate the gravity of the move. He continued to prattle away about high protective tariffs, which was the main reason he voted for Lincoln. Bernhard also betrayed his own attitudes toward blacks for the first time:

The times are just as we deserved them given our exuberance during the good times. On top of this comes the realization that we have plunged into this evil by our own fault and stupidity— now that there is no commercial cause. The American people now resembles the donkey that kicked back when things got too comfortable. It will not be easy for us to come to our senses until we are hit where it hurts most, by an economic slump, which has already happened to some extent. You have no idea how dispirited everyone is after being spoiled for so long by easy success. We are in the middle of a crisis that America has never seen before, nor, I hope, will see again as long as I live here. My bank Angelrodt & Barth is said to have lost more than $4000 a few days ago as a result of the failure of Bredlow & Co. in New Orleans.

It is too bad that you don't have your liquid assets here now. You could buy up property in and around St. Louis and become independently wealthy in a few years. A great deal of property in and about St. Louis belongs to business people who have been hit by the crisis and are trying to get rid of it as if there were no future for this great nation. It is really a shame that one can't take advantage of this situation, because we will never experience a better time to speculate. Unfortunately, all our money is currently tied up.

In politics everything is still in a state of confusion, "all blue," and there is nothing important to report. To give you a better understanding, I have been sending you copies of the *New Yorker Criminal-Zeitung*. We get 3 copies of it in this post office, but they are never picked up, and so I send them to you. It doesn't cost me anything except postage. On Wednesday the U.S. Senate officially announced Lincoln's election. Lincoln is now on his way to Washington, and his trip is a real triumphal march. In general, people expect that conditions will improve after his inauguration.

I cannot agree with the political portion of your last letter. You are rushing to conclusions much too quickly without having adequately considered the matter of high tariffs. You are judging America as if you were dealing with the 33 small German states without considering that you are dealing with a great and powerful continent that has all these natural resources and energy, which have been used up in Europe, and which we have in 1000-fold greater abundance. You state that labor and therefore goods (which are one and the same since the latter is dependent on the former) constitute national wealth. That is also our opinion, though not in the way you think. Purchased products, or Nuremberg baubles, as you rightly call them, which are bought by a nation as luxury items and are used within a few months, i.e., disappear, can, in my opinion, never be considered national wealth. You say that that constitutes America's wealth and advantage, that you sell the above-mentioned items overseas and therefore exploit the poor German workers and send more money abroad than you will ever get back. In that case, I would like to know where the excess goes and how you want to explain it. No, precisely because we know very well that labor and the goods it creates constitute national wealth and must constantly renew itself, that is precisely why we want to manufacture these goods in our own country.

You yourself say that each country must produce what its soil and climate are best suited for. That is exactly what we want. Think about it; this is a continent whose as yet untapped natural resources we want to mine and put on the world market. It is a country whose various parts contain every imaginable climate and bring forth all manner of agricultural products. Such a country has never existed before, and don't let yourself be convinced from bygone examples. If I tell you that the tracks of the Iron Mountain Railroad, which runs from St. Louis to Pilot Knob, are made of English iron, i.e., that English iron is used in preference to our own solid iron ore, which is so rich that any smith can in short order turn it into usable iron on his anvil, do you still maintain that that is our advantage and shouldn't be changed? I could easily pile up more examples.

England and France like to boast, and they preach free trade. But let us not forget that for many years they had a very well-conceived system of protective tariffs and were therefore able to perfect their factory methods to such a point that they can now stand before all the nations of the world and challenge them to competition. Americans are the last people in the world who would want to create another China, isolated from the world. Who can take exception if they want to take advantage of their country's riches? And how else can they better do it than with protective tariffs? Give us a protective tariff, and we will put many factories in Saxony and Switzerland that produce almost exclusively for us out of business. Then their impoverished workers will come over here and do the same work here for substantially better wages. So, there is profit on all sides. Currency stays in the country; the state gains good citizens, and the individual gains materially. When we have reached the same point as England, you will see what kind of free trade people the Yankees are.

Above everything else, we must resolve the slavery question somehow, and "henceforth keep the nigger out of congress." But, enough of this political stuff. You seem to still be in the dark about the interest rates here and the security of capital investments. Ten percent is as common here as 4% is over there. One seldom hears less, but 12–15% is not that uncommon. Only the banks pay 6%, i.e., if the money stays for 6 months or more, otherwise, 4% on deposits on call, which is most frequently the case. Some pay nothing, but for that, they make it easier for their customers to change money.

On 23 February 1861 Bernhard reported on the birth of his first daughter, and on 13 March about the return of spring and with it an upturn in his egg business:

Egg sales are once again almost in full swing, and I can hardly get them off my neck as fast as the orders come in. I send them all to New Orleans via St. Louis and people down there sell them on consignment for me. Hubert drives eggs to St. Louis twice a week now, mostly in a 4-horse wagon, and we still can hardly get rid of them all fast enough.

Spring has come very early this year, and many farmers have already planted summer barley and some have even sown oats. We will sow next week; I think that is soon enough. It promises to be a good year. The wheat is coming up like never before, and we might even get a double harvest. The wheat fields here look almost like your fertile fields in May.

But then,

Prairie du Long
10 May 1861

Dear Theodor!

Please excuse the tardiness of my answer to your last letter, but I really could find neither the time nor the desire to write. We have also received letters from Mother, Adolph, Agathe, and Franz, and I will answer them today as well. As you can see, I have a good day's work ahead of me.

Politically, everything is now up in the air. One has no idea what will happen, and commercially things look even sorrier. Volunteer companies are being organized all over and placed at the president's disposal. There are probably 100,000 men under arms right now prepared to defend and preserve the Union. The South is also arming itself, and if people don't come to their senses soon, this stupidity will turn serious. A business slump and a scarcity of money for trade (a result of fearful restraint on investment and metals, leading to a devaluation of our paper money, particularly that whose security is based on Southern stocks), are the logical consequences. Exchange in New York now costs a 10–12% premium in St. Louis; gold and silver the same against our best paper money, Missouri bankable funds. Up to now I have actually seen some benefits from this confusion, but I'm sure it won't be long before the damaging effects are felt. For 6 weeks there has been no shipping on the Ohio to New Orleans, and even though the Mississippi has also been declared blockaded at Cairo, nobody has paid attention yet: St. Louis is still shipping products south as be-fore, including my eggs, which last week shot up to an enormous price. Thus, I made about $170 clear on the last 32 barrels, about a 70% profit.[3] Yesterday, unfortunately, I read in the papers that the blockade will now be put into effect, which will be catastrophic.

This entire political humbug is getting in my way. If the Mis-sissippi stayed open, I would quickly be able to get my groceries, sugar, coffee, etc. direct, but now I can't even think of it and will have to develop new contacts. On the whole, though, I am much happier in my business now that I am alone; I am also far more active, even though we have to deal with many difficulties and unpleasantries. For example, last week I found myself up against a roadblock in Freedom in the form of the brother-in-law of the man who owns the house the store is in. They are now trying to make my life as miserable as possible. So, for example, they rented the house right adjacent to the store to a family of filthy Jews who had fled from St. Louis to the free state of Illinois. This, even though I had offered a higher price if only so that the house could remain empty and I could at least insure my goods, which I now cannot do since all the buildings are frame houses. I am in a com-pletely desperate position and constantly upset. Now I will have to build my own store, cost what it may, even though my lease runs another two years. I certainly can't stay without insurance.

If the times were not so desperately bad, building would not present any problems. But the way things are, we will soon be very tight for money. The people in this region now have absolutely no money and cannot pay, even with the best of intentions. I have been trying, without success, to collect the ca. $500 in debts that are outstanding, and so everything will have to be put off until after the harvest. Anybody who wants to sue or use force to get his money will only end up harming himself most of all.

Luckily, the prospects for the next harvest look as good as can be. The wheat is 2 feet high and looks magnificent; that is the main thing, since it will bring money into the country. Hubert has been in St. Louis with a load of eggs since yesterday morning. Maria and our little daughter are well, especially the former, who is once again up and about.

The young Dobbelmann from Nijmegen, who has no job and no prospects, is staying with us now and earns his keep by doing odd jobs in the store and around the farm.[4] We also have two maid servants and a farm hand; every now and then we hire day laborers as well. So that's our entire household.

Now that it is too late, Jansen has received money from his father, but as he told me, he intends to use it to settle accounts with his creditors.

I'm sending you several editions of the *Missouri Democrat,* a more political paper than the *New Yorker Criminal-Zeitung,* and it will give you a better picture of the situation in this country than I could in my letters.

So, dear Theodor, my best wishes to you. The paper is now full, and I don't have the time to add another one to it. I have to travel to St. Louis tomorrow. Hubert keeps promising to write, but he never gets to it. The poor lad is embarrassed.

He and Maria send their regards; give my best to Lina and the children.

Your Bernhard

The Unrest in Missouri

Why might a "family of filthy Jews," as Bernhard put it, or anybody else for that matter, want to flee St. Louis in early 1861 and settle in a tiny rural Illinois settlement? Missouri was a slave state, not a "free" state like Illinois. But it was also divided and contested territory.

In the state as a whole, only about 5 percent of the population owned slaves, and the total number of slaves was only 10 percent of the population. The counties with the largest proportion of slaves in 1860 (25–37 percent of the population) were in what has been called "Little Dixie," a strip of counties ranged along the north bank of the Missouri River, west of Hermann. There were also counties north of St. Louis along the Mississippi that had slave populations approaching 25 percent.[1] But in St. Louis itself, where the slave population had been about 10 percent in 1840 and had dropped to less than 1 percent by 1860, slavery was unpopular. This may have had more to do with the influx of immigrant labor and the influence of eastern capital than with idealism.[2] Most Missourians were motivated neither by the abolitionists nor by the Southern "fire eaters." Nevertheless, abolition was a matter of principle for at least one segment of the population: politically motivated Germans who still identified in one way or another with the ideals of 1848. Germans allied themselves with Republican unionist politicians like Congressman Frank Blair and even organized a private militia called the "Wide-awakes," made up primarily of Germans, that acted as bodyguards and enforcers.

This was not a peaceful time. Under the heading "City News," for example, the *Missouri Democrat* ran the following ad on 8 September 1860:

ATTENTION, WIDE AWAKES
You are notified to appear at headquarters on the corner of Seventh and Chesnut streets this Saturday evening at 7 o'clock, punctually, for the purpose of joining in a demonstration of the Republicans at Illinoistown.[3] All Republicans are cordially invited to join.

C. P. M. Johnson, Pres't.
Henry Almstedt, Major.

The newspaper's account of "the Republican Gathering at Illinoistown" two days later included this description:

An interruption of another kind was at one time occasioned by a few Douglas bullies on the opposite side of the square. They entered upon the happy task of expelling certain recuperating Wide-Awakes from a beer saloon, but were themselves expelled instead, though without serious harm on either side. At this juncture, one of them thought proper to discharge the contents of a loaded pistol through a window into the saloon! The charge passed through the lowest pane of glass, over the counter, and lodged in the wall behind the bar. Almost miraculously, no person was hit. But the miscreant was at once seized, forced to release his pistol, and severely punished for his atrocity. Another individual then drew and cocked a pistol, but the weapon was instantly wrested from him by Captain Almstedt, whose utmost exertions were then needed to save the foolish fellow from merciless punishment.

In early 1861 Governor Claiborne Fox Jackson, a Democrat who identified with the South and supported secession, called for a state convention "to consider Missouri's relations with the Union." At this point Frank Blair realized that the governor fully intended to pull Missouri out of the Union, and he thereupon reorganized the Wide-awakes and members of the German *Turnverein* into an armed Home Guard or militia that began to drill. By some contemporary accounts, they were not always strictly disciplined. In any case, the city became increasingly militarized and unsafe.

Governor Jackson's call backfired on him. On 18 February Missouri voters elected the entire slate of unionist delegates to the convention, and even though 80 percent of the ninety-nine delegates were slave holders themselves and many of them not firm unionists, the outcome was a stinging defeat. The vast majority of Missourians (110,000 "no," 30,000 "yes") were simply not prepared to leave the Union and all that that would entail.

Jackson then tried another tack. He and Confederate President Jefferson Davis agreed that St. Louis must be taken since it was the key to control of the state. Whatever the outcome, the rest of the state would probably follow in the footsteps of the victor. With this in mind, Jackson determined to gain control of the federal arsenal in St. Louis.

After Confederate troops attacked Fort Sumter in Charleston Harbor, South Carolina, on 15 April 1861, Lincoln asked the states to send seventy-five thousand volunteers to defend the Union. Jackson refused to meet Missouri's quota of four thousand, stating that the request was "illegal, unconstitutional, and revolutionary." However, Blair offered to send members of the Home Guards, and in short order they were sworn into federal service as "Missouri Volunteers."

At this point Jackson decided to take the arsenal in a surprise assault from the hills overlooking it; however, when his Missouri State Guard arrived, the hills were already occupied by federal troops, and Jackson was once again thwarted. The State Guard then set up its own encampment, Camp Jackson, near the western edge of the city. By early May about nine hundred militiamen began military exercises there; many, if not most, would eventually serve the Confederacy.

When on 9 May a steamer sent by Jefferson Davis carrying guns destined for Camp Jackson arrived, forces loyal to the federal government were set to act, and next day several hundred regular soldiers along with four regiments of Missouri Volunteers commanded by Frank Blair, Nicholas Schüttner, Heinrich Börnstein, and Franz Sigel, another '48er, and under the overall command of Gen. Nathaniel Lyons, surrounded the camp. Outnumbered nine hundred to seven or eight thousand, the State Guard surrendered and were marched out of the camp. Apparently there was no shortage of troublemakers in town, and according to William Tecumseh Sherman, who witnessed the scene, a drunk with a pistol tried to break through the line of soldiers. In the ensuing melee, Volunteer Capt. Constantine Blandowski was shot and killed. The Missouri Volunteers then opened fire, killing about fifteen onlookers.

After Camp Jackson there could be no more reconciliation. Within days Governor Jackson absconded from the state capitol, Jefferson City, taking the state seal and important records. Shortly thereafter Lyons, Blair, Börnstein, and about two thousand troops were on their way to the capitol. Börnstein was installed as commandant of the capitol, and the others followed after Jackson, defeating his State Guards at Boonville. Jackson then set up a temporary capitol at Neosho, in the far southwest corner of the state. In July the unionists recalled the state convention, which elected Hamilton Gamble as governor. Lincoln immediately recognized the legitimacy and outcome of this electoral process. With that, the threat of Missouri's secession was over.[4]

Bernhard did not write Theodor about any of this; however, the newspapers he sent him were full of these events, especially the *Missouri Democrat* (the Republican paper), the *Westliche Post*, and the *Anzeiger des Westens* (Heinrich Börnstein's paper). If Bernhard had written about these momentous happenings, it is probably safe to assume that he would have seen them in light of how they affected his business's bottom line. And although we have none of Theodor's thoughts, we may assume that his sympathies were with Blair, Börnstein, and the Missouri Volunteers.

The Civil War According to Bernhard

The war had begun on 12 April 1861 with the shelling of Fort Sumter, a federal fort on a small island in Charleston Harbor, South Carolina. Thirty-four hours later, it surrendered to the Confederacy. Despite the quick seizure of the fort, many observers believed that the Southern uprising would be of short duration and that the superiority of the free Union forces, which some have claimed was a four-to-one advantage, and the North's industrial might would soon put an end to it.[1] Instead, the Battle of Bull Run on 21 July put an end to that delusion. As picnicking spectators looked on in horror, the Union victory turned into an ignominious rout.[2]

Wilson's Creek, which is the Missouri battle that Bernhard described in his letter of 19 August, took place on 9 August and was a disaster of almost equal proportions:

> The situation here is now so bad that I hardly dare to describe them. There hasn't been any business at the store for a while. I send Cunitz around every day to try to collect, but people just don't have any money. Products of all sorts are so cheap that it hardly pays to work. Wheat 40–60 cents, oats 20 cents, corn 21–23 cents, etc. However, tobacco is in great demand and is about 40% higher than usual. You should have held on to yours a while longer.
>
> For the past few days, St. Louis has been on a war footing. Gen. Frémont has been named commander of the Western Division, as I'm sure you already know. He is supposed to be a very dynamic man, and since his arrival the military administration has really come to life. But what does it matter; for the time being, not at all. Up to this point, the South is superior to us. Wherever our troops attack, they are met by forces three times as large and find themselves pushed back, as the affair at Bull Run, which ended in a shameful rout, demonstrated. We saw it again a little while ago where General Lyon felt he had to attack an enemy numbering 23,000 with his 1000-man force.
>
> The battle was bloody on both sides, and Lyon lost his life. General Sigel is now commanding and is retreating toward Rolla. The most shameful corruption is plaguing the entire administration, as, for example, the recruitment of three-month troops makes

clear. What were they supposed to do in three months? Now that their time is up, most of them are going home, and we are left in the same position we were in three months ago. It is true that things will probably improve since the troops are now sworn in for 3 years or the entire war. There has never been a better time than now to make a quick career in the military. In two weeks you can go from plowman or clerk to captain, and 6 weeks later you can be a brigadier general, no problem. My former partner, Jansen, just returned day before yesterday from Springfield with the rank of 1st lieutenant. I was even being considered for organizing a company in these parts—as captain. If one knew for certain that one would eventually be drawn into the conflict, one would do better to go in now as an officer than later as a foot soldier. That is for certain. But presumably Uncle Sam is still getting enough volunteers; they are well paid, and the poverty of the working classes is such that half the army consists of married men. Where will this all lead? I am convinced that we are witnessing the beginning of the end of the Republic as it exists today. Of course, not much would be lost; things couldn't continue for long as they have.

In the past few years—and it is true now as well—we have had a form of despotism, a despotism of which one cannot even dream in Europe, namely a despotism of the masses, the worst form of all. No! If there is to be despotic rule, let it rather be by a privileged educated class than by the unwashed masses, whose rule opens the door to the crudest corruption. The South seems to have understood this; nevertheless, whatever happens, we will get a stronger government, perhaps with a 10–12 year presidential term, which would probably be better. In any case, this is far off in the future, and it is certain only that times are bad, that the future promises a great deal, and that we have nothing to lose. So, forward. . . .

Bernhard was a little off on his figures; perhaps he was trying to impress Theodor with the gravity of the situation or the incompetence of the Union. Although the Union generals estimated an enemy troop strength of twenty thousand, the Confederacy had no more than twelve thousand troops, and these mostly poorly armed. The Union had about six thousand troops under General Nathaniel Lyons. The battle consisted largely of troops facing each other at close range on the firing line and shooting. As one line went down, they were replaced by a fresh contingent; the loss of life was immense but was soon overshadowed by the bloodletting of later battles.[3]

General Franz Sigel was a veteran of the Revolution of 1848, but although he looked good on a horse, he was rather incompetent on the field. His troops were to attack the Confederate forces from the rear, but as soon as they encountered resistance, they broke up and fled. That was the "retreat toward Rolla." Nathaniel Lyons, an abolitionist and competent general who was much respected by the Germans, died during the battle.

General Frémont, a favorite of the Germans, had run for president in 1856, and the Germans had given him their unstinting support. Not particularly effective as a military administrator, he was relieved of his duties by Lincoln not long after being appointed.[4]

On 15 January 1862 Bernhard wrote a letter that revealed a great deal about his inability to connect with others or command their loyalty. It represents a personal side of the war:

> I have experienced some unpleasant business recently, which is probably why I have had so little desire to write.
>
> For example, with regard to the post office. The friends of Jacob Fricke, the new merchant in Freedom, have succeeded in getting him a position as postmaster, thereby laying me off. Even though this fellow Fricke can barely read and can write even less, that seems to be no reason why in the land of the free, where all men are created equal, he should not be entitled to the highest office in the state rather than a more appropriate drudge job. I wrote you in my last letter that I was asked to raise a company of soldiers in this area to fight for Uncle Sam against the Southern rebels. Maria didn't want to hear of it, and so I rejected the idea. Well, then the Fricke family (a very large German family of day laborers that has gained influence by sheer numbers) took advantage of the situation, and our neighbor Fricke and a bankrupt bar keeper from Freedom set to work raising a company. The one became captain, the other 1st lieutenant. Since very few wanted to participate and I held myself neutral, they managed to gather together an army of 35 men (mainly cripples), instead of 100. With these, they set off and joined the independent Körner regiment that had been organized in Belleville. However, much to the administration's credit, the two of them were sent back home after 6 weeks duty, i.e.,

only the officers, captains and lieutenants, for an overabundance of lack of ability. They kept the troops and filled out the company from other parts.

As you may imagine, they turned all their anger for their lack of success on me, calling me an "aristocrat" (always the first thing people think of) and "secessionist," etc. It was out of this that the movement started to get the post office, and they only succeeded because I didn't think it was worth the effort to remonstrate. Everybody who has any sense of honor and decency is repulsed by this ugly corrupt mobocracy, and the better classes of the population stay out of all public movements. Instead of a reasonable policy aimed at suppressing the revolution, we get nothing but the most shameful corruption from almost all branches of the administration. We see fraud in deliveries to the army, ugly intriguing among the officers, trying to push each other out of their positions, etc. It has gotten to the point that the best commanders, like Gen. John C. Frémont, who has the trust of the nation, have to ruin others to succeed, and some who are just as capable, like Gen. Sigel, hand in their resignations. Truly, anybody who read the classics and ancient history in his school years and still has a warm place in his heart for republican institutions should come over here and be cured. In my opinion, these events of the last 12 months have at least managed to bring about a complete revolution; I have learned that a republic without republicans is absolutely ridiculous.

At this remove we cannot know how Bernhard acted when called upon to step forward in time of war. By his own admission, he suffered the consequences of not stepping forward. He does not seem to have been able to defend himself from a smear campaign, perhaps because he felt he had few friends to rally to his cause. In this he was his father's son.

In spite of his setbacks and those of the Union, Bernhard went ahead with plans to build a new store, as this letter dated 16 May 1862 testifies:

As I mentioned earlier, we have been building a new store in Freedom for the past 3 weeks. It will be a good strong brick building, 32′ along the front and 65′ deep. However, it is just one and a half stories high, nothing but a store, no apartment. It will cost about $2000, and we hope that it will be completed by harvest time.

The harvest will be early this year; the wheat will be ready by June 20 at the latest. Everything looks good and promises high yield. Today we are planting our last corn. If only we didn't have this miserable war. You have no idea how ruined everything is. It takes away all desire to do anything; even writing is too much. But I promise you that when the new store is finished, I will write you diligently. At the moment, everything is topsy-turvy, and I just don't get to it, unless, like today, I stay home for that purpose.

You write that you want me to tell you more about politics, but it seems to me after reading the paper from Cologne that you and Adolph sent that there isn't much more to tell. The Union troops have been victorious almost everywhere; New Orleans has been taken by the navy, and our gunboats have already reached Vicksburg. Memphis is still in the hands of the secessionists, and our gunboats have not gotten downstream much further than Island #10 (which we have taken).

So, the Mississippi isn't open yet. And, of course, there is now the awful heat and the unhealthy season, both of which are mighty allies of the Southerners. We get daily reports of sicknesses in our camp. One has to feel sorry for the boys; the war is being fought bitterly enough and exacts a terrible toll in dead and injured. Most of the latter die anyway because their wounds are inflicted by buckshot, which is very hard to take care of. Add to this the poor quality of medical care in most instances. The *Merrimac* is supposed to have been blown up and the *Monitor* victorious. Once again, Yankee ingenuity has proved itself. The last great battle took place on the 6th in the morning near Pittsburg Landing, Tennessee. Naturally, our papers trumpeted it as a victory; however, it was anything but.

Dobbelmann, the standard bearer for the 49th Illinois regiment, writes that if there are a few more days like that, it will be farewell to the Union.[5] We are awaiting a decisive battle near Corinth, Tennessee. I hope it will decide whether the Mississippi will open again.

It is really something what this war has cost in terms of money. Just try to imagine that each common soldier is paid $15 per month, with everything else paid for. Jansen, who is a 1st lieutenant in the cavalry, gets $150. Is that not horrendous! It cannot be denied that the accomplishments of last year have been almost unbelievable: an army that barely existed has grown to 600,000 men; our fleet, which hardly had 10–12 ships, now has more than 300. We are rightfully amazed; but where is all the money coming from? And how are debts going to be paid by such an insecure system of government? But enough of this loose talk.

Bernhard's reporting was generally accurate. New Orleans had surrendered after the superior Northern navy had all but destroyed the ships defending the city. The Union officers who walked into city hall came with an ultimatum: New Orleans could surrender peacefully or they would return with troops and "not leave as long as one brick remained upon another." And although the Union Navy reached Vicksburg, they were unable to take the city, so effectively was it fortified. Island #10 was also an important victory. Lying in an S-bend in the Mississippi, just inside Tennessee and immediately upstream from New Madrid, Missouri, it was a key choke point for the Confederacy. As long as they controlled it, Union warships could not proceed safely downriver.[6]

Bernhard's information about the battle at Pittsburg Landing, more commonly known as Shiloh, was also basically correct. To get an idea of the destructiveness of this battle, the number of casualties (killed, wounded, and captured or missing) totaled 23,741. This was more than the total for the Revolutionary War, the War of 1812, and the Mexican War combined. Although Shiloh was counted a Union victory, it made clear to generals, politicians, and the public that this would be a long and very bloody war.[7]

Naatje Reygers, Bernhard's mother, was the subject of a June letter. It is completely detached and businesslike:

What you found out from Aunt Naatje about the institution in Utrecht seems quite acceptable and much cheaper than I had expected. From what you said, the total cost for the institution, minus clothing allowance, would come to about fl. 500; with clothing and miscellaneous not more than fl. 600, about $240. That is not an insignificant outlay for us if we don't get something for it in return later, which I'm sure we will. Anyway, we can pay it. If worse comes to worst, this is the best way to proceed since the plan to house her with Aunt Julia and Mietje won't work, if I know them. There was only one thing I didn't like, namely that the institution retains the right to send the suffering woman home at any time. If I'm not mistaken, that was the case with the institution in Zutphen as well, otherwise Mama would still be there and we wouldn't have this trouble. If you have paid the fl. 139.58, let me know so that we can reimburse you.

Yesterday's newspaper brought glorious news, the first in a long time, that will make a dollars and cents difference. Memphis has been captured, and so the Mississippi is open from source to mouth. Even though there are certain restrictions and great risks involved, the first heavily-loaded boats left St. Louis today for New Orleans, the first in 13 months. In anticipation of the event, I wrote to my commissionary in New Orleans yesterday, and I hope for good business in the fall.

The harvest looks to be very good except that the wheat has a lot of rust again. However, experienced farmers tell me that it will do relatively little damage this year. Hubert is working hard with the field hands in the corn field, i.e., when he's not on his way to St. Louis, which he is frequently. Winter barley is ripe in these parts, but we don't have any. At the end of next week, we will start harvesting wheat.

Maria and Agathe are well, as are Hubert and I. Maria is knitting a large travel bag for me, and I am still awaiting my house shoes from Agathe. We are also awaiting news of a happy family event from you. Maria is preparing for a similar event in several months.

Give our regards to Lina, Agathe, Uncle Wenzel, and Aunt Annette. And write again soon.

Unfortunately, Bernhard soon realized that his optimism had been premature:

Prairie du Long
24 October 1862

Dear Theodor!

At the moment I am very busy, but I just must make the time and write a few lines to you so that you won't think I'm lazy or don't want to answer your letters punctually. I think you are un-just when you accuse me of not writing often enough and then too little. For example, I wrote you a long letter on 10 July, which you have received but don't give me credit for. After all, you refer to it in your letter dated 7 September, although you say it was the 10 May letter. I wrote about the steamer that left for New Orleans, which as it turns out was complete humbug. Steamers can't get past Memphis. The Mississippi won't be open for quite a while; Vicksburg is still in the hands of the Southerners and probably will be for some time.

Nevertheless, the economy is very good again. As I'm sure you are aware, the government has printed an enormous amount of paper money. Everybody has their pockets full of the stuff and wants to get rid of it, which makes for good business. Of course, the paper money has completely replaced gold and silver since it is legal tender and is under fixed valuation. But it doesn't matter as long as one can buy goods for it, even at highly inflated prices. In some respects, our wealth is imaginary because things that used to cost $1 now go for $2.

As I said, we are all doing good business, and I am swimming along in the stream like everybody else. However, I am careful not to have too much of this money on hand; instead, I immediately buy more goods, which, come what may, will always have value. This is another reason why the new store could hardly have been built at a better time. The store was completed a few days ago, and it is undeniably the largest and most beautiful in the district. I am sure you will understand that we have a great deal to do (moving will take 8–10 days), and so please forgive me if this letter is shorter than you would like and there is white space left over.

I went to Fayette, Missouri, and St. Louis last week on a buying trip. I covered both at a shot and was away for 14 days (my longest trip yet), but I had a great deal to buy in St. Louis because a store such as ours has to carry just about everything, so it was no small task. Goods are very expensive, but I buy in the expectation that the prices will go even higher. Cotton goods are insanely high, e.g., calico goes for 16–17 cents per yard, plain unbleached cotton cloth is 25 cents, etc. Coffee is 30 cents per pound; tobacco, $20–26 per 100 pounds. All these prices are wholesale.

It would have paid you to keep your tobacco growing. Next year plant a good-sized plot; it will keep its value well, even if the war ends because the South has grown very little this year. The shortage is therefore very great.

Bernhard's calculations concerning the cost of goods and the return on investment led him to consider how the financial dislocations caused by the war economy could be put to good use:

Freedom, 14 January 1863

My Dear Theodor!

Even though I have not received an answer to my letter of 24 October of last year, I just must write you at the turning of the year. First, Happy New Year to you and Lina and also my best wishes for your upcoming birthday. I hope there will be many more. I would have written before, but in November and December I really had no time. And then again, you always ask for such lengthy descriptions that when I do have a moment, I can't make up my mind if it is enough to begin a letter. If you were satisfied with less, you might get news more often.

Thank God I was not in a position to describe our current political and social circumstances since my time can be better spent than in relating this disaster. Apart from the market reports, I hardly have time to read the most important articles in the newspaper. Also, the situation, particularly the miserable handling of the war by the North, are hardly worth a detailed report. My only hope is that the resurgent Democratic party will put an end to this fraud, and soon, by recognizing the South and its demands and thereby ending this senseless war. It shouldn't have to come down to principles as we are well beyond that in this country.

A few days ago I completed our books for the year, and since I wrote you the results last year, I will not keep them from you this year.

Last year's profit, after subtracting all outlays for living expenses, etc., comes to exactly $1431.68. Considering the circumstances, I am satisfied, and if things continue as they have, I think that this year's profits will be even better.

Life here is horribly monotonous and dependent, but if our business continues to improve for a few more years then I might be able to move to St. Louis and open a wholesale business; perhaps later, much later, I could even return to Germany. Right now the farm is giving us the most trouble and brings in the least, mainly because it is nearly impossible to find workers. Can't you send us a few good people?

Just think, the maid gets $7 per month, and a second girl gets $4. We pay a boy who is not yet as strong as your Grädeske was back then $100 per year. A worker I wanted to hire recently demanded $200, with laundry and everything else free.

29 January 1863

I had to put the letter aside again because of business, and then I had to go to St. Louis where people are in a continual state of financial upheaval. Our greenbacks (so called because they are printed in green on both sides, but particularly the back) depreciate in value every day; or as our financiers say it so artfully, "Gold is becoming more expensive!" In yesterday's edition of the *Republican,* I saw gold quoted at a 60% premium, i.e., it costs $1.60 to buy $1 in gold. In short, Uncle Sam's money loses value every day. And, because it is the only legal tender, we are forced to accept it.

To run our business with the means at our disposal has made it necessary, indeed desirable, to carry a total running debt of about $6000 with the St. Louis concerns at which I buy. I can now pay off these $6000, for which I have bought merchandise since the end of October, and which have since risen 25–40% in value (because the value of our money has dropped), at par with greenbacks. In order to pay these $6000, we would need 5217.11.9 thalers (at Barth's quoted rate of 1.15). This would result in a pure profit of 3115.28.3 thalers, since the rate that we customarily got was $.72 ($6000 would be equal to 8333.10 thalers).

This idea has been coursing around my head, and I can't get rid of it. This is the situation, and I'm not exaggerating. Five thousand thalers would yield you a pure profit of 3000 thalers. Then the idea came up that you have many relatives in Germany whose situations are such that they could take advantage of such a proposition. Many times I thought of writing to Uncle Jacob, Uncle Wenzel, or Bennert, but each time I decided against it for fear of being misunderstood. This I did not want in any case. Hubert's and my situation is such that anybody could entrust three or four times that amount to us without fear. I don't dare offer it to you, for well-known reasons. But do you think that one of the people I have mentioned would extend a credit of 4–5000 thalers? Do what you feel you can. I want nothing more than credit for the amount I must borrow, and I will only make use of the money as long as greenbacks remain as low as they are. If our Northern troops were to win a decisive victory, against all expectations, and the greenbacks went up in value, then I wouldn't draw on them at all. Also, I want their money only until we have a new monetary system or greenbacks are valued at par.

4 February 1863

I almost have to steal time in order to finish this letter. My chief clerk, Cunitz, is away for 10–14 days, and I am alone in the store with my second clerk, Peter Waring. And, since business is good, in spite of the times (much better than last year), I really have little time to write.

As of 1 January, Hubert and I have entered into a formal contract. We capitalized our assets at a low rate of interest and then divided it equally and placed it in two accounts.

We will continue to run the entire business, store and farm and everything else, as before. *All* costs and outlays will be borne by us together 50–50. However, since I earn more than Hubert, I will receive ⅔ of all future profits and Hubert ⅓. So, we are in a private partnership; the store will go by the name B. van Dreveldt. We and Hubert are very satisfied with this arrangement.

If you are able to come up with money for us, even 3–4000 thalers, please let me know quickly. We can draw on it for 30–40 days, which won't inconvenience anybody. We just don't know how quickly economic conditions can change. I don't want to let this opportunity to earn a few thalers slip through my hands, and I give you my word of honor that as soon as the situation has straightened out, I will be punctual in repaying the money.

You probably do not know that I was ill all fall and winter. For a time I even had consumptive edema and other nonsense. But it was nothing more than the fever, which, as you know from experience, can really bring one down. For the past few days, it hasn't visited me, but I am still pretty weak.

Maria, Hubert, and the children are all well, especially Tonia. The baby had the fever a few times. Tonia speaks English and German very well already; she is a clever child and a great deal of fun.

Maria, who is *supposed* to maintain correspondence by herself, sends her regards and excuses herself with a very convincing "too lazy to write."

Other than that, there is nothing new. Tomorrow I will send you several editions of the *Missouri Republican* (which I now subscribe to). Pay particular attention to the market and financial reports.

Are cotton goods as expensive over there as here? Here they go for almost four times the normal. Today, raw cotton was quoted at .83 per pound. Tobacco is also incredibly high: $18–23 per 100 pounds. Whatever you do, plant a lot of tobacco this year. Tobacco will stay high, no matter what.

So, Good Night, dear Theodor. Maria is asleep, and I have to go to bed as well. Regards to Lina, Uncle Wenzel and Aunt Annette and Johanna as well as the children from your nephew and brother-in-law,

B. van Dreveldt

Theodor was not impressed with Bernhard's currency speculations and rejected them out of hand. In a letter to her sister, Maria noted that, "the rejection was not totally unexpected as I had drawn Bernhard's attention to how difficult it was to get only 1-200 thalers in Germany just on one's 'good face,' and how seldom one is loaned capital without security and a mortgage." Still, Theodor had also commented on Bernhard's profits and noted that his own would probably not be as good, which Bernhard took as a slap. Bernhard inferred that Theodor meant that if Bernhard was doing so well, perhaps the money should be flowing in the other direction—back to Germany.

In spite of his evident disappointment and anger, Bernhard was eager to tell Theodor about local conditions and keep him abreast of Grierson's Raid and Lieutenant Jansen's heroic deeds. Grierson's Raid, which was key to the Union capture of Vicksburg, was basically a diversionary maneuver, one of a series devised by Grant. Leaving LaGrange, Tennessee, on 17 April 1863 with about seventeen hundred troops, Grierson led a sixteen-day slash-and-burn campaign through Tennessee, Mississippi, and Louisiana, all east of Vicksburg, which diverted Confederate troops away from the defense of this key city on the Mississippi. Meanwhile, Grant swooped down on Vicksburg from the north. Even with this element of surprise and the numeric advantages in troop strength brought about by the success of the feints, the siege of Vicksburg took forty-eight days. The surrender of the city on 4 July is often viewed as the beginning of the end for the Confederacy.

Hecker P.O. Ill

20 July 1863

Dear Theodor!

I received your last three letters dated 5 and 25 March and 16 May after making inquiry with the postmaster in Freedom, Ill. (in LaSalle County in the northern part of the state). The first two had sat there several months waiting to be picked up. I can't imagine how you can address your letters to Freedom Ill. instead of Hecker. I hope you will be more careful in the future since the loss of time is very annoying. I won't even comment on the content of the above-mentioned letters, except to make a few remarks, since the subject is old and half forgotten and to bring it up again would only occasion bad feelings.

Still, I'm sorry that I ever broached this matter and that I *ever* asked for help; my entire past experience should have taught me that it would come to nothing and that I must simply rely on myself. You may rely on the fact that I will doggedly continue to strive for the goals I have set myself without ever asking *any* of my relatives for help again. Whether I will attain my goal depends on circumstances, and it is impossible to predict, although the present gives some reason for hope. Even though it may take a long time, I will do everything in my power to attain my goals.

I can assure you, dear Theodor, that I am not annoyed with you because I did not succeed in getting the money. I never expected any from you directly, and I thank you for your efforts and well-intended advice. But look, unlike others my age, I have had to do everything on my own, and I expected short, direct answers rather than advice since I am in the habit of doing my own thinking and contemplating before I act. If you hadn't addressed your letters to Freedom, I would have let go of the idea much sooner, and the entire matter would have gone the way of all projects for which one discovers that one does not have the means. I would have set it aside or dropped it completely. So, I got no direct answer to my repeated requests, and this circumstance caused me to expect something very different. But then I read between the lines in your long letter, mostly copies of letters from Herr Bennert [Annette Höynck's son-in-law, the owner of the meat firm Liebig Fleischcompagnie in Antwerp] and Uncle Jakob, what you would have done better to tell me in a few lines yourself.[8] That is the nub of it, namely that Hubert's and my credit with you, amounting to 3000 thalers, is not quite sufficient, and then, instead of copies of Bennert's letters, you could have filled out the rest of your letter with your own words. Finally, when I received all these copies instead of a short answer, I realized that I had profited very little from that mercantile eminence in Antwerp. I take the liberty to suggest that if you take the time to observe the chain of events here, you will soon come to the conclusion that I, whose knowledge is restricted to a one-horse town in the North American backwoods, a store keeper who weighs sugar and coffee and measures calico by the ell, understand more about American finances than does Herr Bennert. A mercantile eminence from Antwerp, my foot!! He should know, having experienced it, that what is happening here now is the same as happened in South America 20 years ago. Apart from the tastelessness of comparing the United States with South America, such eminencies would do much better if they didn't make themselves look ridiculous by giving off opinions, particularly of the self-important, Solomonic sort, on matters about which they know nothing. Perhaps this sounds a little overbearing, given such an authority. However, Herr Bennert says himself, and it remains a universal truth, that one only profits from one's own experiences, not from those of others.

You ask in your letter whether Hubert would have to serve in the military. Yes, he certainly will, we all will; however, military service has not yet been enforced in Illinois. I am also fairly certain that Hubert will be exempt because of his hernia, and even if that should prove not to be the case, one can always buy oneself out for $300. Whether military service will ever be enforced is doubtful. In any case, the authorities will have to take last week's events in New York into consideration.

The enclosed newspapers have a short article about the lynch court that took place in this county. To all appearances, the criminals who were hanged belonged to the same gang that recently broke in and robbed my store of about $300. The gang is said to have had 30 members, and more of them are being caught every day; just yesterday in Prairie du Rocher, two of them were taken out of the sheriff's hands and hanged. The entire country around here is overrun with riffraff, and the population as a whole is terribly demoralized by this war, which unleashes unimaginable passions. Human life is worth almost nothing, and one hears everywhere about murders of the most upsetting sorts.

I have heard nothing from my former partner, Jansen, since I forwarded your letter to him. Postal connections were problematic for a long time because of the distances and the detour that the mail had to make via New Orleans. But now that Vicks-

burg and Port Hudson have been captured—Jansen was lately involved at Port Hudson—I read about him almost daily. Jansen
has really done himself proud, particularly the famous cavalry
march through Mississippi under Col. Grierson, about which you
have read.

In terms of people, we have a good farm hand and a half-grown
boy who can do almost any kind of work, like plowing, already.
The farm hand is paid $175 per year and the boy, $90, with everything free. Maria still has the two maids that she always had.

What you write about the Catholic clergy and their propaganda
is in evidence here as well. The Catholic clergy is active everywhere and is making great progress. We have enough examples
of this nearby; however, here they are mainly striving for money
and property, and they seem to be pulling all the levers, i.e., by
reaching into believers' money bags through their emotions. In
this, they usually succeed masterfully. We often have the opportunity to observe this here in the Catholic church in Freedom. We
have rented a seat in this church for $15 per year and go to church
as often as is advisable, perhaps once every 3–4 weeks. But unlike
you, I don't get upset at helping the clerics to celebrate their tri-
umphs, but see it more as a business opportunity, much as they do.
That is the only reason I go. I no longer have this love for mankind
in general for which I enthused when I was younger. I have found
that people really aren't worth it, and because of that, I cannot see
a reason why I shouldn't help the clerics celebrate, so long as my
own interests are furthered. The individual cannot fight against
the current of the times in which he lives, and in my opinion, he
does best in most cases if he goes along with the stream. It is different after he has attained a social position from which he can
exert his own influence as a result of this flexibility. Then, he may
live his own ideals, if they are good, and act according to them.

During the next eight months, Maria carried on the family correspondence, several times defending her husband to Theodor. Bernhard
finally wrote his uncle again:

Hecker, Illinois
30 March 1864

Dear Theodor!

I am reading your lovely letters of 18 and 26 February. The reasons our correspondence came to a halt are ancient, and, I hope,

a thing of the past. If I was wrong, I beg your forgiveness. We are all well and are happy that you and your family are too. As you know, since 1 January of this year, I have a new partner in the store, Mr. Nathaniel McKee, and the firm is now called B. van Dreveldt & Co. I took this step in order to expand my business and put it on a firmer footing. Financially it wasn't necessary; our business was very good last year, and on 1 January, I was very satisfied with the books.

McKee has a ⅓ share of the store, for which he invested $6111.90, one-half of our total capital in the store, which on 1 January came to $12,213.80 so that we now have a working capital of $18,325.70. To this point I am very satisfied with this decision, and it appears that my expectations were not wrong: since the New Year, our sales are about double what they were at the same time last year. In spite of the war, business is good, a natural result of paper money; everything costs twice, even three and four times what it did before. Wages and salaries for clerks are correspondingly higher as well. The fact that gold stands at $1.65–1.70, in other words that a paper dollar will only buy 60 cents worth of gold, no longer frightens us as we are used to it. Business and trade are lively, and that is all that one asks for here.

What is uncomfortable about our present situation is the lack of workers and the resulting shameless demands that they make in order to work for somebody. This in spite of inflated wages. Hubert suffers the most because of this. The poor boy has to work from early morning to late in the evening, and so farming is turning into a drudgery for him. Because of this, we have decided to sell the farm at the earliest appropriate opportunity. Aren't there any wealthy farmers in the area around Elten and Emmerich who want to emigrate to America? This would be the ideal time since land has not risen nearly as much as gold. Our farm would be an ideal investment for people like the Frankens who have many children and who aren't too lazy to work.

As far as Franz, Hubert, and Wolter's coming over is concerned, I do think that this would be the time to emigrate, but don't speak a word about it. I could not tell you whether the boys would fit in here; you would be a better judge of that. I have not advised anyone; if I had wanted to, I would have done so 4 years ago.

If this letter should arrive before the boys leave, tell Franz not to concern himself with things that he doesn't understand. The best thing that he can bring along is the conviction that he must work here. If he has more money than the trip requires, tell him to turn it into gold in New York or certificates redeemable in gold. He needs to be careful, otherwise he will get greenbacks, which are our legal tender.

Yesterday, gold was sold in St. Louis at an 80% premium, and as a result, goods of all sorts rose in price. One has no idea what to ask for things because what you sold yesterday would have been worth much more today. Business is, of course, very lively, but damned risky as well. To someone like yourself, who quietly watches these goings-on from afar, it must look absolutely reckless. However, it is not as dangerous as it appears, and the careful person who swims with the stream will always stay on top, if he knows how to swim. In the end, that is all that matters. The wealth of this country is too enormous—I almost want to say inexhaustible—to be ruined, otherwise the mighty efforts that our government has made over the last three years would have succeeded! Of course, one shouldn't wonder, as Jansen does, that greenbacks are discounted. But these military people have entirely other ways of reasoning, and I am reminded that when a person puts on a uniform, he often takes off his reason.

Maria's three brothers arrived in Freedom in the summer of 1864. They were immediately put to work, as this letter from Maria testifies:

Hecker, P.O.
4 August 1864

Dear Lina!

Brother Franz was with us until today. He only stayed in St. Louis for a short time in June and returned because he wasn't feeling well. He was sick for three weeks, but the illness never became serious. He probably became overheated in St. Louis and then contracted this bilious fever by drinking cold drinks. Ice water and lemonade, which are sold on every street corner, are very appealing to a foreigner. Brother Hubert complained about the same thing a few days ago, and as a result, he missed work in the store yesterday and today. He plans to work tomorrow.

Wolter has managed to stay healthy. He worked industriously during the entire harvest and took the heat of the sun well every day. Our harvest began at the end of June, and barley, wheat, and oats came in such rapid succession that the entire harvest was completed in 30 days, including hay. Workers were even harder to find this year than last, and the daily wage for the grain harvest, which lasted 13 days, was $3. Haying paid $1.50. Bernhard ran the machine; our new Buckeye machine worked very well, and everybody liked it. Wolter bound the sheaves with Mr. Cunitz, who is also no farmer. But I never heard a word of complaint from him, not about the heat nor about his hands hurting. By the end, Cunitz was completely exhausted and probably would not have held out much longer; Wolter, on the other hand, went haying next day with gusto. Only once did he ask Franz to take his place so that he could get some decent sleep. But even though Franz, who is generally so good to little Wolter, didn't want to, he went out next day with his usual enthusiasm, and I was pleased that he wasn't at all sullen about it. He gets along very well with his brother-in-law Hubert and soaks up the lessons he teaches and his way with horses and work in general. Bernhard has given him special permission to ride our beautiful 3½ year old Olga. The boys love to ride and hunt; we bagged our first squirrels, and Hubertus got off a few good shots.

I hope that Franz soon finds a good position; he can always find employment in the workshops for $3–3.50 per day. However, he won't want to do anything before September, and I wouldn't recommend it because of the heat. Nevertheless, it would be bad if he were loose in St. Louis for the whole month with nothing to do. From here, he wouldn't be able to find a position easily. He has made good progress in English.

Wolter is back in the store again today, but he is going to help with threshing again. Bernhard is going to have them thresh at the end of the month, and it will probably go on for 14 days. At that point, the hard work of summer will be over and the beautiful fall season will begin. Sarah helped me during the harvest, and I would like to keep her until we are finished with threshing. But I doubt that they will want to postpone their marriage that long. I don't know how I would have managed with a new girl; I was always so tired and had to take a nap every afternoon.

Bernhard has rented some land to a family from Missouri. The husband had a 160-acre farm, but he got called up for service and was captive for over a year. In the meantime, his wife and children, the oldest 10, lived completely alone in the bush and were exposed to innumerable dangers. At the first opportunity he sold the farm, including horses, cows, etc., for about $800 and left the region. Such people have been hit hard by the war, and they will almost certainly vote for peace. But these people are lucky compared to many who sacrificed their sons and brothers. In times of war, 1-year service is doubly unpleasant, and your son Carl must try to get out of it however he can. If nothing else works, he will have to emigrate as well.

Soon you will be telling us of a new family event, and willy-nilly, I must concede you priority since our son is not yet on the way. Write again soon. Fondest regards to Theodor and you from

Your Maria

In September 1864 President Lincoln ordered a military draft, the fourth such conscription, to be implemented in every town or election district that had not made up its quota with volunteers. This draft, which called for five hundred thousand men, was no more popular than the others had been. A number of features were particularly troubling. At various times and to varying degrees, it had been possible to pay someone to serve in one's stead or to pay the government a sum, usually $300, for an exemption. Substitution brokers placed ads in newspapers: "Six hundred dollars cash paid for substitutes." Naturally, such a policy benefited the wealthier middle classes. Bounties from $300 to about $700 were also paid for volunteers; however, government agents in many locales became notorious for shorting recruits and pocketing large sums themselves. This substitution loophole had been eliminated in the September draft.[9]

The net effect was that in many parts of the country, conscripts resisted the draft by evading it, organizing resistance, and finally, as in the case of the 1863 New York draft riots, rebelling openly. No such thing happened in the tiny backwater town of Freedom, Illinois, although a group called the Sons of Liberty organized active resistance in Illinois. This potential for civil disturbance during the Civil War prompted the governor of Illinois to request in August 1864 that the state be made a military district and an officer put in charge.[10]

In response to a previous draft, the *Waterloo Advocate,* the local paper that Bernhard would have read, carried the following "bold and manly utterances" from the *Neue Zeit* in St. Louis on 19 February 1864:

> FIVE HUNDRED THOUSAND MEN MORE! — We call the most serious attention of every friend of freedom and patriotism to the astonishing fact that Abraham Lincoln orders another draft of 500,000 soldiers — conscripts — for the army and for the term of three years, or as long as the war lasts. . . . In the most laconic style of a European despot — "Thus we command!" this remarkable document presents itself before our eyes: 500,000 men more! Do our readers know what this signifies? For three years, or during the war! Can they perceive the vast possible consequences? This is an astonishing event!

Making liberal use of the exclamation mark, the editorial continued in this vein. The *Anzeiger des Westens,* identified as "an administration paper" in the *Advocate,* weighed in with these cynical but perhaps justifiable remarks:

> If this new order were really intended to draft more men, we should be induced to ask astonished and anxiously: In face of all the recent rose-colored reports concerning the near end of the rebellion, for what is this immense increase in the army? Has any misfortune happened, or is there any in prospect? But it is well known that the old conscription law has furnished very few men. The new and worse law is made to bring still less men, but more money. The men between thirty-five and forty-five, now called into the field, will rather part with a number of greenbacks than with family and business. Hence this new draft, it may be expected, will furnish a great deal of money for bounties.

It may seem surprising, but by 1864 a large part of the German press had turned against Lincoln, whom they perceived as betraying the anti-slavery and unionist cause. Many Germans pinned their hopes on John C. Frémont for president. The *Missouri Republican* was not slow to exploit this disunity in Republican Party ranks, publishing translations of German attacks on Lincoln almost daily under the heading, "The Spirit of the German Press."

The war and the manpower it required also created a significant labor shortage, which is a subject of almost all of Bernhard's and Maria's letters during this time. In the cities, where the war economy was booming, women, the young, and the elderly often took the place of experienced workmen. In small towns such as Freedom, however, the shortage was acute, and with the demand for labor outstripping supply, wages spiraled upward.

In general, Americans were extremely weary of the war and the dislocations and casualties it had caused. The war was not going well for the North, and to many observers it appeared that it might drag on and bring down the entire country. Lincoln became increasingly unpopular, and that unpopularity is reflected in the following letters. George B. McClellan, a popular general who had been dismissed by Lincoln in November 1862, became the Democratic candidate for the presidency in 1864. The Democratic platform, which not once mentioned slavery, contained a peace plank that is worth quoting because its popularity reflects what the mood in the country must have been:

> *Resolved,* that this convention does explicitly declare, as the sense of the American people, that after four years of failure to restore the Union by the experiment of war, . . . justice, humanity, liberty and the public welfare demand that immediate efforts be made for a cessation of hostilities, with a view of an ultimate convention of the States or other peaceable means, to the end that, at the earliest practicable moment, peace may be restored on the basis of the Federal Union of the States.[11]

On 16 September 1864 Bernhard wrote:

Hubert v. Weise was very sick with a bad case of bilious fever, but he is getting better. He is still weak, and so I will take him to the doctor in St. Louis next Monday. He hasn't been in the store for 4 weeks. Wolter is very healthy and makes himself useful on the farm by helping our Hubert plow. In order to avoid a great deal of work, we are sowing much of our land with timothy this fall. We rented out a portion of the farm again. We only have one farm hand, and Wolter and my brother Hubert have quite a bit to do. The two of them seem to have become fast friends, which pleases me. Wolter is a good fellow. Workers are not to be had here, and since Cunitz married Sarah, Maria has a maid problem. Not only does one have to pay enormous wages for a job done only half right, if that, rather, the people have to like you in every respect, otherwise they won't work for you, and even if they do they won't stay. May the Devil take this life; the whole world order is out of joint. The boss is the servant, and the servant stands at the head, both in the house and in the state. Anybody in Germany who sympathizes with the working classes should come over here and take a close look at this fraud. I bet that they will change their views. This is the main reason why we want to leave here.

Brother-in-law Franz was here a few days ago and then left suddenly when he heard about a position he wanted. I gave him a letter to take to an acquaintance who might have some influence. We don't know yet whether he has been successful. Franz will have to go through quite a lot before his ship finds a safe haven. The other two will have an easier time.

The weather is extraordinarily dry this month, and the nights are cool, which is unhealthy and brings on fevers. Doctors are doing well. Since McClellan's nomination, the price of gold has fallen, and in general, people seem to be more optimistic about the possibility of peace. If McClellan is elected (and his prospects are not bad) then we will get peace. In any case, they will do everything possible, and shortly after his inauguration, they will make a truce, and I believe that this is peace. If we get peace, then everything will be all right again; there will be a lasting peace, even if the nigger has to be the scapegoat. The white man in America will never again wage a war on his behalf. I don't believe in conditions like those in Mexico as Jansen describes them. In general, these military people have received their political views as from a cookie cutter. Our population was and is very different from the Mexican. Our population is still overwhelmingly healthy European, and not the degenerate mixture that lives in Mexico. This is the foundation of my hopes. In addition, the country is new and its various resources hardly tapped. I can hardly imagine a government that would be so bad that the country would fail to prosper. The best proof of this, in my opinion, is our current condition and Mr. Lincoln's miserable administration. It appears that conscription will go ahead in earnest; the lottery is set for next Monday. This is a bitter pill for the American people and will not help Mr. Lincoln in the next election. So far there hasn't been that much of an uproar because those who have money can buy themselves a proxy. Those who do not, must do what people everywhere must: suffer.

Your nephew B. van Dreveldt

At some point in 1862, the family had switched newspapers, subscribing to the *Missouri Republican,* the newspaper supporting the Democratic Party. Both Maria's comments on race and Bernhard's more intemperate outbursts, which give voice to his general animus, are consistent with the coverage and editorial policy of that paper. Short items such as the following from 30 September 1864, which may seem transparent and ludicrous today, were not uncommon and both influenced and reflected the attitudes of many readers:

THE "NIGGER."

"The Richmond *Examiner* complains that the negroes are the most luxurious class in that city, dressing better than the whites and monopolizing the delicacies in the market. Strangers are struck with the leanness of the white men and the fatness of the black men in Richmond, and the *Examiner* says the negroes get their money by stealing and burglary and are rich enough to bribe the police and judges."

This is a curious revelation. Taken in connection with what is visible in most places north of the Mason and Dixon line, it shows that about the only people benefited by this war, either North or South, is the negro. Suppose the South consents to end this war, and thus give another chance to white men?

Maria gave an indication of this influence toward the conclusion of the following letter:

Hecker, P.O.
19 October 1864

My dear Lina!

The long-threatened draft has finally become a reality. Bernhard had already prepared himself, sure that he and Hubert would be taken. Both of them were lucky.

Last Friday, 14 October, our district held a lottery, and of every 5 eligible men, 3 were drawn; everyone was afraid that they would draw a bad number. Cunitz is clear. In Freedom it mainly hit people who are really having a hard time; 18 men were chosen, all married men with small children. They are mainly carpenters, cobblers, and smiths, people who hardly possess more than they earn in a day. It is horrible to hear about it. Yesterday, the men marched off to go before the examination commission in Alton. After that, the ones who are chosen will be given 5 days of vacation, which most will not be able to take because of the costs. Then they will be put in uniform and march immediately to Springfield.

On Friday and Saturday, Bernhard was in Alton and witnessed the departure of such a newly formed company. Order was kept by older soldiers with fixed bayonets. It must have been painful to see. In Freedom there is an eerie silence now that the men are gone. The brother-in-law of our maid has to go as well. He is a cooper and has a good income. A few weeks ago, his wife had her third child. How is this poor woman supposed to survive? Uncle Sam is slow to pay, and the conscripts don't get a bounty. What will the next elections bring? The Democrats are hopeful, but Lincoln has better prospects. The soldiers have the vote, and we know what influence officers have on the political views of the troops. Then again, the draft is pulling the most votes from predominantly Democratic regions. Gold, which only 14 days ago had fallen markedly, which was already having an effect on prices, has risen rapidly again. The maids' wages go up every month, and I now have to pay the 17-year-old $8 per month. The other one wanted the same, but I put my foot down, and she only gets $6. That is an awful lot of money, $16 per month. I just wonder what is going to happen in the summer if this continues and so many people leave. The girls will probably demand men's wages.

I won't write much about the brothers; I'd much rather let them do it. Hubertus wants to write today, and Wolter too, if he gets some time. The apples have all been brought in, although no cider has been made yet. We will only get 10–12 barrels, 2 of which will be cooked down for syrup. Wolter will help with that. Then there are also small chores that can be done in 2–3 weeks, and then Wolter will go back to the store. He has offered his services for slaughtering. It is amazing how little the boy's hands have suffered; the skin peels off and remains thin so that he has had neither blisters nor calluses.

If Lincoln is elected, there will be no end in sight, and everything will be done for the Negroes. If the Democratic papers are half-believable, Lincoln & Co. give great preference to the black troops. They are well fed, warmly clothed, and ride the best horses, while the whites are poorly clothed and often starved. The whites are sent into the field while the blacks stay behind in the cities as guards and make pests of themselves. In the end, it may go so far that the blacks get the vote while the whites are denied theirs.

But, I have to end this letter. Farewell, dear Lina. Give your littlest one a kiss and the others one as well. Best regards to Theodor, Mother, and Agathe, and keep your sister in your thoughts,

Your Maria

Bernard began a letter shortly afterward:

Hecker, Illinois
28 October 1864

Dear Theodor!

My best belated wishes to Lina, the happy mother as well as to you, the father, upon the birth of your new daughter Louise. And I wish you both all the joys of parenthood. We are also quite well; Antonia is getting big and smart and speaks both English and German fluently. Little Agathe is a sweet, healthy, and fat little thing. Wolter is still working on the farm helping my brother Hubert. Hubertus v. Weise is healthy again and is working in the store. For the past several days, Franz has been visiting us; he still doesn't have a position. Next Monday I will be going to St. Louis on business, and I will take Franz along and see if I can't procure a position for him.

Since the day before yesterday, I have the store in Freedom to myself again as Mr. McKie and I parted ways amicably. I will pay Mr. McKie for his ⅓ participation, and his profits for the year come to $2305. I am happy to go it alone again even though I think I made a good deal. Our business was very good throughout the entire year, and I am looking forward to a pleasant profit come 1 January.

A few weeks ago we survived our first compulsory conscription. All of us made it through, i.e., neither Hubert, Cunitz, nor I were drafted. My former partner, McKie, however, was signed up, and he was able to get out of it on account of physical weakness, but at great cost and effort. Here in Monroe County, 538 men had to become soldiers, which is an enormous number for such a small population as ours, almost ⅖ of the able-bodied men between the age of 20–45. It didn't matter what their status or situation was; married or unmarried, they were all shorn with the same shears. In my opinion, this is the most irresponsible and unjust form of conscription, especially, as is the case here, when a proxy can be sent. This opens up the door to trade in white flesh. There were terrible scenes here on account of this. I know people who would rather give up everything than leave their families. And all this for the damned niggers! This has gone a little too far in this glorious land; our freedoms are in jeopardy! But the mob keeps clamoring for war, and old Abe (Lincoln) will most probably be reelected for another four years.

11 November 1864

That is as far as I got in my letter of last month before I was interrupted. I haven't had any time until now to finish it. I was in St. Louis last week, and Franz is there now but, despite prospects, he is still unemployed. We hope that he will succeed this time. If Franz had set himself to it as he should have, he would have had a position long ago. But one time it was too warm to work, and another time the work was too dirty for him, etc., etc. He simply wants a position in which he can start out as a gentleman, which strikes me as unlikely given his field. Of course, those are just German prejudices that I am absolutely convinced will disappear with the last German money. What's the difference if he has to do some hard work for a time as a lowly worker? We all had to do this, and luckily there is no shame in it; if he has talent and capabilities, he will make his way.

To the shame of the nation, Lincoln has been reelected president of the United States of America for another four years, much as expected. Thus, we cannot think about peace any time soon. And the nation's freedoms are in jeopardy as well. Many view the jubilation of the abolitionists as the death knell of our freedom. God help us that they be wrong. We hope for the best, and await what will come. Gold is up at 260 again. Only God knows where this will lead, but even the wisest doubt they can find a credible solution to our problems. Not another word about it; let's all observe what happens and draw our own conclusions.

We organized a deer hunt for Hubertus, and we actually bagged two, a fat buck and a doe. With all my lack of skill, I managed to bring down both of them. I got a good shot off on the buck from 62 paces right in the breast. The animal weighed at least 175–180 pounds. When I shot the doe, Hubertus also got a shot off and hit the animal in the hind leg.

Business is picking up in the store just now, and so I will close this letter, otherwise I will be interrupted again and it will lie around for a few more days. Maria and the children send their greetings, so do Hubertus and Hubert and Wolter, who are both in St. Louis picking up merchandise. Hubert is driving a four-horse wagon and Wolter a two-horse. You see, the boys have to work, there's no talking their way out of it.

Your Nephew
B. van Dreveldt

The government ordered a fifth draft in early 1865, which Bernhard managed to avoid, although "evade" might be closer to the truth. In his previous letter, Bernhard had made a point of how unjust and corrupt a draft system was that allowed for proxies and the "trade in white flesh." No one could accuse him of the latter:

Hecker, Illinois
10 March 1865

Dear Theodor!

I finally have the opportunity to answer your letter of 14 November of last year. I haven't had time to write at all. Even though I'm not feeling well today, I went to the store this morning but soon returned home. I hope that I'll get over the illness soon because I'm supposed to go to St. Louis as soon as possible to negotiate an offer on the farm, which has still not been sold. Last Monday we held an auction on the farm and sold off things we don't need anymore: 4 young and old horses, sheep, pigs, agricultural equipment. The proceeds from the auction came to about $1100. We kept 5 horses as well as 2 wagons with harnesses, a carriage and buggy, a couple of cows, sheep, pigs, etc. We have once again rented the fields out for ⅓. We get ½ the profits from the crops we planted the previous fall, such as wheat and barley. That goes for the pastures as well. We will keep the fruit gardens ourselves. At the same time we are offering the farm for sale, and we should succeed by fall given our continuing efforts. The lease of the fields is in effect until next harvest. At the moment, our lives are relatively quiet and pleasant; we have only 1 farm hand and 2 maids and don't need any more help. Brother Hubert provides the main manpower and regularly drives the produce to the store in St. Louis twice a week, usually in a 4-horse wagon. You see, we are always up to here in work, even though the farm is leased out. There was no choice; we can't find workers because there are no people around. When the farm has been sold we will move to Freedom where we plan to build a house this summer. This will also be better for the store because of all the time I waste right now going back and forth.

Hubert and I are out of danger in terms of military duty. Our numbers were both drawn. Hubert was deemed unfit, and I found a proxy for three years, a big, strong escaped nigger, or to express myself more artfully, "a free American citizen of African descent." The whole thing cost me $850; still, cheap enough. Let someone else get shot. Since November, I have been running the store alone again. Once we have sold the farm we will sell the store as quickly as possible. It is very profitable, but I yearn for something bigger. A few years may go by, but I will do it in any case. I don't see these things with that old youthful enthusiasm any more that believes that nothing can fail, but I do feel capable of running a larger store and earning more money.

Our politics appear to favor the North. With Charleston and Wilmington in our hands and Sherman victorious in South and North Carolina and pressing on to Richmond, which is also encircled from the other side as well, success is no longer in doubt.

The price of gold falls every day in the same way as our armies advance, slowly but surely. It seems to me that once the Northerners accepted conscription so patiently, the fate of the Southern Confederacy was sealed. And, if the signs are not deceptive, we will have peace within half a year. Should this be the case, the United States would once again take an impressive role in the world, and I don't think that Maximilian's dynasty in Mexico would last long. I can hardly imagine a better application of the Monroe Doctrine nor a better occupation for our army, a large part of which would be better off in Mexico than here. But enough of politics, which we can neither steer nor change.

Of the brothers-in-law, only Wolter is still here, working in the store. Hubert v. Weise has been gone since New Year's; he became fresh and the thing couldn't go on any more. As a result of the way he departed as well as a very crude letter that he wrote me a few days later without any provocation, things between us are such that there can be no question of a friendly relationship. I did not stoop to answer his letter.

Franz visited us last Sunday. He is working in St. Charles, Missouri, for the North Missouri Railroad Co.; Hubert is also supposed to be working there as a clerk in the County Clerk's office. It is a source of no little pleasure that I had the boys, Hubert as well as Wolter, earn their livings from the first day they arrived. The advantage of having done so is completely theirs, even though Hubert had the arrogant impertinence to suggest that I had gained advantage from them. The ridiculousness of this claim should be clear to everyone. Even so, the whole thing is not very encouraging, especially where Wolter is concerned. Wolter still has a place here as a relative as long as it is advantageous to him and he can get something out of it. Nevertheless, given what we experienced with Hubert, we assume that there will be unpleasantness. Not that he ever gave cause for complaint; on the contrary, he always tried to make himself useful. However, I just don't have the desire to take him in as I once would have. But enough of this matter, which must be very unpleasant for his mother.

Bernhard

Although the last Confederate troops would not surrender until late May 1865, Lee's surrender to Grant at Appomattox Court House, Virginia on 9 April marked the collapse of the rebellion. Just five days later, President Lincoln was assassinated. Bernhard commented on the assassination, and his political assessment was astute.

But the constant trickle of racism from Bernhard finally prompted Theodor to take him to task. From Bernhard's response one can gather how little he heard what he had been saying. He may have been astute in some areas, but he was not wise. In addition, his falling out with Maria's brother Hubert was simply a continuation of an old pattern. One may well imagine that Bernhard's arrogance, political opinions, and even hypocrisy might have been hard for the boys to accept:

Hecker, Illinois
19 April 1865

Dear Theodor!

I have some free time, and I want to use it to write a few lines to you. I received your letter dated 26 February. Since Sunday, we have been living in the most horrible political upheaval. You will know the cause of this when you read this letter; I am speaking of the murder of our president, Mr. Lincoln. This incident is the worst shame that could have befallen our nation.

From the above-mentioned letter, I see that you misunderstand my political views. I am not a politician and want to be nothing more than a businessman. Nevertheless, I want to try to justify myself. I find most politics boring because I know that it seldom accomplishes more than hot heads and that the end result is that people simply hold more firmly to their various opinions. In addition, the layman and the uninitiated can do nothing to alter the course of events. In fact, he runs the risk of completely misunderstanding political rules because in politics it is often the case that things are undertaken in order to effect precisely the opposite policy than one would assume from appearances. Between you and me, the idea that the people rule in a republic such as ours is usually humbug.

The leaders of the major parties also steer politics. Depending on how they seek advantage and put an opponent at a disadvantage by being able to perceive and make use of the trends of the times, one party or another will be stronger and win.

I myself belong to none of the major parties and keep myself independent of party platforms. If I can't be a leader, I at least don't want to be a follower. If I had had the opportunity in my youth to satisfy my intellectual curiosity, things might be different. If I vote at all, it is for the candidate whose personality and political ideas are most in line with my wishes. Thus, four years ago, I voted for Lincoln; in the last elections for McClellan. If Lincoln had acted before the last election the way he has in the past six weeks, I would have voted for him this time as well.

I just don't understand where you get the idea that I am pro-slavery and belong to a party that you would want to see disappear. I don't think you could have gotten it from my statements. If my young brothers-in-law represented this opinion to you, I must tell you that they understand too little of our circumstances to even comprehend my views.

Their politicking, and they love to do it, is to this point just the urge, which they share with many people, to wag their tongues about what they understand least. They like to be in opposition to everything and everyone.

It won't surprise you that this behavior led to quite a few arguments between us, sometimes sharp ones. Actually, our political opinions are the same, and I think this will be proven once they have become familiar with the institutions here, have knocked off a few rough edges, and given up this tendency to oppose.

In general, I hold that in public life it is best to keep one's political ideas to oneself, and I think I live according to that principle. And, of course, a lot of politicking would harm my business, since I have to deal with people holding the most varied views. I probably wouldn't even be understood by most people here because it is well known that Germans are at least 100 years behind the Americans. I am neither pro-slavery nor a secessionist, and that is that. But it does not follow that I am therefore an abolitionist or even one of the radicals, who want nothing more than tumult and murder and a similar cleansing process in this beautiful country of the sort experienced by France during the reign of terror initiated by those bloodhounds. I am nothing more than a conservative who wants to conserve the Union and institutions of this country, concentrate power in a central government, and have a moderate aristocracy, as much as this is compatible with our institutions, all this as a counterweight to the rule of the mob. Honestly, I can't see how a reasonable person in this country could be anything but a conservative. To want to take a system of government that was bequeathed to us by Washington, Jefferson, Franklin, and whoever the others were, and tinker around with a bunch of radical experiments to try to make it better, is a little too much. From this it follows that one must be against the kind of war that this party wanted to wage against the South and actually has waged for a time. This sort of war is aimed less against slavery than it is a sort of defensive war aimed against the better class of whites in the South.

Slavery is secondary, just a pretext. As you yourself stated, the general tenor of the times is against slavery. Of course, and justifiably so. Even Russia is freeing its slaves. Why should one not expect that so free and noble-thinking a people as the Americans, especially those in the South, would not eventually do the same with their slaves?

But that isn't what the radicals want. It is less the Negro that they want to free than his master whom they want to oppress. As long as he or his heirs live in the South, with or without slavery, and make themselves felt, at least those scoundrels would not be able to take the rudder with their revolutionary doctrines. This is precisely why Lincoln's death is so terrible coming at this moment and so regrettable. Now, at just the moment when he was in the process of turning his political opponents into friends through his conciliatory policies toward the South, when the military might of the South was broken and the rebellion at an end for all practical purposes, now is when we need a man like Lincoln, a man who has climbed as high as a citizen can in this republic, whose ambition cannot take him any higher except to devote his term in office to the great task of reconstruction. We needed a great statesman whose name would ring for all generations to come and rise to immortality. His political actions and final speeches evince this quality in my opinion, and I would not venture to surmise whether his successor, Andrew Johnson, will pursue the same policy of reconciliation. For the time being, he has declared that he will not undertake to make departmental changes. This man's personality and past are such that one must harbor the most serious fears. He is himself a Southerner by birth (Tennessee) and a former tailor who has worked himself up to his present position from his lowly beginnings by both straight and crooked political means. He appears to represent those who see their salvation in the downfall of the party now in power in the South, and now that the battle has been won on the field of war intend to carry it on in the houses and palaces of the well-to-do and rich. Yet we hope for the best. If Seward lives and Johnson falls into his hands, then the future will not be so gloomy. Up to now, the price of gold has not risen since Lincoln's death and currently sells at a 45–46% premium.

Enough of these miserable politics. I don't understand how I could have spilled so much ink about it. But you will probably read it anyway, although it makes me feel foolish, as if I were trying to instruct wiser people than myself about politics.

Next Saturday we will go to St. Louis to have photographs taken of the children, something we have been talking about for a long time.

Your nephew and brother-in-law
Bernh. van Dreveldt

Did Bernhard harbor racialist ideas, and was he a Southern sympathizer? The answer is almost certainly "yes" to the former: "Our population is still overwhelmingly healthy European, and not the degenerate mixture that lives in Mexico. This is the foundation of my hopes." Still, it is easy to judge him from where we stand today. But let us consider what Maria wrote to her sister on 30 March 1865 regarding the latter. Her letter, a staunch defense of her husband, demonstrates her own political interests and thinking, but also the complexity of the war and the issues around which it was fought and the passions it aroused:

> Theodor is wrong (pardon my saying this) in his opinions about American politics and calls them by the wrong name. I consider Theodor as little an abolitionist as Bernhard a rebel. Not all of the members of the former Republican Party have gone along with the radicals who are now in power, and if Theodor knew the Jesuitical and despotic ways and means that this party allows itself to employ, which he could only know if he were here, then he would feel sorry for every time he had called himself an abolitionist. The radicals lie, yell, curse, and try to deceive foreign and domestic observers, and in this they often succeed because they are in power. Basically, Theodor and Bernhard share the same political principles. Do you think that Bernhard could be against the abolition of slavery? Absolutely not; just don't let it be at the expense of the whites. Would Theodor want to join the radicals in labeling everyone who disagrees with them a traitor? During the Missouri Convention, didn't Mr. Folmsbee declare that there was only one loyal party, and that he would take by the neck whoever did not belong to it, etc.? Where is the political freedom in this? I don't believe that Bernhard ever backed the South, if only because of his business dealings, which he always based on the idea of the equivalence of greenbacks and gold. If the North were to lose, this would probably never occur. One can respect the tenacity and skill with which Southerners have fought this war without sympathizing with the South.

Whatever else one might be tempted to think of Maria's defense of Bernhard, she certainly understood her husband's motives.

Bernhard's Death

When the Civil War was over, Bernhard was able to turn his attention to his wider business ambitions, which included starting a grocery store and then expanding into shipping and financial services. Maria was not opposed to the idea of moving to St. Louis, but she was not particularly enthusiastic either, as this excerpt from her 28 August 1865 letter indicates:

I am sure that you think I am yearning for the city life, but this is not the case. I myself was amazed that the sale left me feeling quite indifferent since I know that we will miss our cool house, the large porch, and the grassy yard planted with shade trees. In all my visits, I can't say that I've liked St. Louis, and I generally like its people even less. And I've been there in all seasons. On the other hand, I can see that we own a lot of capital in the form of buildings and land that brought in little rent, that Hubert is increasingly irritated at the amount of work he must do with little help, and that Bernhard lives too far from Freedom to run his business as he would like to. I am also convinced that Bernhard will provide the comforts of home in excess of my requests, and under such circumstances one could certainly live anywhere. I would have preferred that we kept the store and built a nice house nearby and then a garden and kept the horses. But I feel that Bernhard is probably right when he says that we would not be able to stand it for long. Where we are is neither city nor country; we have no circle of friends, only neighbors, and what a bad lot they are! Even Mary is getting on my nerves. Three Sundays in a row she danced until dawn, and she stays out until 11:00 3–4 nights of the week. When I try to talk to her about it, she says, "I do my work." What am I supposed to do? I certainly won't find a better one to take her place.

Bernard reported that by November, all of their property in Prairie du Long and Freedom had been sold:

Hecker, Ill.
7 December 1865

Dear Theodor!

We have now moved into Freedom for the time being. The buyer of our farm is already settled in there, and my former business was taken over by a partnership on 1 November. Adam Roth, the buyer of the store, has taken my former clerk August Cunitz and his brother-in-law Jacob Heine as partners, both without capital. The two of them run the store here while Roth stays in St. Louis. After subtracting expenses and outlays as well as 10% for Adam Roth's capital investment (about $25,000), they each get ⅓ of the profit. Because of outstanding debts, I was forced to spend the winter here, and so when I sold the store, I retained the right to keep my office. My only occupation consists of writing out bills and talking to my former customers about payment. I do this with great energy, and I hope that I can get satisfaction from most of them without resorting to the justice of the peace or the constable. In the spring we will move to St. Louis, and by that time I will have a better idea of what I will do. I will probably open a wholesale grocery similar to the one that Angelrodt, Barth & Eggers had in your time. But this is just between us.

In April the family finally moved to St. Louis. Bernhard had written Theodor in February 1863 that he had been ill all fall and winter. Maria reported that in St. Louis his illness returned and then took a decided turn for the worse:

St. Louis, Mo.

20 May 1866

Dear Lina!

After receiving your letter and Mother's short note in mid-March, I wrote to Mother immediately, and so you know about Bernhard's illness. I couldn't write to you earlier, and you will have heard about the course of the illness from our brothers. As of 10 days ago he is out of danger, and he can go out. He is regaining his strength rapidly, and unless he has a relapse, we can count on a full recovery in 14 days. Unfortunately, relapses are always to be expected, and his recurring high fevers make daily visits from the doctor necessary. If I am not mistaken, I wrote Mother that we had a doctor from Belleville whose treatment led directly to amelioration. He diagnosed the illness as chronic dysentery secondary to abscesses in his intestines brought about by suppressed, poorly treated fever. However, he did not dare to undertake a course of treatment and considered it necessary to visit the patient once, even twice daily. So, we had to move here as fast as possible and had the good fortune of finding a skilled young doctor who was able to treat him successfully. Curiously, he had had the illness himself when he was a military doctor in the field. Ill for four months, he treated himself, and so he has experience. The illness is extremely painful and the treatment almost more so. He has had continuous blood in his stools and pus 30–60 times a day, and this for six full weeks. He has no appetite and gets no rest except by artificial means. The treatment consisted largely of injections of lunar caustic and warm baths. You can't imagine how weak and exhausted Bernhard has become. When he took his first bath, I was truly shocked by his gauntness, which was every bit as pronounced as Father's in 1860. However, he has been gaining weight steadily since his appetite has come back. But reading and writing are still too much for him and leave him exhausted.

Our brother Franz has visited us several times. He spent the Easter days in Freedom, which was all the better because I had to go to Waterloo on Easter Sunday, and then I returned to St. Louis on Monday. Wolter took over Bernhard's care at night while I got the house in order during the days. He did a good job keeping the patient comfortable and satisfied. Brother-in-law Hubert was supposed to help me, but he didn't feel like it and made himself scarce. When I got here on 2 April, the previous renters were still in our quarters, and there was no sign of cleaning. Everything was filthy. Tuesday the 3rd was a lost day; I hired women to clean. On Wednesday and Thursday we cleaned, whitewashed the pantry, stairs, kitchen, and dining room. On Friday we papered two rooms and put stoves in the kitchen and bedroom. On Saturday carpets were laid down in the salon, living room, and our bedroom. Then two wagons arrived with bedding, valises, and kitchen ware, which I had to unpack. Hubert moved in. Sunday was a rest day. On Monday Hubert drove out to Freedom to pick up Tonia, Agathe, and Mary; Hubert von Weise slept in the new house and helped on Monday when the new furniture arrived. By midday the house was in order. I had bought provisions and burned out the pots, so I could cook right away. Bernhard arrived on Monday the 9th at about 4:00; Wolter had driven him in the buggy via Waterloo, and the trip took two days. He looked drawn but was still able to negotiate the stairs with little help. The first two days he came down and sat with us at table, but after that, he couldn't any more.

Once the initial excitement had worn off, his exhausted state became all the more apparent. Dr. Junghanns held that it would be more comfortable for him to lie, and so he remained in bed until the beginning of May. Then he began to get up for a few hours, and as soon as he was able to climb the stairs, he was allowed to go outside. I am using his momentary absence to write this letter, and I am in a rush. Please excuse my handwriting. Antonia also had some sort of dysentery and was quite sick. She even had to be medicated. Agathe is healthy, but she has a stuffed nose, for which she takes daily salt baths. Johanna, too, but without the salt. As you see, I have enough to do; things are going much better though. Mary had the fever for three weeks, and I was overcome with homesickness and annoyance at having no help. However, I do have a quick and competent baby sitter who, although she is only 12, keeps the bedrooms, stairways, and halls nicely in order. I take care of the two salons; we bathe the children together, and Mary sees to the kitchen and dining room. I recently had to hire someone to do the laundry. Every day I go to market at 6:00 in the morning. It is close by, which is fortunate because it is already quite hot, and it is absolutely necessary to go to market daily.

Johanna is an extraordinarily quiet and lovely child. She has allowed me to write this letter without my having had to pick her up even once. She is obviously thriving, which I find curious because I haven't had a moment's rest since she was born. I've also had headaches and toothaches; a few days ago, I had to have four molars removed.

Wolter will begin a new job in a wholesale grocery owned by Miss Bockhoff's brother-in-law.

Farewell, dear Lina. Give my regards to Theodor, and ask him to write. Also, give regards to Mother and Agathe. Kiss your children for me, and don't forget

Your Maria

The medicine Bernhard was given, lunar caustic (a medicinal name for silver nitrate, the substance used to coat photographic film), was used primarily in the treatment of "epilepsy, chorea, angina pectoris, and other spasmodic afflictions," and was also "among our most efficient remedies in chronic gastritis, attended with pain and vomiting." It was also used to treat inflammation and ulceration of the ileum secondary to typhoid fever.[1] Just as medications were what we would call "broad-spectrum," so were diagnoses. It is probably impossible to determine precisely what Bernhard's affliction was.

On 7 July 1866 Bernhard tried to write one last time:

St. Louis
7 July 1866

Dear Theodor!

I want to try at least once more to let you see a sign of life from me. Whether this will be my last in this world or the beginning of a regular correspondence, only the future can teach us. As for myself, I am without courage or hope. I have suffered horribly, and if it were not for Maria and the children— truly, life is not worth one-tenth of what I have had to endure. Thanks to Dr. Junghanns's wonderful treatment, my original illness, neglected chronic dysentery and intestinal ulcers, is completely cured. Other doctors would have just let me expire; the doctors in Freedom treated it as hemorrhoids for months. However, as if my suffering were not complete, I have had a congestion of the liver for about a month. This is the most horrible pain that a human being can have, and whoever hasn't experienced it cannot imagine what it is like. Even as I write, the pain is sometimes so severe that I want to cry like a child.

The letter stops here; Bernhard evidently requested that it not be sent until he finished it. In the meantime, Maria reported on the course of his illness:

St. Louis
30 July 1866

Dear Lina!

We heard from Adolph about the birth of your little girl on the 2nd. We hope that she stays healthy and gives you double the pleasure in compensation for your loss.[2] Unfortunately, your and Theodor's well wishes for Bernhard's recovery were premature. Just as the main illness disappeared, it looked as if a complete recovery would occur. The doctor prescribed a two- to three-month stay in St. Paul, but because of Bernhard's weakness and side pains we kept having to postpone it. Finally, on 2 July, when I was all packed up and ready to go, the doctor declared the trip an impossibility. Naturally we were completely demoralized, and it took repeated efforts by Dr. Junghanns to get our courage back up. He explained the pus had accumulated from the back and chest and was slowly draining downwards and would either dissipate or would have to be lanced. At the beginning of July, this accumulation of pus was sitting on the liver, which is what caused the great pain and was also very dangerous. If the pus had drained more internally, the consequences would have been dire. As it is, it has drained just beneath the skin, and one can observe the reduction of the painful areas daily. Since 1 July, the doctor has forbidden all walking or riding, anything that requires movement. It seems best since any motion causes greater pain. It will take a few more months, and God knows when Bernhard will be well again and have regained his old strength.

The heat is terrible. Even early in the morning at 6 it is usually about 84° Fahrenheit. At midday between 94–96°, in the shade of course. And for the past three weeks it has regularly hovered around 92° at 9 in the evening. Such weather makes healthy people sick and is particularly hard on Bernhard. Hearty meals and much wine and brandy are therefore the main medicines.

Adolph's plans to emigrate are and remain rather unusual since he is really too old and has gotten used to too much comfort to like the life over here. Nonetheless, he probably won't be happy until he has at least seen the United States, and in the worst case, he can look at the trip as a pleasure or educational trip. We look forward to his visit, especially Wolter who is very excited by the thought.

Don't address your letters to us to South 5th St. 178 as I recently wrote you. All the numbers in the city changed recently, and we are now at No. 725. We want to leave this house as soon as possible because it is situated too low, and the kitchen, dining room, and garden are damp and the air and mist feverish, which is particularly bad for Bernhard. Address it "care of Messrs. Haenschen & Orthwein." Our daughters are well as is brother-in-law Hubert, who fears cholera.

In the hope that you, Theodor, and the children are in the best of health, I greet you from my heart.

Your sister Maria

On 7 August 1866 Maria sent off Bernhard's final letter, adding the following words:

From day to day I had to let my letter sit because Bernhard thought he wanted to finish his. He is no longer able to. The pain is becoming more intense and the medicines used to allay it less and less effective. So, more has to be used, and when Bernhard finds relief, he feels nothing and sleeps. Then at midday he has high fever, for which the doctor has ordered baths. His appetite has also suffered, but he still manages to eat enough, mostly meat. For the past two days he has been suffering from bedsores and his feet have swollen, both signs of great weakness. The doctor is nevertheless optimistic and asserts that the course of the illness is propitious. Bernhard always wants to read my letters, which is why I couldn't write you just how I felt. I'm going to seal this letter before he wakes.

Herr Haenschen, who is a good friend of Dr. Junghanns, wanted to open a business with Bernhard on 1 January 1867 and withdraw from the company that he now heads. Although Bernhard had not yet given his approval, I think that he would have gotten around to it. Now Haenschen doesn't talk about it anymore and dedicates himself completely to his old business. Others who would gladly have had him as a partner now no longer send word. Nobody comes to visit us anymore; people would rather visit someone on the mend than a sick man. It is as if the entire world has given up on us. Don't mention any of this in your letters; I write this only so that you will understand how things stand with the illness. Write soon

Maria

Bernhard finally died on 18 September 1866; his brother-in-law Franz von Weise informed the family in Europe:

St. Louis
18 September 1866

Dear Theodor!

The sad event has come. Bernhard left us peacefully this morning at 3 o'clock. Maria and I pressed his eyes shut. Recently, he had suffered a great deal. For the past 14 days diarrhea was so bad that it took away all his strength. He was nothing more than bones. I have been here for the past eight days as Maria was not well and Hubert van Dreveldt had to go to Freedom. The poor fellow hasn't returned yet. He will only see the cold, lifeless body of his brother again. Bernhard said that he liked having me around and liked being cared for by me. On Saturday I had to promise to stay with him to the end, and yesterday morning, sensing the approach of death, he asked me to stand watch all night. Maria spelled me for a time.

Please give the relatives the sad news. I can't write more now. We send you our regards. Lament with us this bitter fate.

Your brother-in-law Franz von Weise

Bernhard's death certificate gave the cause of death as "Pyaemia/abscess of the liver." Regardless of what the cause of death was, the fact remained that his widow and three children were now without support in America, though not without family. Her brother Adolph arrived shortly after Bernhard died, joining his three younger brothers. All of them remained in America and raised families. And Carl van Dreveldt, the first of Theodor's four sons to emigrate, arrived shortly thereafter. Of the four, he was the only one to return to Europe, taking over Voorthuyzen after Theodor's death.

Maria remained in St. Louis until early summer 1869, when she returned to Voorthuyzen.

Almost nothing is known about Hubert's activities after Maria's departure. He is buried in the family plot in Bellefontaine Cemetery.

Conclusion

These are the people for whom I have come to feel a good deal of affection. Even when I disliked them, I liked them. I have tried to do justice to their complexity insofar as I have been able to imagine it. I have seen Theodor's easy-going, footloose radicalism mature, and although he may have become a pillar of the community and certainly of his large, extended family, he retained the idealism that made him restless. I have shaken my head at Anton's perverseness and irresponsibility but still found that I could respect him for breaking his ties with Europe and making a new start. It is a respect that he probably was rarely accorded during his lifetime. Bernhard irritated me constantly, and yet, when I looked at the circumstances in which he grew up, I could not but feel compassion for him. Perhaps I would not be so generous if I had known him personally.

What is too often neglected in the history of American immigration is the terrible price exacted upon people who wrenched themselves away from their families and familiar surroundings in order to remake themselves in a new land. It was not as simple as immigrants happily clearing the forest and hewing logs to make cabins and finding their efforts inexorably crowned by success, making them sovereigns of a new democratic nation. Their best efforts were as often as not crowned by hardship, loneliness, and failure. People died trying. That struggle — and failure — is a crucial component of the American experience.

Apart from the unforgiving wilderness, immigrants had to deal with what they could never leave behind: themselves. At one level, the story of the van Dreveldts is an epic of hope and good intentions colliding with personal flaws and an unforgiving land. Through their eloquent letters, they have opened themselves up and allowed us to witness their struggles as they tried to make their way.

The van Dreveldts were also a recognizably modern family struggling with the opposing demands of family and individualism. Theodor, Anton, and Bernhard were never joiners who sought safety within a group. That might have made things considerably easier for these men; immigrants who made common cause with each other generally did better than those who did not. Despite their independence, the pull of family and the need to belong and to have family support were intense. When Bernhard, who in some ways best gave expression to the family's inner dynamics, wrote Theodor, "I'm sorry that I ever broached this matter and that I *ever* asked for help; my entire past experience should have taught me that it would come to nothing and that I must simply rely on myself. You may rely on the fact that I will doggedly continue to strive for the goals I have set myself without ever asking *any* of my relatives for help again," he was giving voice to his frustration at being not just an immigrant but also a sort of exile alienated from the family fold. As were they all. Both Anton and Theodor expressed almost identical sentiments at one time or another, alienated as they were from each other and their family of origin.

Theodor overcame the alienation to become the respected hub of a large, extended family that included not just a wife and eleven children, nine of whom reached adulthood, but also the von Weises. And though Bernhard swore he would never ask family for help again, the prospect of Theodor's return to America filled him with visions of creating "a very strong family in every respect," perhaps even a successful family dynasty.

Were the van Dreveldts successful in their endeavors? Clearly, they did not leave a major mark on American history. But that is true of the vast majority of people at all times, whether they are passing through a place as transients or settling in to make a living and find their place. The van Dreveldts were all part of the unruly, anarchic striving that built the country. Perhaps the entire question of success and failure is wrong.

The van Dreveldts have left behind a remarkable body of articulate letters that let us, descendants and strangers, know who they were. Their cumulative story is a sort of morality play that beckons us to react and take sides. We may blame and defend, feel righteous anger at faults and prejudices, compassion with shortcomings, and solidarity with their strivings and overall purpose.

This is a rich legacy for their descendants, creating a family myth for subsequent generations to struggle with and find their places within. Few families possess such rich documentation of their history. In many cases few letters were written. Most families have not saved letters; "useless" letters were thrown in the trash so that a crate could be reused or a desk sold. War and forced emigration obliterated other family records. The fact is that most Americans do not see themselves as historical beings and have only the vaguest notion of where they really came from. Stories like those of the van Dreveldts, to the extent they are even known, are often not passed on because they are not seen as "positive" or "uplifting." This robs descendants of a sense of historical and personal complexity and perspective. Even facing these hindrances, many Americans dig around in genealogy and "roots," searching for clues about themselves. Family history tugs at us in a way that our television culture, for example, rarely does. Readers who have entered into dialogue with the van Dreveldts through their letters may well have responded to that tug.

Two days before his death at Voorthuyzen in 1880, Theodor, a life-long opponent of what he saw as the fundamental hypocrisy and irrationality of organized religion, wrote a lengthy letter to an old university friend, a Catholic cleric. To my mind it is a summation of the man he had become in the thirty years after his failed immigration. These are the words of a man deeply at peace with himself:

> I don't think the chances look good for our meeting in the Hereafter. However, I would like to spend a few hours in leisure with you, to look once again into my old friend's honest eyes.
>
> It is a singular but comforting feeling to get together with a friend from my youth after nearly half a century, a friend with whom I do not always agree, but for whom my feelings of friendship have not diminished.
>
> Dear Rütjes, if I could, I would visit you. However, my doctor has prescribed total rest for me. I used to be able to go out for a half an hour each day, but even this much exercise proved damaging. At this point, I am imprisoned indoors, tied to a nice little spot by the door. We could spend a few happy moments there together. Come here and visit your dying friend. You will be well received by my large family, and you will not come to see the day that you performed this service of love as one of the wasted days of your life. Come soon, my dear Hennemann, come and visit your old friend.

Afterword

Before leaving Anton, Theodor, and Bernhard, I would like to return for a moment to the founder of their line, the proud and unconventional Johann Anton Goossens tot Voorthuyzen. Goossens's gravestone on the Eltenberg is inscribed with a poem, which he probably wrote himself, that may give some sense of his spiritual outlook:

> Everything carried by the earth
> Falls prey to earthly time
> But that which moves heart and spirit
> Shares not that fate with the dust.
> Though this memorial may some day fade
> Our love is everlasting
> And friendship's truest sense
> Hopes for reunion there.[1]

These are the conventional sentiments of a Catholic man of his position in the world. Yet, what drove him to found a family, something that ran completely counter to his careful upbringing, not to mention his priestly vows? He had to know that he risked community ridicule. Was he hoping for "everlasting love," something very different from everlasting life?

It is relatively easy to count Anton's birth, the first sin, as a "little mishap," but Goossens went on to have more children. We do know that Goossens was impressed by the Enlightenment and the expectations awakened by the French Revolution. Like many educated people of the time, he had read Rousseau and believed that celibacy would be abolished. These influences and beliefs mark him as a man grappling with the problems of his time. It should be added that his marriage, never made official, was actually nothing out of the ordinary. And yet, in the shadow of St. Martin's in small town Emmerich, it went against public opinion.

Perhaps it is true that the Provost planned to start a family and leave the service of the church in order to make a life as a man of property. However, he could certainly never have imagined that both of his sons would be so affected by the reactionary spirit that took hold of Germany after the Congress of Vienna that they would decide to leave. For the rest of his life, Theodor had mixed feelings about not having remained in the United States. He had a good life in Germany, but he probably regretted what he would have seen as a loss of freedom. It was Theodor who influenced his wife's brothers to emigrate. Without his strong backing, they probably would have stayed safely at home in Cologne. Four von Weise brothers made their way to America. Caroline's brother Wolter perhaps made his way best of all. The business that he founded in Pocahontas, Illinois, was so successful that his children, living in Greenville and Rockford, Illinois, could count on family backing to found their own successful businesses. In this sense they fulfilled Bernhard's desire to build a "strong family in every respect."

Theodor's son Carl also spent a number of years in the United States before he too returned to Voorthuyzen. His letters to his father have been saved as well, and they document vividly the struggles of this young man to make his way.

Finally, there is Hubert, who in many ways was Bernhard's right hand man, but of whom so very little is known. He apparently made a good living, good enough that he could afford to recuperate from an illness in California in 1910 and 1911. A letter written on 19 May 1913 by Adolf Stille documented his death:

> Hubert van Dreveldt died yesterday afternoon and his body will be shipped to St. Louis to be incinerated in accordance with his instructions. As soon as I return to St. Louis, I will have his will probated and will send you a copy of the same as well as a copy of the inventory, as soon as the same has been completed and filed.

With Hubert's death, the van Dreveldt line died out in America. His remains are interred in Bellefontaine Cemetery in St. Louis, next to his father and brother.

C. HANS VON GIMBORN

Notes

INTRODUCTION

1. Germany did not exist as a nation-state until 1871, when Otto von Bismarck brought together a number of German states and William I of Prussia became kaiser of the Second German Reich. This Germany did not include Austria. The van Dreveldts came from Emmerich, which was part of Prussia. However, during Theodor's time, anyone was considered "German" who spoke German. Thus, German-speaking Austrians and Swiss who emigrated to America were usually called Germans. The terms *Germany* and *German* will be used here to denote a language area or group rather than a state.

2. Gottfried Duden, *Report on a Journey to the Western States of North America,* ed. James W. Goodrich (Columbia: University of Missouri Press, 1980) 236.

3. The size of Voorthuyzen varied over the years. In November 1860, Theodore attempted to sell it, and an ad for that sale noted its dimensions at that time: "1185 Morgen, 114 Ruthen in addition to 11 bunder, 97 roeden, and 20 ellen." A Prussian Morgen equaled 2550 m² (about ⅔ acre); a Ruthe, 14.1 m². A Dutch bunder equaled about 10,000 m². Thus, the property was approximately 800–850 acres in 1860.

THE TOWN OF EMMERICH

1. Ferdinand Goebel, *Emmerich einst und jetzt, ein Heimatbuch für Schule und Haus* (Emmerich: Bürgerblatt Druckerei, 1934), 101–4.

2. L. Hütten, *Wirtschaftsgeschichte der Stadt Emmerich von 1770–1914* (Emmerich: n.d.), 17. This work contains a wealth of information about freight transport on the Rhine, specifically in Emmerich.

3. E. Wassenberg, *Embrica* (Cleves: Tobias Silberling, 1667), 62–64.

PROVOST GOOSSENS

1. Carl von Gimborn, *Johann Anton Goossens: Eine Familiengeschichte* (Emmerich am Rhein: 1965), 7–17. All documents and letters in this chapter are from this work.

THE FRENCH REVOLUTION

1. W. Elcker and H. Goldschmidt, eds. *Aus der Geschichte des Herzogtums Cleve: Festschrift zur Jubelfeier zur 300 jährigen Zugehörigkeit des*

Herzogtums Cleve zur Krone Brandenburg-Preußen (Cleves and Berlin: Franz Ebhardt, 1909), 150.

2. Heinrich Weber, foreword, "Erinnerungen des Abbé Baston," *Beiträge zur Landes- und Volkskunde des Kreises Coesfeld* (Coesfeld: Bocholt, 1961), 62–65.

THE "LITTLE MISHAPS"

1. Von Gimborn, *Goossens*. All documents and letters in this chapter are from this work.

VOORTHUYZEN

1. Elizabeth Terhorst, *Das Eyland* (Cologne: Staufen-Verlag, 1943), 7.
2. Quoted in Hütten, *Wirtschaftsgeschichte der Stadt Emmerich*, 26.

THE TWO BROTHERS

1. Quoted in John L. Snell, *The Democratic Movement in Germany, 1789–1914* (Chapel Hill: University of North Carolina Press, 1976), 22.
2. The *Volkisch* idea, based on the conception of a distinct people or stock tied to the land in an organic, ancient, and mystical way, is exclusionary. Those people seen to be not of that stock are outside the community, no matter how long they have lived in it.
3. Jacob Katz, *Die Hep-Hep-Verfolgungen des Jahres 1819* (Berlin: Metropol, 1994). Anti-Jewish riots in which the rallying cry was Hep! Hep! (a cry used to herd livestock) took place throughout Germany and as late as 1844 in Geseke, Westphalia, where my own ancestors lived. See Margit Naarmann, " 'Daß Jude und Christ ihr Brot gemeinsam in Eintracht brechen . . .': Die antijüdischen Ausschreitungen in Geseke und Störmede im Jahr 1844 als historischer Hintergrund für Else Lasker-Schülers Drama *Arthur Aronymus und seine Väter*," *Menora: Jahrbuch für deutsch-jüdische Geschichte* (Munich: Serie Piper, 1991), 339–70.
4. Snell, *The Democratic Movement in Germany*, 23.
5. Kurt F. Reinhardt, *Germany: 2000 Years* (New York: Frederick Ungar, 1961), 2:523.
6. Reinhardt, *Germany: 2000 Years*, 2:465–67.
7. Carl von Gimborn, *Theodor van Dreveldt, aus dem Leben meines Großvaters* (Emmerich, 1969). Documents and letters in this chapter come exclusively from this work.

EMIGRATION

1. Carl von Gimborn, *Aus der neuen Welt: Familienbriefe 1844–1869* (Emmerich: 1968), 4.
2. Mack Walker, *Germany and the Emigration, 1816–1885* (Cambridge MA: Harvard University Press, 1964), 1–41.
3. Walter D. Kamphoefner, *The Westfalians: From Germany to Missouri* (Princeton NJ: Princeton University Press, 1987), 16–20.
4. Gottfried Duden, *Report on a Journey to the Western States of North America and a Stay of Several Years Along the Missouri (during the Years 1824, '25, '26, 1827)*, trans. and ed. James Goodrich et al. (Columbia: University of Missouri Press, 1980) 82.
5. Duden, *Report*, 57.
6. Duden, *Report*, 122.
7. Kamphoefner, *Westfalians*, 50.
8. Quoted in Antonius Holtmann, *Ferner thue ich euch zu wissen . . . : Die Briefe des Johann Heinrich zur Oeveste aus Amerika 1834–1876* (Bremen: Edition Temmen, 1995), 12.
9. Walter D. Kamphoefner, Wolfgang Helbich, and Ulrike Sommer, *News from the Land of Freedom: German Immigrants Write Home*, trans. Susan Carter Vogel (Ithaca NY: Cornell University Press, 1991), 27.

THEODOR IN AMERICA

1. Alexander de Conde, *This Affair of Louisiana* (New York: Scribner's, 1976), 57–62.
2. De Conde, *This Affair of Louisiana*, 145.
3. De Conde, *This Affair of Louisiana*, 103.
4. U.S. Department of Commerce, *Historical Statistics of the United States: Colonial Times to 1970*, part 1 (Washington DC: Bureau of the Census, 1975), 27–33.
5. William Lee Miller, *Arguing About Slavery* (New York: Knopf, 1996), 48.
6. Miller, *Arguing About Slavery*, 190.
7. Like many Germans who left their homeland for political reasons, Theodor became an abolitionist, as opposed to slavery in America as he was to tyrannical rule in Prussia. Although living in a slave state, most Missouri Germans who had black workers hired them—but not all. Duden's friend Eversmann, for example, owned slaves. And Wilhelm Noot, Theodor's companion, apparently came to support the institution, although he would fight for the Union in the Civil War.
8. Distance measured in hours refers to the distance that could be walked

in that amount of time, generally three kilometers or two miles per hour.

9. The steamboat *Maria,* a 692-ton sidewheel, was built in 1844. On 21 November 1846 it collided with the *Sultana* seven miles south of Natchez, Tennessee, on the Mississippi River and sank within five minutes with a loss of thirty to fifty lives. Such accidents and loss of life were not uncommon on the Mississippi and other major rivers. See Edward D. Jervey and James E. Moss, eds., "The Journal of Elizabeth Ann Cooley," *Missouri Historical Review* 60 (October 1965): 188–89.

10. The Reaumur temperature scale sets the freezing point at 0° and boiling at 80°. Centigrade equals 5/4 Reaumur; therefore, 25° Reaumur equals just over 31° Centigrade or 88° Fahrenheit. However, temperatures below freezing were not labeled as such; in winter, 30° Reaumur was simply understood as 30° Reaumur below zero.

WHAT WAS GOING ON IN GERMANY

1. *Der beste Censor*
   Der beste Censor unter allen,
   Des Weisheit Alle macht zu Spott,
   Und den man gern sich läßt gefallen,
   Des Censor ist der liebe Gott.

   Wer sieht es nicht mit Wohlbehagen,
   Wie er sein Censoramt betreibt?
   Er läßt uns Alles schreiben, sagen,
   Was man auf Eiden sagt und schreibt.

   Es gibt kein Ding, was ihn geniret,
   Und wär' es auch ein Fluch, ein Schwur,
   Er streicht Nichts aus, was nur passiret,
   Passirt vor ihm auch die Censur.

   Ja, ob man seiner selber spotte
   Und gegen ihn zu Felde zieh'
   Ihn kümmert aller Feinde Rotte
   Mit ihrem Widerspruche nie.

   Und ob er gleich läßt Alles gehen,
   So sieht man doch sein Regiment
   Jahraus, jahrein so wohl bestehen,
   Daß man nicht seines Gleichen kennt.

2. *Warte Raabenpack!*
Zum Herbstmanöver durch den Wald
Zog König Leu und machte Halt
Vor einem Thal, wo, wie er wußte,
Ein breiter See erglänzen mußte.
Verwundert fand er Sumpf und Moor,
Und wo die Klare Fluth zuvor,
Drin munter einst das Fischlein schwamm,
Da saß der Frosch in seinem Schlamm.

Wodurch, rief Nobel fast bestürzt,
Ward so des Fisches Recht verkürzt?

Der Raabe Staatsminister nahm
'Ne Pris' und sagte: Herr, es kam,
Weil auf dem Reichstag jeder Frist
Der Fisch vom Frosch vertreten ist.

Wie? rief der Leu in seinem Grimme,
Hat denn der Fisch nicht Sitz und Stimme
Gleich jedem andern Thiergeschlecht?
Warum verficht er nicht sein Recht?

Der Raabe, dem's am Herzen lag,
Nahm wieder eine Pris' und sprach:
Der Fisch hat freilich Sitz und Stimme
Dort auf dem Reichtag, doch das Schlimme
Ist, daß der unbeholfene Mann
Nicht sitzen und nicht sprechen kann,
Und, ob die Schulen auch floriren,
Noch immer ist am buchstabiren;
So kam's denn, daß im großen Rath
Sein Nachbar Freimund ihn vertrat.

Wohlan, sprach Nobel, reinigt schnell
Vom Schilf und Schlamm den alten Quell,
Und einen mächtigen Damm erbaut,
Daß wieder er zum See sich staut;
Denn meiner Fische fromm Geschlecht
Entbehre nicht sein gutes Recht!

Nun hättet ihr sie sehen sollen,
Die Frösche, wie vor Wuth geschwollen
Sie vor den Löwen sich gesetzt;
Die Charte, schrien sie, wird verletzt!
Was wir verfassungsmäßig dort
Erlangt, soll hier ein Königswort
Vernichten? Warte, Raabenpack,
Dir sei's vergolten! Quak, quak, quak!

Doch Nobel hob die Herrscherpranken,
Daß rings erzitterten die Schranken,
Und sprach: Ihr deputirten Herrn,
Was Ihr beschließt, vollzieh' ich gern;
Doch wer noch selber nicht vermag
Für sich zu sprechen auf dem Tag,
Für den, so lang er buchstabirt,
Bin ich, der König, deputirt.

G. Pfarrius

3. Steven Rowan, "The Continuation of the German Revolutionary Tradition on American Soil," in *Germans for a Free Missouri: Translations from the St. Louis Radical Press, 1857–1862*, selected and trans. Steven Rowan (Columbia: Missouri, 1983), 23–45.

THE REVOLUTION OF 1848 AND THEODOR'S RETURN

1. St. Hubert (d. ca. 727) was the patron saint of hunters. The bishop of Liège, he was, according to legend, an avid hunter until a stag appeared to him with a shining cross between its golden antlers. The day of his elevation, 3 November, was celebrated with elaborate hunts and hunting feasts, especially by the nobility. His clerical stole was considered the best remedy for the bite of a rabid dog.

2. James Neale Primm, "Missouri, St. Louis, and the Secession Crisis," in *Germans for a Free Missouri*, 7.

3. Alfred Vagts, *Deutsch-Amerikanische Rückwanderung* (Heidelberg: Carl Winter-Universitätsverlag, 1960), 7, 20–21.

4. Snell, *The Democratic Movement in Germany*, 81–83.

5. Marshall Dill, *Germany, a Modern History* (Ann Arbor: University of Michigan Press, 1961), 110; John E. Rodes, *The Quest for Unity: Modern Germany 1848–1970* (New York: Holt, Rinehart and Winston, 1971), 34–35.

6. U.S. Department of Commerce, *Historical Statistics of the United States,* 106.

7. Thomas M. Lindsay, *A History of the Reformation* (New York: Scribner's, 1907), 460–69.

8. Wilhelm van Rossum, "Das Revolutionsjahr 1848 in Emmerich," in *1964 Heimatkalender Landkreis Rees* (Wesel: Kreisverwaltung Rees, 1964), 180–82.

9. In handwritten autobiography of William Noot written sometime after the Civil War, Minnesota Historical Society Manuscript Collection, #P939.

ANTON IN AMERICA

1. In December 1883 a death card was printed in Dutch to commemorate the passing of "Antoinette Elisabeth Charlotte Reijgers, weduwe van Antoon van Dreveldt." It consisted of passages from the Bible, as was the custom. The first four from the Hebrew Bible are about suffering and evince a great deal of compassion for her. For example, the first passage says, "I only tasted a little honey." That was certainly the truth. Of the two passages from the Christian Bible, the first looks to a happier reunion, the second asks for a prayer. Some of the passages appear to be composites and do not correspond exactly to the Vulgate.

1. Ik heb slechts een weinig honi[n]g geproefd. (1 Kings 14:43)

2. Ik heb ellendige maanden gehad en moeilijke nachten geteld; mijn leven is geëindigd in pijn en mijne jaren verliepen in zuchten. (Job 7: 3-6)

3. Waarom was mijne kwaal ongeneeslijk en was er niemand, die mij helpen kon? Omdat Gij, o Heer, gehandeld hebt volgens uw welbehagen. (Jer. 15:18-20)

4. Wilt niet treuren, waat de dood is beter dan een bitter leven en de eeuwige rust beter dan eene voortdurende zickte. (Sir. 30:17)

5. Ik zal u wederzien en uw hart zal blijde zijn. (John 16:22)

6. Ik smeek u door onzen Heer Jezus Christus en de liefde des H. Geestes, dat gij mij door uwe gebeden bij God ter hulpe komt. (Rom. 15:30)

2. Oscar Handlin, *The Uprooted* (Boston: Little, Brown, 1973), 46; Raymond L. Cohn, "Mortality on Immigrant Voyages to New York, 1836–53," *Journal of Economic History* 44 (June 1984): 289–300. The latter study examined the passenger lists of 1077 ships that listed deaths. Although ship captains were required by law to account for on-board

deaths and there were penalties for not doing so, one can imagine ways of maintaining a clean record as well as reasons for doing so.

3. See Terry Coleman, *Going to America* (New York: Pantheon, 1972), 89–120.

BERNHARD: FROM VOORTHUYZEN TO NEW VOORTHUYZEN

1. "Illinois," vol. 161 (Monroe County), p. 26, R. G. Dun & Co. Collection, Baker Library, Harvard University Graduate School of Business Administration.

POLITICS IN BLACK AND WHITE

1. Rowan, "The Continuation of the German Revolutionary Tradition on American Soil," 37.
2. Kenneth M. Stampp, *The Imperiled Union: Essays on the Background of the Civil War* (New York: Oxford, 1980), 107.
3. Stampp, *The Imperiled Union*, 109–10.
4. Stampp, *The Imperiled Union*, 110.
5. Stampp, *The Imperiled Union*, 111.
6. Stampp, *The Imperiled Union*, 116.

BERNHARD AND MARIA IN AMERICA

1. Peter J. Parish, *The American Civil War* (New York: Holmes & Meier, 1975), 68.
2. David M. Potter, *The Impending Crisis, 1848–1861* (New York: Harper and Row, 1976), 496.
3. The eggs were packed in barrels filled with straw.
4. Louis Dobbelmann was a Dutchman who lived and worked with the van Dreveldts for a time. After Bernhard died and Maria returned to Europe, Dobbelmann married her. In Holland, he founded a tobacco company.

THE UNREST IN MISSOURI

1. R. Douglas Hurt, *Agriculture and Slavery in Missouri's Little Dixie* (Columbia: University of Missouri Press, 1992), xii.
2. Primm, "Missouri, St. Louis, and the Secession Crisis," 4.
3. Illinoistown is now East St. Louis, Illinois.
4. Primm, "Missouri, St. Louis, and the Secession Crisis," 6–22.

THE CIVIL WAR ACCORDING TO BERNHARD

1. Parish, *The American Civil War,* 107.
2. Shelby Foote, *The Civil War: Fort Sumter to Perryville* (New York: Random House, 1958), 82.
3. Foote, *The Civil War,* 91–95.
4. Rowan, "The Continuation of the German Revolutionary Tradition on American Soil," 28–29.
5. Louis Dobbelmann wrote many letters to his family in Holland about his experiences in Civil War. See Liesbeth Wezelaar-Dobbelmann, *Louis Dobbelmann 1837–1901. Yankee en Rotterdammer* (Amsterdam: van Soeren, 1997). An American edition is being prepared.
6. Foote, *The Civil War,* 307–8.
7. Foote, *The Civil War,* 346–51.
8. Herr Bennert was Annette Höynck's son-in-law and the owner of the meat firm Liebig Fleischcompagnie in Antwerp.
9. John Bach McMaster, *A History of the People of the United States during Lincoln's Administration* (New York: D. Appleton, 1927), 449–53.
10. McMaster, *A History of the People of the United States,* 453.
11. Quoted in McMaster, *A History of the People of the United States,* 522.

BERNHARD'S DEATH

1. George B. Wood, M.D., and Franklin Bache, M.D., *The Dispensatory of the United States of America* (Philadelphia: Lippincott, 1867), 2:1008–11.
2. The loss to which Maria refers is the infant death of daughter Luise.

AFTERWORD

1. Alles was die Erde trägt
    Fällt der ird'schen Zeit zum Raub
    Doch was Geist und Herz bewegt
    Teilt das Los nicht mit dem Staub.
    Sinke einst dies Denkmal hin
    Unsere Liebe dauert fort
    Und der Freundschaft treuer Sinn
    Hofft auf Wiedersehen dort.

Index